Governing China in the 21st Century

Series Editors
Zhimin Chen
School of International Relations and Public Affairs
Fudan University
Shanghai, China

Yijia Jing
Institute for Global Public Policy &
School of International Relations and Public Affairs
Fudan University
Shanghai, China

Since 1978, China's political and social systems have transformed significantly to accommodate the world's largest population and second largest economy. These changes have grown more complex and challenging as China deals with modernization, globalization, and informatization. The unique path of sociopolitical development of China hardly fits within any existing frame of reference. The number of scientific explorations of China's political and social development, as well as contributions to international literature from Chinese scholars living and researching in Mainland China, has been growing fast. This series publishes research by Chinese and international scholars on China's politics, diplomacy, public affairs, and social and economic issues for the international academic community.

More information about this series at
http://www.palgrave.com/gp/series/15023

Yijia Jing • Alvaro Mendez • Yu Zheng
Editors

New Development Assistance

Emerging Economies and the New Landscape of Development Assistance

palgrave
macmillan

Editors
Yijia Jing
Institute for Global Public Policy
School of International Relations and Public Affairs
Fudan University
Shanghai, China

Alvaro Mendez
London School of Economics
London, UK

Yu Zheng
School of International Relations and Public Affairs
Fudan University
Shanghai, China

ISSN 2730-6968 ISSN 2730-6976 (electronic)
Governing China in the 21st Century
ISBN 978-981-13-7231-5 ISBN 978-981-13-7232-2 (eBook)
https://doi.org/10.1007/978-981-13-7232-2

This Palgrave Macmillan imprint is published by the registered company Springer Nature Singapore Pte Ltd.
The registered company address is: 152 Beach Road, #21-01/04 Gateway East, Singapore 189721, Singapore

The original version of the book was revised: Series print and electronic ISSN have been updated. The correction to the book is available at https://doi.org/10.1007/978-981-13-7232-2_12

Acknowledgments

The book is supported by the National Social Science Foundation of China under Grant 15ZDA031, the National Science Foundation of China under Grant 71490735 and the LSE-Fudan Research Centre for Global Public Policy.

Contents

Notes on Contributors

Chris Alden is Professor of International Relations at the London School of Economics and Political Science (LSE), and is a research associate with the Global Powers and Africa Programme, South African Institute of International Affairs (SAIIA). He is author/co-author of numerous books, including *Mozambique and the Construction of the New African State* (Palgrave Macmillan 2003), *South Africa's Post-Apartheid Foreign Policy* (2003), *China in Africa* (2007), *Land, Liberation and Compromise in Southern Africa* (Palgrave Macmillan 2009), *The South in World Politics* (Palgrave Macmillan 2010), *Foreign Policy Analysis: New Approaches* 2nd edition (2017), and co-editor of *China and Africa: Building Peace and Security Cooperation on the Continent* (Palgrave Macmillan 2017), *China and Mozambique: From Comrades to Capitalists* (2014), *China Returns to Africa* (2008). He has written numerous articles in internationally recognised journals. He has held fellowships at Cambridge University; Institute of Social Science, University of Tokyo; Ritsumeikan University, Kyoto; École Normale Supérieure (Cachan), Paris; and University of Pretoria.

Elena Dobrolyubova holds a PhD in Economics. She graduated from the Russian Economic Academy (MA in World Economy). In 2015, she defended a thesis on governance statistics. She has worked in the World Bank during 1999–2007 on various public sector projects in Russia. Since 2007, she is the Head of Center of Economic and Financial Consulting, a Russian consultancy firm specializing in governance reforms, performance management, and fiscal affairs. Since 2011, she is also the Deputy

Director of the Center for Public Administration Technologies in the Russian Presidential Academy of National Economy and Public Administration (RANEPA). She has about 100 publications on economic and public sector issues.

Jing Gu is the Director of Centre for Rising Powers and Global Development, and a senior research fellow at the Institute of Development Studies. She is a senior consultant to the Center for International Knowledge on Development at the Development Research Center of the State Council in China. She is a political economist with extensive experience in research and advisory work of governance, business and sustainable development. She has led many interdisciplinary research projects involving multi-country teams, including the groundbreaking pioneering research on China's outward investment in Africa. Her teaching, research and advisory work focus on China's international development strategies, BRICS and South-South Cooperation. She is a member of the International Editorial Board of *Third World Quarterly*.

Yijia Jing is a Chang Jiang Scholar, Seaker Chan Chair Professor of Public Management, Dean of the Institute for Global Public Policy, and professor of School of International Relations and Public Affairs, Fudan University, Shanghai, China. He holds his BA/MA degree in Economics from Peking University, MA in Sociology from the University of Maryland, College Park, and PhD in Public Policy from the Ohio State University. He is the editor-in-chief of *Fudan Public Administration Review* and co-editor of *International Public Management Journal*. He is the founding co-editor of the Palgrave Macmillan book series *Governing China in the Twenty-First Century*. He serves as a vice president of International Research Society for Public Management.

Daniel Large is an assistant professor at Central European University's School of Public Policy. He is also a senior non-resident fellow of the University of Nottingham's China Policy Institute, and a fellow of the Rift Valley Institute. His publications include *New Directions in the Study of Africa and China* (2018), co-edited with Chris Alden; *Sudan Looks East: China, India and the Politics of Asian Alternatives* (2011), co-edited with Luke Patey; and *China Returns to Africa: A Rising Power and a Continent Embrace* (2008), co-edited with Chris Alden and Ricardo Soares de Oliveira.

Alvaro Mendez is the co-director of the Global South Unit at the LSE, where he is also a senior research fellow in the International Relations Department. He is a senior fellow at Fudan University; a research associate at the University of Bristol; and a former editor of *Millennium-Journal of International Studies* at the LSE. He lectures at the LSE on courses such as China and the global South and foreign policy analysis. LSE's International Relations Department awarded him its 2003–2004 Teaching Prize. Mendez is an associate academic at the LSE Latin America and Caribbean Centre and an International Advisory Board member of the Observatoire Politique de l'Amérique latine et des Caraïbes (OPALC) at Sciences Po. His most recent publications include *Colombian Agency and the Making of US Foreign Policy* (2017); *Global Governance in Foreign Policy* (2018); and *The China-Latin America Axis: Emerging Markets and Their Role in an Increasingly Globalised World* (co-authored, Palgrave Macmillan, 2018).

Zhe Ouyang is a graduate student and research assistant for the Center for Global Governance at the School of International Relations and Public Affairs, Fudan University. His research interest is mainly in international public policy. His work has been published in leading Chinese journals.

Rogerio F. Pinto a Brazilian national, is an international consultant in public management and institutional development with extended experience in international development as a staff of the World Bank, the Inter-American Development Bank and the Organization of American States. He has worked in different capacities in 45 different countries in four continents around the world (mostly in Africa and Latin America). After retirement from the World Bank, he taught at the Brazilian School of Public and Business Administration of the Getulio Vargas Foundation. He has delivered consulting and teaching assignments with governments, NGOs, universities and international organizations.

Neil Renwick is a professor in the School of Humanities, Coventry University, UK. He specialises in international relations with a particular interest in human development challenges. A graduate of Durham University and the Australian National University, his published work includes a number of monographs and edited books and numerous journal articles. His work focuses on East Asia and the Pacific, and he has delivered many lectures and research seminars at universities and research institutes across the region over two decades. He is a consultant to the UNDP Pacific Region, to the T20 Think Tank Forum for the G20 Leaders' Summits in China and Germany and to a number of NGOs. He is a member of the International Institute of Strategic Studies, an elected committee member of the International Political Science Association and an associate of the British Academy of Social Sciences. He is an invited member of the CCTV Group of International Experts and has contributed to international and Chinese media on a regular basis.

Eswaran Sridharan is Academic Director and Chief Executive of the University of Pennsylvania Institute for the Advanced Study of India, New Delhi. He is a political scientist and the author, editor or co-editor of nine books. His published work includes over 80 journal articles and edited volume chapters. He has held visiting appointments at the University of California, Berkeley; London School of Economics; Institute for Developing Economies, Tokyo; and Institute of South Asian Studies, Singapore. He is the editor of *India Review*, a refereed journal. He holds a PhD in Political Science from the University of Pennsylvania.

Chris Tapscott is an emeritus professor at the School of Government, University of the Western Cape, South Africa. As a sociologist, he has extensive applied policy research experience in the fields of administrative reform and governance in developing states. His research focus is on the local state and on the political and administrative challenges which confront the development of substantive participatory democracy and services delivery in countries of the global South. His publications in this field include *Citizenship and Social Movements, Perspectives from the Global South* (2010) co-edited with Lisa Thompson, and a forthcoming volume on *The Democratic Development State: North-South Perspectives*, co-edited with Tor Halvorsen and Teresita Ceuz-del Rosario.

Denghua Zhang is a research fellow at the Australian National University. He completed his PhD on Chinese foreign policy and aid at the Australian National University in 2017. Prior to that, he had a decade-long work experience as a Chinese diplomat. His research focuses on international relations, development studies, Chinese foreign policy, Chinese foreign aid and China in the Pacific. His articles have been published widely including recently in *The Pacific Review*, *Third World Quarterly*, *Asian Journal of Political Sciences*, *The Round Table*, *Asia and the Pacific Policy Studies* and *Security Challenges*.

Jianzhi Zhao is Associate Professor of Economic Policy and Deputy Director for the Center for Global Governance at the School of International Relations and Public Affairs, Fudan University. His research interests are international political economy, public economics, development economics, and development finance. He has worked at multiple international organizations, including the World Bank, Asian Development Bank and Inter-American Development Bank. Zhao was also a visiting researcher at the Bank of Finland. He has been invited to present his research paper at the Congressional Budget Office (CBO) of the United States government. He has consulted with World Bank, Chinese Ministry of Commerce, Chinese Social Science Foundation and USAID. He has served as an ad hoc referee for many international journals. His work has been published in many leading journals. Zhao was Shorenstein Postdoctoral Fellow at Stanford University and holds his PhD in International Economic Policy from the University of Maryland, College Park.

Yu Zheng is a professor at the School of International Relations and Public Affairs (SIRPA), Fudan University, Shanghai, China. He holds a PhD from the University of California, San Diego, and taught at the University of Connecticut, USA. He is the author of *Governance and Foreign Investment in China, India, and Taiwan: Credibility, Flexibility, and International Business*. His publications have also appeared in journals such as *Comparative Politics*, *Public Opinion Quarterly*, *Socio-Economic Review*, *Studies in Comparative International Development*, and others.

Jiejin Zhu is an associate professor at the School of International Relations and Public Affairs, Fudan University, China. His research interests include international institutions and global governance, especially the BRICS and G20. His published work includes 3 books and over 30 papers on these topics. He is doing research on Rising Powers' Strategy for Changing the International Institutions.

List of Figures

List of Tables

CHAPTER 1

New Development Assistance in the Making: An Introduction

Yijia Jing, Alvaro Mendez, and Yu Zheng

New Development Assistance: A New Agenda

Many emerging economies have been gradually evolving from recipients of Official Development Assistance (ODA) to new donors. While statistical information of their contribution varies due to heterogeneous definitions, criteria, and data availability, the impacts of emerging economies' increasing engagement in international development have become visible. Their growing role in international development does not just reflect a shift of the center of gravity of the global political economy toward the South and East, but has paved the way for rethinking and reforming ODA.

Y. Jing (✉)
Institute for Global Public Policy, School of International Relations and Public Affairs, Fudan University, Shanghai, China
e-mail: jingyj@fudan.edu.cn

A. Mendez
London School of Economics, London, UK
e-mail: a.mendez@lse.ac.uk

Y. Zheng
School of International Relations and Public Affairs, Fudan University, Shanghai, China
e-mail: yzheng@fudan.edu.cn

Y. Jing et al. (eds.), *New Development Assistance*, Governing China in the 21st Century,
https://doi.org/10.1007/978-981-13-7232-2_1

In early 2017, scholars of Fudan University and the London School of Economics and Political Science (LSE) with a common interest in international development assistance launched a joint project to explore the changing landscape that is stemming from the increasingly prominent donor roles played by emerging economies. The project evaluated the current practices of development assistance and their effectiveness; identified new patterns and challenges; and sorted out new concepts, norms, and activities to deliver policy advice to national governments, aid agencies, and multilateral aid organizations. In April 2017, scholars from both institutions met in the Old Building of LSE and coined the concept of New Development Assistance (NDA), with the ambition to establish a new analytic framework that would capture the attributes of emerging-economy development assistance realized so far which fundamentally diverge from those of conventional ODA. The following September, a forum on Development and Governance in BRICS was held at Fudan University with a roundtable on NDA. Members of the research project enthusiastically presented their research, which had been structured according to a general understanding of the ideas and practices of NDA. It was concluded that the changing global political economy had laid the socioeconomic background for reasonably definable and distinct patterns of development assistance to emerge that merit serious academic attention and exploration.

The New International Political Economy and New Development Assistance (NDA)

The post-WWII global political economy has undergone fundamental changes that have created new momentum and challenges for development assistance. ODA was first a response to a war-damaged Europe, then shifted its focus to developing countries, most of which had been European colonies before WWII. For a long period, ODA reflected the hierarchical global economic structure by being a major responsibility of developed countries in the Global North. Beyond a historically forged moral obligation, ODA brought with it economic, political, cultural, and other purposes and implications. As its magnitude continued to grow, ODA began to assume the function of "global redistribution" contributing to development and sociopolitical stability in the Global South.

In the second half of the twentieth century, ODA passed through incremental changes and improvements. The economic boom of the 1960s and 1970s brought still more developed countries into the donor group. The

Development Assistance Committee (DAC) of the Organisation for Economic Co-operation and Development (OECD) was established in 1961 to promote development assistance, coordinate cooperation, guide operations, and harmonize standards. In 1969, DAC first defined ODA to include three basic components: an official sector contribution, an economic development focus, and concessional financial terms. For decades, over 90% of world's ODA came from DAC members. Unsurprisingly, most ODA reflected the ideas, specifically neoliberalism, of the developed Global North regarding effective and legitimate ways of assisting development. Even though OECD was encouraging its member states to enhance borrowers' ownership through the Paris Declaration and the Accra Agenda for Action, the OECD's value-laden ODA practices still tended to reflect Western views of global political-economic governance. ODA conditionality, driven by a value consensus on economic marketization and political democratization, often confronted aid-receiving countries with a tension between external rule adoption and autonomous development. Although ODA alleviated some of the economic difficulties of aid recipients and brought them new opportunities, it was incapable of exerting a major influence that would empower countries with ingrained weaknesses in market infrastructure and political stability. ODA was based on the experiences of the Global North, and hardly provided an effective prescription for the North-South hierarchical political-economic structure.

The rise of emerging economies in the late twentieth century blazed alternative paths of development and subsequently new directions and resources for international development. In 2017, emerging economies accounted for 9 of the top 20 countries in terms of GDP, and their average GDP was 70% of the latter group's. Amazingly, China's GDP rose from 19% of Japan's in 1980 to 247% in 2017. The G20 has been replacing the G7 as the world's main scheme of global economic governance. Despite their vast internal variation, the development paths of emerging economies have one thing in common, their deviation from the accepted Western precepts. The values underlying their development achievements were nicknamed the "Beijing Consensus" in 2004 by Joshua Ramo (2004), a scholar at Kissinger Associates, to designate it as an alternative to the "Washington Consensus".

The growing productive capacity of emerging economies has significantly expanded their role as development assistance providers. The leading ones are big regional countries such as the BRICS, starting to provide development assistance long ago despite being recipients of it at the same time. Aside from regional geopolitical concerns, common motivations driving emerging economies to become donors before they were really rich enough were economic integration, trade benefits, cultural ties, and humanitarian rescue. Usually, the engagement of emerging countries was gradual in terms of aid amount, geographical coverage, and institution and capacity building. The Belt and Road Initiative (BRI) launched in 2013 and the Asian Infrastructure Investment Bank (AIIB) established in 2015 as part of China's grand global political economic strategy had a huge component of international development. As China and India are expected to have a GDP bigger than that of the US by the middle of this century (OECD, 2018), the development assistance potential of emerging economies is hardly negligible, and will surely become an important resource for bridging the huge gap between the supply of and demand for development assistance.

Notwithstanding that emerging economies have obviously learned from DAC rules and aid practices, their perceptions of development and of appropriate ways of external intervention are different. They usually lack strong market and social infrastructure and institutions, and their development trajectories may not distinguish a clear boundary between the economy and the state. Their political systems have difficulty in adopting and stabilizing Western democracy. Consequently, their aid actions are pragmatic and devoid of a value focus. As the new donors themselves had emerged from a history of colonial rule by Western powers, their assistance to other developing economies was not restrained by the moral obligations that traditional ODA carries, and tended to emphasize South-South cooperation and mutual benefit, which, in turn, was critical for domestically justifying their aid engagement and spending.

Systematic adoption of DAC rules by emerging countries was proved practically impossible. Although there is a clear trend of increasing engagement, they have not yet reached consensus on a given proportion of GDP as the goal for assistance inputs, unlike DAC countries. The standard of concessional ODA of 25% grant elements was not widely followed. International development funding from emerging donors was often unconditional, and lacking multilateral cooperation and due transparency by DAC standards. While a deficiency of institutionalization and good governance partially explains these differences, a better preference match between new assistance providers and recipients is also in play. The increasing aid from emerging countries has been a response to the fundamental limitations put upon aid governed by the DAC rules. The sustainable effects of New Development Assistance lie in its appropriate shaping of the relations between state, market, and society in recipients. The development philosophy of emerging donors may provide viable models complementary to the prescriptions offered by DAC.

The new donors, though an overall blessing for international development, bring complicated issues and challenges in their wake. The first issue is their aid governance capacity. A lack thereof will negatively affect aid effectiveness, and may cause a backlash from both donors and recipients. Emerging economies are still in need of better developed aid management institutions, more experienced aid experts and personnel, stable policy commitment, and adequate risk analysis and control. This is especially important for countries that are quickly expanding their engagement in international development assistance. The potential to learn from DAC is limited by the important differences mentioned above. A related issue is how development assistance can be coordinated in a way that maximizes the benefits to aid recipients. Due to their preference for bilateralism in their aid practices, coordination of new donors is as much needed as of developed donors in order to avoid unnecessary overlap, crowding-out, or competition, and to reduce "gaming" behavior that may end up in welfare loss or corruption.

Along with the practical issues is that of the theoretical limitedness of the widely used concept of ODA. ODA was coined in the 1960s and is not very helpful in describing or informing the engagement of new donors in international development. A new conceptual and theoretical system to reflect new practices is to be explored, notwithstanding the difficulties due to their newness, rapid evolution, and profuse variation. This raises the central theoretical mission of this book—to explore an alternative approach capable of developing positive and normative theories concerning the new practices of international development assistance.

A New Development Assistance paradigm is proposed and explored in this edited book, based on the joint research of Fudan and LSE. NDA has certain general features. It is, first, a response to the limitations of ODA, such as its insufficient supply and narrow rules; it also reflects the changing global political economy, especially the rise of emerging economies with their own geopolitical interests; it is informed by the new donors' shared colonial history and their philosophy of development and international cooperation; and it is dynamic, learning from both DAC and its own practices. In the next section we will comparatively analyze the conceptual ramifications of NDA and ODA.

New Development Assistance as a Concept and Practice

The current ODA system faces two major challenges. One is the declining share of ODA in international capital flows. In 1970, ODA flows were four times Foreign Direct Investment (FDI) inflows into developing countries. In 2015, FDI inflows in the same countries were more than four times ODA inflows. During the same period, developing countries' exports increased from 12 times to 43 times ODA.[1] Since ODA has become a less important source of capital inflows, developing countries have relied more and more on other sources of capital in pursuit of their development goals.

The second challenge is aid effectiveness. One of the most controversial issues in the field of international development is whether foreign aid actually helps developing countries grow. Although OECD donors have spent more than $3.5 trillion on development assistance since 1960, the results are disappointing. Numerous empirical studies (Doucouliagos & Paldam, 2009; Easterly, 2001; Rajan & Subramanian, 2008) have found that aid has had no significant impact on economic growth whatsoever, suggesting that the current ODA system fails to incorporate an incentives structure conducive to development.

In tandem with the declining role and disappointing performance of ODA, the rise of the emerging economies has created great potential for additional development finance and new ideas for development. An emerging economy is broadly defined as a national economy that is progressing toward being advanced but is not as advanced as developed countries. In other words, emerging economies are a subset of middle-income countries (MICs), a large and diverse group by size, population, and economic performance. This definition has given rise to various classifications of emerging economies which sometimes lump together countries at very different development stages.

Emerging economies have become the primary drivers of global economic growth, which explains why even OECD-DAC donors "are moving towards Southern development norms and modalities" (Mawdsley, 2017, p. 111). The contribution of emerging economies and developing countries to this growth has increased from 18% in the 1970s to 70% in 2016.[2] With their growing financial wealth, some emerging economies have evolved from aid recipients to aid donors. Between 2005 and 2015, emerging donors' aid increased six-fold whereas DAC members' ODA increased by only 40%. Emerging donors' share of other official flows (OOF) mainly consists of non-concessional loans (e.g., export credits), which increased from 10% to 81%. Moreover, developing countries have accounted for ever more FDI outflows, rising from 11% to 29% of global total FDI.[3] Their own development experience in the framework of South-South cooperation is yet to be fully exploited.

Emerging economies increasingly see themselves as development *partners* rather than *donors* as customarily defined. A new framework of international development cooperation is therefore called for to engage emerging economies more as contributors and less as recipients. Three main features explain the relevance of emerging economies as key players in development assistance: (1) the outstanding size of their economies, and their increasing significance in world economy; (2) regional power, demanding a stronger political voice in regional and global governance; and (3) active engagement in providing assistance to other developing countries.

Over the years since foreign aid was taken up by the West, the definition of ODA has been continuously redefined to ensure the greatest possible consistency among OECD donors. The recent Busan Forum, however, has marked a paradigm shift in predominant donor-recipient relations and a transition of power within the architecture of global development governance. Yet these changes still have not adequately addressed the changing global development landscape. The current DAC system does not put emerging donors' aid into the same category as ODA, nor does it recognize non-concessional financial flows as ODA. Estimated by the dimensions of ODA, emerging donors have yet to attain the levels of generosity achieved by OECD donors. The median ODA/GNI ratio for OECD donors is around 0.3% whereas emerging donors have a median ratio of 0.09% (Gulrajani, 2017).

Emerging donors, however, differ noticeably from traditional donors in their ways of providing assistance. First, emerging economies prefer a loosely defined South-South cooperation that stresses mutually beneficial assistance without the typical conditions imposed by traditional donors. Second, they do not have an aid strategy as clearly specified and institutionalized as that of traditional donors. Third, the development finance provided by emerging economies often combines aid, loans, and investment, and is less concessional in nature than traditional ODA.

It is important that the participation of emerging donors should be rightly measured and assessed, as this is crucial to the credibility of a framework of development cooperation that is truly international, and is a necessary step to improving effective development cooperation. We therefore propose the following principles for conceptualizing NDA.

First, the concept of NDA should be more inclusive than ODA with respect to sources of finance, categories of assistance, and degrees of "concessionality".

1. Multiple sources: NDA should include not only designated government expenditure on aid, but also private finance subsidized or guaranteed by the government.
2. Broader categories: Many emerging donors' primary contributions consist of non-monetary support in the form of technical assistance or shared development knowledge. They have also developed a number of innovative financing schemes that may not fit the current categories of ODA.
3. Less concessionality: A strict application of the DAC criteria would have disqualified many loans by emerging donors to be counted as ODA because they are less concessional. Relaxing the criterion of concessionality might not only encourage emerging donors to give more aid, but also better capture their actual contribution in development finance.

Second, given the heterogeneity of developing countries, the NDA should promulgate differential aid goals to accommodate various development priorities. The use of aid conditionality in the allocation of bilateral ODA has been characteristic, as traditional donors seek to induce the recipient to pursue certain goals and to adopt certain policies. Since the 1990s, aid conditionality has been extended from economic aspects (e.g., financial accountability and structural reforms) to political aspects (e.g., governance and institutional reforms). But these conditions have been a subject of controversy and debate. Aid conditionality indicates a best-practice model of economic development drawn from developed countries' experiences.

Developing countries, however, face greater challenges and more constraints in their own development paths. This suggests that appropriate conditions for development may vary from country to country (Rodrik, 2008). A consensus among emerging donors is that recipients' own systems rather than donor-mandated processes are the best ways to ensure integrity in the use of donor funds (Shah, 2017). A central feature of this consensus is the goal of strengthening the capacity of recipient countries to manage their own development programs and drive donor coordination at the country level, as opposed to being driven by the donors. The

NDA should try to help developing countries find their own development paths, not to impose a standard package on them without regard to the variation among them.

Third, the NDA should encourage linkages between aid, trade, and investment. DAC has discouraged the use of "tied aid" because it was regarded as a form of protectionism that undermines aid effectiveness. But there is no concrete evidence to support this claim.[4] In recent years, both traditional and emerging donors have become more willing to use aid to leverage investment in various forms of blended finance. In fact, the debate over tying versus untying aid is not just about aid effectiveness; it also reflects a controversy among the development philosophies of developed countries and emerging economies, as between growth promotion and poverty reduction.

Traditional and emerging donors have converged on several orientations that aid should be pursuing. These include the centrality of investment-driven growth for poverty reduction, the need for infrastructure development, and the imperative for broad-based cooperation to mobilize all available financial and other resources. This convergence may lead traditional and emerging donors toward a middle ground that is more inclusive and development-oriented. It is time to move beyond the traditional donor-recipient relationship toward a model where NDA is viewed more as a mutual partnership than merely an exchange of money and knowledge.

New Research Agendas and Directions

As the world changes, so must the research agendas of empiricists and theoreticians in the field adapt to new realities. The previous sections have illustrated how dramatically development assistance landscape has changed in the past decades. Non-traditional donors from the Global South such as China and India have partially broken into the "cornered market" once held by the members of the Organisation for Economic Co-operation and Development and its Development Assistance Committee (Schmaljohann & Prizzon, 2015).

At the last high-level meeting in Busan in 2011, for instance, which was oriented toward measuring development, emerging-economy donors like China became more vocal about their views (Watson, 2014). The term "aid effectiveness" was replaced by "development effectiveness" to signify that not only aid but "other policies of donors and partners [are] important if development is to make progress" (Klingebiel, 2013, p. 72). It was simultaneously decided that from the end of 2012, the Global Partnership for Effective Development Cooperation (GPDEC) would take over from OECD-DAC as the new multilateral forum for continuing the global dialogue on aid effectiveness (Abdel-Malek, 2012).

Two high-level meetings under the aegis of GPDEC have taken place so far: the first one in Mexico in 2014 and the second one in Kenya in 2016. The OECD (2016) reports that the Global Partnership has been an improvement because it has an "inclusive, multi-stakeholder character [that] enables a broad range of development stakeholders to make strong contributions to the implementation of the [UN] 2030 Agenda" (OECD, 2016, p. 3). Some analysts, while not disagreeing, also claim that emerging-economy donors in particular have "gained a more prominent place within the Partnership, reflecting the changing global context" (Mahon, 2017, p. 351). Others, however, see things much more critically, arguing that the new forum had "a congenital defect: it lacked the support of major emerging economies like China and India, which felt it did not take proper account of their views" (Lanzet, 2017, p. 17). There remain "many challenges to partnerships, both in terms of defining their form and operation, but also achieving sustainable, mutually beneficial partnerships for development" (Schaaf, 2015, p. 68).

This continuing debate has had an impact on the research agendas of scholars looking into the role of emerging-economy non-DAC donors in development assistance. Several new directions are visible in the literature, ranging from critical studies to studies of particular regions of the emerging world and their role in NDA. The following section summarizes the current research that has influenced the debate. It is not meant to be an exhaustive literature review, but only a sampling of some of the relevant literature since 2016 which the reader may find helpful.

Inclusion of the "Agency" of Emerging Countries

This important new direction in academic research into NDA has been driven by the ongoing problem of the (lack of) inclusion of emerging-market donors as "drivers of development theory and practice" (Mawdsley, 2012, p. 218). The consensus is that it is no longer possible to debate development assistance without taking account of the agency of countries like Brazil, Indonesia, or China that bring "new ideas, concerns and perspectives" into the sector (Klingebiel, 2013, p. 16; Sumner & Mallett, 2013).

Original work is being expanded and recent publications have been advancing the academic debate in this direction. Of note was the 2017 special issue of *Development Policy Review* which was dedicated to examining the diverse perspectives on NDA by emerging donors (Pickering, Davies, & Prizzon, 2017).

Mawdsley (2018) notes how conventional donors from the North seemed to be adapting to the discourse and ethos of their counterparts in the South. She calls this new direction the "Southernization" of development. It is partly based on earlier work by Alden, Morphet, and Vieira (2010, p. 8), which considered the "role of agency [by the South] and the possibility and impact of change on the prevailing international system [of the North]". She identifies three types of Southernization: firstly, donors of the North have discursively (if not necessarily operationally) reframed their ODA in terms of the ethic of a bargaining game with win-win outcomes and equilibrium. Secondly, they have reinstated economic growth as the most important metric of aid effectiveness. Thirdly and finally, they have accepted as a new normal Southern donors' insistence on counting trade and investment as legitimate aid on a par with finance conditional upon Northern social engineering agendas (Mawdsley, 2018).

The New Development Banks

Another important new direction in research is to study the new multilateral investment institutions of the South and their role in promoting development without (Northern) conditionality. Most of these works focus on China's newly minted multilateral development banks. It is a broad trend and there is room for only a few vignettes from the most recent literature.

One is research into the role of the New Development Bank (NDB) as a provider of NDA assessing the implications of the emergence of the BRICS and NDB for the global financial architecture (Qobo & Soko, 2015). Another investigation studies the NDB's important features, concluding that it is unique, owing to its "principle of equality with respect to the NDB's members' rights and obligations [which] marks a distinctive shift in the application of the tenets of global governance" (Cooper, 2017, p. 276; see also Cooper & Farooq, 2016; Westra, 2017). A third study sweeps in both the NDB and the AIIB with the aim of assessing their impact on multilateral lending (Reisen, 2015).

Many studies put forward by a variety of academics have focused on the AIIB alone. One early work by Wan (2016) merits attention for detailing the origins of the institution and the dynamics of its creation. Other more recent works inquire into the challenges to global governance posed by the AIIB (Hameiri & Jones, 2018). Particularly useful for anyone doing research into the impact of the bank on NDA is the recent work of Lichtenstein, which details its inner workings (Lichtenstein, 2018).

More recent work focuses on the role of the AIIB on specific regions of the world. Some studies analyze the impact of the AIIB on Africa, which is becoming important now that the AIIB has four full members from Africa including Egypt, Ethiopia, Madagascar, and Sudan (AIIB, 2018; Fatile, Afegbua, & Ejalonibu, 2016). Other studies look at how the AIIB has gone out of its way to attract Latin American countries to join by granting "prospective membership" to seven of them, including Brazil, Peru, Venezuela, Bolivia, Chile, Argentina, and Ecuador (AIIB, 2018). Yet not one of them has paid up their dues for lack of internal political and strategic clarity (Mendez, 2018).

Specific Country and Regional Case Studies of NDA

The third and final new research direction to be noted focuses on specific emerging donors or regions of donors from around the emerging world. As might be expected, the research agenda is dominated by studies of Asian countries, but it is refreshing that some are researching the role played by actors from other emerging regions such as Africa and Latin America.[5]

The literature on Asia is dominated by the case of China, though some accounts give the reader a broader view (Sato & Shimomura, 2013; Watson, 2014). Some works investigating Chinese practice have given great insights into the inner workings of its engagement. Warmerdam (2014) in particular makes a convincing case that Chinese NDA complements, rather than challenges, the existing system. Some investigations have an interesting take on the Chinese aid apparatus, arguing that it is "characterized by fierce and ongoing competition for influence among [domestic] actors" (Zhang & Smith, 2017, p. 2330). The findings suggest that the reality of politics in China is not exempt from the "pulling and hauling among various groups within the government" (Allison, 1971, p. 158). Finally, other studies provide a pertinent account of the long history of Beijing's involvement in development assistance and argue that the recent establishment of the China International Development

Cooperation Agency is bound to transform China's implementation of foreign aid (Kitano, 2018).

Africa seems to be "ground zero" for the NDA movement (particularly South Africa). Some researchers have looked specifically at the region's prominent role in the evolution of NDA, as the case for Johannesburg's use of foreign aid as a soft power tool in its foreign policy (Piknerová, 2014; Sidiropoulos, 2014). A more recent account identifies the significant challenges South Africa faces as an emerging donor and provider of NDA, due to its "outdated narrative and capacities ill-suited to compete with traditional donors" (O'Riordan & Stulgaitis, 2016, p. 24).

Latin America, of course, is also important with some reviewing how South American states have tried to use discourses to break out of the traditional global governance structures of development aid. They have found that this strategy almost never changes the reality (Kern & Pauselli, 2017). Two Latin American countries in particular stand out in the literature as providers of NDA. One gives an account of Chile as an emerging donor (Gutiérrez & Jaimovich, 2017). Another relevant study focuses on Brazil as a new actor on the NDA scene (Farias, 2018). More new directions seem to be emerging in our rapidly changing times which have yet to develop a profile clear enough to be characterized in any systematic way. They must therefore be left out of this account.

A Road Map of This Book

The book is divided into two parts, each having five chapters. The first part attempts to develop a framework for NDA, and the second part details the NDA practices of the several BRICS countries.

In Chap. 2, "The Western Way of Development: A Critical Review", Chris Alden, Dan Large, and Alvaro Mendez survey the evolution of the Western way of development and its policies, and analyze its transformations in the way donors approach development and foreign aid, with special reference to the OECD-DAC rules. Their review of the recent changes to the global political economy provides the background to understanding the trajectory of the evolving ideas and practices of the West's development policy. This chapter expounds the decline of the idea of aid that has been replaced by the more constructive and mutually beneficial concept of cooperation.

In Chap. 3, "The Emergence of New Development Assistance: Conceptual and Operational Frameworks", Yu Zheng identifies 13 emerging economies that have been playing a key role in transforming the development cooperation agenda. He proposes three principles for conceptualizing and measuring NDA, and then summarizes the key differences between NDA and ODA, including motivation, intercountry relationships, patterns, distribution channels, and geographical and sectoral allocation.

Jianzhi Zhao and Zhe Ouyang, in Chap. 4, "The Aid Management Systems in BRICS Countries", review the aid management systems of Brazil, India, China, and South Africa. By analyzing official documents, government declarations, academic publications, and online databases of the four countries, they compare the characteristics of their aid management systems, evolution, as well as merits and drawbacks.

In Chap. 5, "Two Approaches to Institutionalizing the New Development Assistance: A Comparative Analysis of the Operational Institutions of NDB and AIIB", Jiejin Zhu analyzes why the New Development Bank and the Asian Infrastructure Investment Bank have adopted different models of development assistance. He argues that NDB has taken up a borrowing country-oriented operational modality, while AIIB's operational modality is still donor country-oriented. This chapter makes use of the historical institutionalism perspective to explain these structural differences.

In Chap. 6, "Is Development Assistance Getting Better Due to the Widening Role of Emerging Economies?", Neil Renwick and Jing Gu examine the impact and implications of the increasingly central role played by emerging economies (EEs) in international development assistance. This chapter considers their evolving relationships with the existing system and assesses the character and quality of value-added that the EEs have contributed to the system. The authors argue that while there is potential for friction in the process of change, the transition will be more of a "peaceful rise".

Rogerio F. Pinto, in Chap. 7, "International Development Assistance: A Case Study of Brazil", provides a country report of the development assistance practices of Brazil. Rogerio examines the evolution of Brazil's international development assistance, its current trends, and the role of its lead agency, the ABC (*Agencia Brasileira de Cooperação*). This chapter highlights some comparative advantages and weaknesses of the Brazilian system, and argues that the ideal way to chart a path going forward for an entity such as ABC is to base it on the results of an evaluative effort.

Elena Dobrolyubova, in Chap. 8, "Russia's Contribution to International Development Assistance", identifies Russia's dramatic role change from a borrower to a donor in the past two decades. The author argues that Russia has been switching from “traditional” multilateral mechanisms to novel South-South international development instruments, and has steadily increased bilateral assistance as a share of its international development assistance. It is believed that the effectiveness of Russia’s contribution will largely depend on improving interagency coordination and managing capacities.

In Chap. 9, “India as an Emerging Donor: Political and Economic Determinants”, Eswaran Sridharan describes and analyzes the emerging Indian development cooperation program. Situating the assistance program in the larger context of India’s foreign policy and India’s trade and investment relationships, the chapter focuses on the quantity, direction, modalities, and institutions of Indian development assistance. The author concludes that the Indian development cooperation program in Asia is largely political and security-motivated, while the emerging shift in focus to Africa is intended for long-term relationship building.

In Chap. 10, “Chinese Foreign Aid and Financing: An Example of New Development Assistance?”, Denghua Zhang examines whether and how Chinese aid differs from traditional donors’ assistance. This chapter deconstructs Chinese aid programs and examines seven main aspects, including amount, destinations, patterns, motivations, organizations, impact, and future directions of Chinese aid. The author argues that Chinese foreign aid has demonstrated distinctive features that could enrich the category of NDA.

In Chap. 11, “South African Development Assistance in Africa”, Chris Tapscott examines the NDA practices of South Africa. South Africa, by embracing the ideals of Pan-Africanism, has sought to distance itself from traditional modes of development assistance by positioning itself as a development partner rather than as an aid donor. Support is provided in response to requests for assistance and without any conditions attached. South Africa provides a range of direct and indirect forms of assistance not typically classified as aid. The author argues that South Africa’s aid policy remains inchoate and much of its assistance is of an ad hoc nature.

Notes

1. Estimated based on information from World Development Indicators.
2. International Monetary Fund, World Economic Outlook, April 2017: Gaining Momentum? 2017: 67.

3. Estimated based by OECD DAC Statistics. http://stats.oecd.org.
4. A widely cited paper published by the Development Centre of OECD estimates that tied aid raises the direct cost of products by 15% to 30% on average, but the finding was tentative, and no specific source was provided.
5. For other emerging donor regions such as the Middle East, see: ODI (2017).

References

Abdel-Malek, T. (2012). The Global Partnership for Effective Development Cooperation. *Development and Cooperation: D+C, 39*(9).

AIIB. (2018). *Members and Prospective Members of the Bank.* Retrieved from https://www.aiib.org/en/about-aiib/governance/members-of-bank/index.html

Alden, C., Morphet, S., & Vieira, M. (2010). *The South in World Politics.* Basingstoke: Springer.

Allison, G. T. (1971). *Essence of Decision: Explaining the Cuban Missile Crisis.* Boston, MA: Little, Brown and Company.

Cooper, A. F. (2017). The BRICS' New Development Bank: Shifting from Material Leverage to Innovative Capacity. *Global Policy, 8*(3), 275–284.

Cooper, A. F., & Farooq, A. B. (2016). The Role of China and India in the G20 and BRICS: Commonalities or Competitive Behaviour? *Journal of Current Chinese Affairs, 45*(3), 73–106.

Doucouliagos, H., & Paldam, M. (2009). The Aid Effectiveness Literature: The Sad Results of 40 Years of Research. *Journal of Economic Surveys, 23*(3), 433–461.

Easterly, W. (2001). *The Elusive Quest for Growth: Economists' Adventures and Misadventures in the Tropics.* Cambridge: MIT Press.

Farias, D. B. L. (2018). *Aid and Technical Cooperation as a Foreign Policy Tool for Emerging Donors: The Case of Brazil.* Abingdon, UK: Routledge.

Fatile, J., Afegbua, I., & Ejalonibu, G. (2016). New Global Financial Order and Promotion of Asian Infrastructural Investment Bank (AIIB): Opportunities and Challenges for Africa. *Africa's Public Service Delivery & Performance Review, 4*(1), 118.

Gulrajani, N. (2017, August 4). *The Rise of New Foreign Aid Donors: Why Does It Matter?* [Web Log Post]. Retrieved from http://www.devpolicy.org/rise-new-foreign-aid-donors-matter-20170804/

Gutiérrez, A., & Jaimovich, D. (2017). A New Player in the International Development Community? Chile as an Emerging Donor. *Development Policy Review, 35*(6), 839–858.

Hameiri, S., & Jones, L. (2018). China Challenges Global Governance? Chinese International Development Finance and the AIIB. *International Affairs, 94*(3), 573–593.

Kern, A., & Pauselli, G. (2017). South–South Cooperation and the Governance of Development Aid in South America. In P. Riggirozzi & C. Wylde (Eds.), *Handbook of South American Governance* (Vol. 191). Abingdon, UK: Routledge.

Kitano, N. (2018). China's Foreign Aid: Entering a New Stage. *Asia-Pacific Review, 25*(1), 90 111.

Klingebiel, S. (2013). *Development Cooperation: Challenges of the New Aid Architecture.* Basingstoke: Palgrave Pivot.

Lanzet, P. (2017, February). Aid Effectiveness Deserves More Attention. *Development and Cooperation: D+C, 2.*

Lichtenstein, N. (2018). *A Comparative Guide to the Asian Infrastructure Investment Bank.* Oxford University Press.

Mahon, R. (2017). Gendering Development: The OECD's Development Assistance Committee, 1981–2000. In M. Leimgruber & M. Schmelzer (Eds.), *The OECD and the International Political Economy Since 1948.* Cham, Switzerland: Springer.

Mawdsley, E. (2012). *From Recipients to Donors: Emerging Powers and the Changing Development Landscape.* London: Zed Books.

Mawdsley, E. (2017). Development Geography 1: Cooperation, Competition and Convergence Between "North" and "South". *Progress in Human Geography, 41*(1), 108–117.

Mawdsley, E. (2018). The 'Southernisation' of Development? *Asia Pacific Viewpoint, 59*(2), 173–185.

Mendez, A. (2018, April 27). *The Asian Infrastructure Investment Bank Comes Knocking on Latin America's Door: Is Anyone Home?* [Web Blog Post]. Retrieved from http://blogs.lse.ac.uk/latamcaribbean/2018/04/27/the-asian-infrastructure-investment-bank-comes-knocking-on-latin-americas-door-is-anyone-home/

O'Riordan, A., & Stulgaitis, M. (2016). South Africa as a Donor and Southern Africa: The Sustainable Development Goals (SDGs), Emerging Foreign Policy and Development Themes in the Post-Cotonou Context. *Transformation: Critical Perspectives on Southern Africa, 92*(1), 84–110.

ODI. (2017). *Gulf Country Donorship: Opportunities and Challenges for International Cooperation.* Retrieved from https://www.odi.org/sites/odi.org.uk/files/resource-documents/11390.pdf

OECD. (2016). *Making Development Co-operation More Effective: 2016 Progress Report.* Paris: OECD Publishing. Retrieved from http://www.undp.org/content/dam/undp/library/development-impact/%2D%2D2016%20progress%20report%2D%2DFinal%20(e-book).pdf

OECD. (2018). *Gross Domestic Product (GDP)* (Indicator). Retrieved December 18, 2018, from https://doi.org/10.1787/dc2f7aec-en

Pickering, J., Davies, R., & Prizzon, A. (2017). Development Co-operation: New Perspectives from Developing Countries – Introduction for Special Issue of Development Policy Review. *Development Policy Review, 35*(S1), O1–O9.

Piknerová, L. (2014). The Republic of South Africa: An Emerging Donor. *Mezinárodní Vztahy, 49*(1), 59–82.

Qobo, M., & Soko, M. (2015). The Rise of Emerging Powers in the Global Development Finance Architecture: The Case of the BRICS and the New Development Bank. *South African Journal of International Affairs, 22*(3), 277–288.

Rajan, R. G., & Subramanian, A. (2008). Aid and Growth: What Does the Cross-Country Evidence Really Show? *The Review of Economics and Statistics, 90*(4), 643–665.

Ramo, J. C. (2004). *The Beijing Consensus*. Retrieved from Foreign Policy Centre Website: https://fpc.org.uk/wp-content/uploads/2006/09/244.pdf

Reisen, H. (2015). Will the AIIB and the NDB Help Reform Multilateral Development Banking? *Global Policy, 6*(3), 297–304.

Rodrik, D. (2008). Second-Best Institutions. *American Economic Review: Papers & Proceedings, 98*(2), 100–104.

Sato, J., & Shimomura, Y. (Eds.). (2013). *The Rise of Asian Donors: Japan's Impact on the Evolution of Emerging Donors*. Abingdon, UK: Routledge.

Schaaf, R. (2015). The Rhetoric and Reality of Partnerships for International Development. *Geography Compass, 9*(2), 68–80.

Schmaljohann, M., & Prizzon, A. (2015). Age of Choice: How Partner Countries Are Managing the New Development Assistance Landscape—The Cases of Fiji, Papua New Guinea, Timor Leste and Vanuatu. *Asia & the Pacific Policy Studies, 2*(3), 643–651.

Shah, A. (2017). *Development Assistance and Conditionality: Challenges in Design and Options for More Effective Assistance* [Background Paper]. Paris: OECD Headquarters.

Sidiropoulos, E. (2014). South Africa's Emerging Soft Power. *Current History, 113*(763), 197–202.

Sumner, A., & Mallett, R. (2013). *The Future of Foreign Aid: Development Cooperation and the New Geography of Global Poverty*. Basingstoke: Palgrave Pivot.

Wan, M. (2016). *The Asian Infrastructure Investment Bank: The Construction of Power and the Struggle for the East Asian International Order*. New York: Palgrave Macmillan.

Warmerdam, W. (2014). Beyond the Debates of Which Is Best: Investigating the Complementarity of Chinese and Western Aid, and Possible Lessons from China's Development. *Fudan Journal of the Humanities and Social Sciences, 7*(1), 77–117.

Watson, I. (2014). *Foreign Aid and Emerging Powers: Asian Perspectives on Official Development Assistance*. Abingdon, UK: Routledge.

Westra, R. (Ed.). (2017). *The Political Economy of Emerging Markets: Varieties of BRICS in the Age of Global Crises and Austerity*. Abingdon, UK: Routledge.

Zhang, D., & Smith, G. (2017). China's Foreign Aid System: Structure, Agencies, and Identities. *Third World Quarterly, 38*(10), 2330–2346.

CHAPTER 2

The Western Way of Development: A Critical Review

Chris Alden, Daniel Large, and Alvaro Mendez

Introduction

With the rise of the emerging powers of the South as providers of and participants in development assistance, the landscape of what is conventionally understood to be development is changing. The dominant Western paradigm arose in the context of late colonialism and the Cold War, and reached its zenith with the triumphalism of the neo-liberal consensus. Now, however, the Western way is confronted with challenges on multiple fronts. South-South cooperation, ranging from technical assistance and knowledge exchange to more commercial practices like "tied aid", offers a vision of development based on the recognized success and experiences of countries like China (Fornes & Mendez, 2018). Coupled to this vision are new institutional sources of development finance like the

C. Alden • A. Mendez (✉)
London School of Economics, London, UK
e-mail: j.c.alden@lse.ac.uk; a.mendez@lse.ac.uk

D. Large
Central European University, Budapest, Hungary
e-mail: larged@spp.ceu.edu

Y. Jing et al. (eds.), *New Development Assistance*, Governing China in the 21st Century,
https://doi.org/10.1007/978-981-13-7232-2_2

New Development Bank (NDB) and the Asian Infrastructure Investment Bank (AIIB), which are to provide alternatives to established Western-dominated sources (Reisen, 2015).

What is generally never suspected (let alone ever appreciated) is how much the Western way of development has itself evolved under the "selection pressures" of world politics. Far from any adherence to a grand strategy, as contemporary debates on "neo-liberalism" or the "Washington consensus" tacitly assume, Western development policy has undergone serial changes of position and practice over the last 70 years (Wade, 2015). Understanding the broad trends and drivers of change in the West's conception of development, especially those which have harmonized donor practices, will illumine which ideas and interests have shaped development policy across the West and why. International organizations like the Organization for Economic Co-operation and Development's Development Assistance Committee (OECD-DAC) turn out to have wielded formative influence. This should give pause for reflection on the twin assumptions of ideological distance and practical divergence between OECD-DAC and non-DAC providers which too often cloud analysis of the conventional approach to development.

This chapter will survey the evolution, in context, of the Western way of development and its variable policies, critically engaging with the signature transformations in donor approaches, with special reference to the OECD-DAC. The first section that follows offers a short history of the evolution of Western development aid; the second, a discussion of the differing approaches of OECD-DAC versus non-DAC providers. Third, and finally, it reflects on the slow death of the very idea of aid.

A Short History of Western Development Aid

Scientific inquiry into the origins of the wealth of nations began in earnest with the Enlightenment, but reached a turning point in the twentieth century with its massive political as well as economic upheavals. State-led domestic development propelled the industrialisation of countries like Germany but it was not until the advent of the Soviet Union and its Five Year Planning cycles aimed at producing rapid development that scientific approaches to development gained widespread acceptance. Turkey and Japan drew from these examples to produce their own development successes while, following World War 1, European colonial administrations increasingly focused on delivering sectoral improvements to societies under their suzreignity, a process that intensified under late colonialism (Cooper

2014). By most accounts the idea of development planning that was both centralized and scientific did not take hold in Washington until the crisis of the Great Depression and World War II (Ekbladh 2010). This is the material context that prompted US President Franklin Roosevelt to proclaim his Four Freedoms—of speech, of worship, from want, from fear—as defining what might be called the first universal development goals (Engel, 2016). In the darkest days of the War, the Allies issued the Atlantic Charter, which laid out their ideal of the post-War order: no territorial aggrandizement; no border changes against the will of peoples; political self-determination; restoration of self-government to those deprived of it; the abolition of trade barriers; global cooperation to secure better economic and social conditions for all; freedom from terror and hunger; abandonment of the use of force and the disarmament of aggressor nations (Nolan, 1993). It is notable that all peoples were to be included in these collective and individual freedoms, which undermined European colonialism and rang in a consensus against beggar-thy-neighbour protectionism. Also notable is the earnestness respecting material advancement and social security, which was not necessarily compatible with the classical exemption of private property from the requisition of the state. This declaration formed the kernel of the Western way of development. In the international conferences at Bretton Woods and Dumbarton Oaks, the institutional framework for implementing the goals of peace and development were forged—a political suite consisting of the United Nations, the Security Council and the Economic and Social Council above all, and a financial suite consisting of the International Monetary Fund (IMF) and the World Bank (originally the International Bank for Reconstruction and Development, or IBRD) (Schild, Woods, & Oaks, 1995).

The immediate post-War conception of "development" was economic recovery and reconstruction under the Marshall Plan in Europe and the parallel Dodge Line in Japan: to build a non-militarist Germany and Japan, and to forestall Communist revolutions in the rest of (Western) Europe (McCormick, 1995). As Europe's and Japan's recoveries became established, the parallel challenges of the decolonization of the European empires and rising competition for influence between the US and the Soviet Union came to a head. The US Congress enacted the Agency for International Development (USAID) in 1955; originally called the International Cooperation Administration (ICA), it was built on earlier programmes that had delivered agricultural surpluses and famine relief abroad.[1]

It was in this time frame that a host of new international institutions were set up to coordinate the development process, and in which the IBRD was rebranded as a "World Bank" catering for the newly independent countries and for other developing regions. By 1961 the West had evolved the OECD out of the Organisation for European Economic Co-operation (OEEC), the body which had managed the Marshall Plan, and inside that the DAC was erected to normalize and coordinate the West's development aid to current and former colonies (Leimgruber & Schmelzer, 2017).

The conceptual framework of development was reconceived by American social scientists as "modernization", understood as a universal "singular path of progressive change" to help guide US economic aid and military intervention in post-colonial regions (Gilman, 2003). As articulated by US President John F. Kennedy's Special Assistant for National Security Affairs, Walt Rostow, modernization has evolved over five stages: (1) Traditional Society: subsistence and primary production; (2) Pre-conditions to Take-off: external demand for raw materials spurs change; (3) Take-off: urbanization, industrialization, technology; (4) Drive to Maturity: industrial base diversified via venture capital; (5) Age of Mass Consumption: widespread consumption of high-value consumer goods (Rostow, 1960). Wide-ranging regional programmes based on this paradigm were formed under Kennedy and his successors, most notably the Alliance for Progress in Latin America and bilateral aid to countries in Southeast Asia in the 1960s and onwards (Taffet, 2007).

Given that ascendancy in these regions was being contested by Soviet- and (increasingly) Chinese-backed "nationalist" movements or militant insurgencies, the US and its Western allies stepped up their own assistance to the counter-insurgency level (Freedman, 2000). The oil crisis of the 1970s, coupled with the rise and the fall of commodity cartels in developing markets, compounded developing-country indebtedness, calling for the insertion of the Structural Adjustment Programmes (SAPs) of the IMF (El-Ojeili & Hayden, 2006). The crisis provided an opportunity for East Asian economies to develop rapidly, beginning in the 1980s, through export-oriented manufacturing and targeted access to US and Japanese markets. This introduced a new "growth-orientation" model (Yeung, 2010). The fall of the Berlin Wall in 1989 and the subsequent collapse of the Soviet Union ushered in an era of triumphalism in Western development circles. An uncritical celebration of the efficacy of market democracy to deliver development came to dominate the Western aid landscape. This neo-liberal "Washington Consensus" was reflected in the policies proceeding out of the OECD-DAC countries, focussed broadly on growth-oriented approaches at the expense of social concerns (Mahon, 2017).

A Clash of Institutionalizations: OECD-DAC and Non-DAC Approaches

How is it, then, that the aid industry has become markedly less significant as economic lifeblood to all but a small but persistent cluster of mostly African states? Even in Africa, aid as fallen from 70% of all financial transfers in the 1970s to less than 30% today. Where once Western institutions like the IMF and World Bank, US, European and Japanese aid agencies, and an army of international non-governmental organizations (INGOs) commanded the economic heights of the African continent—buttressed by a network of political and military ties dating back to the colonial period—today entry by China, India, Brazil, South Korea and the like into what used to be the West's exclusive domain has seemingly driven a wedge into that relationship. The newcomers recognized the investment opportunities created by the economic ruptures caused by the structural adjustment programmes of the 1980s and 1990s, with reference to the privatization of state assets in particular (Alden & Sidiropoulos, 2012). The self-styled development partners of the South proved singularly unconcerned with reshaping the domestic norms of African governance, forging, instead, new trade ties and gaining market share in sectors once exclusively Western preserves. It was Chinese relations with war-torn Sudan and Angola, after its entry into the energy sector in those countries, which drew the first Western media attention and criticism; in the meantime, India, Brazil, South Korea, Malaysia and other emerging powers, big and small, were flying under the radar into the same ethically problematic situation. All of them combined prompt allocations of "no conditionalities" finance targeted to Africa's long-neglected infrastructure with a push to acquire petroleum equity.[2] Refreshingly free of the hypocrisies of Western aid, these interest-based forms of engagement, formally predicated on mutually beneficial win-win processes and outcomes, have been greeted with enthusiasm by African leaders because of their direct, results-oriented approach to tackling acute problems in African economies. The consequent disruption of the hegemony of Western multilateral institutions, government aid agencies and non-governmental cohorts, whose capacity to dictate the terms of aid seemed to march in tandem with the relative deterioration of local conditions, has raised concern in Western capitals over the loss of power to shape the political economy of African development.

A signal example of this evolution was the Fourth High Level Forum on Aid Effectiveness held in Busan in 2011, where the senior guidance of the Paris Declaration on Aid Effectiveness was put at stake. The Paris Declaration had been a framework for official development assistance (ODA) by OECD donors, consisting of five principles or "partnership commitments" negotiated in 2005 and elaborated at a follow-up meeting in Accra, Ghana in 2008.[3] The principles had been designed to help achieve the United Nations Millennium Development Goals (MDGs), eight targets agreed in 2000[4] to reduce underdevelopment on points like income and health, through coordinating donor and recipient countries in a universal collective effort. The MDGs focussed primarily on alleviating the conditions of the poorest and most vulnerable, leaving little room for a more muscular priority of enhancing the productive capacity of poverty-stricken countries. J. Brian Atwood (2012), the former head of USAID, has admitted that the Paris Declaration was overly donor driven, and subsequent meetings modified everything from terminology to a commitment to transfer aid directly to developing countries' ministries of finance (despite the occasions for corruption which this might enable).

It should be noted that the emerging powers were signatories of the Paris Declaration, too, but as aid recipients not bound by its principles (OECD, 2005). For decades they have been economically involved on their own account with other developing countries under the rubric of South-South cooperation. Agreements for technical assistance and exchange of personnel, financing and construction of infrastructure projects, and support for what were clearly commercial activities, all counted as the forms of South-South cooperation that had enticed the emerging powers, particularly China, into Africa. These activities were ignored by Western donors, that is, until it became clear in the last decade, from the volume of financial transfers and Africans' revealed preference for commerce, that the emerging powers' approach was on a path to displace Western-led initiatives. Now it becomes clear how different the approaches are, and why African governments prefer the Chinese.

> China's approach to infrastructure abroad mirrors its approach at home. Projects are evaluated more on their impact than on the specific viability of the project in question. The Chinese tend to overvalue the beneficial economic spillover effects of infrastructure projects, while undervaluing the potential harms [*sc.* negative externalities], whether economic, social, or environmental. The Western approach, by contrast, is more transactional and

> focuses on painstaking due diligence concerning the economic, social, and environmental consequences of a given project. These safeguards are in the interests of ordinary people in developing countries. But Western institutions have become so risk averse that the cost and time to implement such projects have skyrocketed. Western governments and the multilateral institutions over which they exert influence, such as the World Bank, must consider making their safeguarding process more flexible if they are not to leave the field open to Chinese monopoly. (Bataineh, Bennon, & Fukuyama, 2018, para. 3)

Reacting to the unexpected challenge, Western-led organizations resorted to deploying strategies of collaboration and convergence in hopes of enmeshing the emerging powers in their established aid practices. For instance, at a UN-sponsored high-level meeting in September 2008, emerging powers were urged to "support current international efforts to harmonize and coordinate donor policies, to make their aid more effective" (Mutume, 2008, p. 6). This strategy lay behind the Memorandum of Understanding of the World Bank with China Exim Bank for joint project funding in three African countries: Ghana, Uganda and Mozambique (World Bank, 2007). The two institutions, however, were unable to settle on common terms and now, if anything, it is China which may be "socialising" the World Bank to acquiesce in Chinese ways of development (Chin, 2012). Another expression of the collaborative strategy was the Memorandum of Understanding of February 2011 between Brasilia and Washington allowing for "peer learning" between the Agencia Brasileira de Cooperação (ABC) and USAID, including secondment of personnel and joint projects in Africa and Latin America (MFAN, 2011). Washington provided US$2 million towards the partnership, funding ABC programmes in agricultural production and nutrition in Mozambique, while Brazil's ABC led cooperation efforts in the agricultural sector, helping USAID in Honduras (USAID, 2015, 2016).

Convergence is the strategy pursued most persistently by the European Union, which probed with its Development Directorate how it might draw China into the established ODA framework, embedding it within the broader Strategic Partnership between the EU and China. Much time and resources were expended on this initiative to engage the Chinese and the Africans in workshops, conferences and related initiatives so as to convince Beijing to bring its financing and investment policies towards Africa in line with OECD standards. The China-DAC Study Group report (2011), though voluminous, makes for thin reading on matters of practical convergence. Initiatives to join up European technical expertise and local knowledge of the Africa continent with Chinese finance—echoing French President Giscard D'Estaing's trilateral dialogue between France, Africa and the newly wealthy Arab states in the late 1970s—produced no concrete outcomes beyond exhibiting Africans' fears that the prospective convergence would turn into a "new Berlin conference", something to be resisted from their perspective. The only thing demonstrated was the weaknesses (if not indeed the delusionality) of European efforts at socialization, a point underscored at the time by the dismissive remarks of Chinese officials involved in the process (Fox & Godement, 2009).

This gambit of the OECD-DAC countries was received with some bemusement in Beijing, Delhi and Brasilia. These emerging powers nonetheless did deign to participate where they could identify tangible gains from collaborating (or appearing to collaborate) with Western donors—whether to allay their sensitivities or for compelling technical reasons or shared interests. This project-based collaboration, called "trilateral cooperation", was not official aid and sat conveniently outside its strictures. But the emerging powers dismissed out of hand the normative framework insinuated by the West that their cumulative experience in aid to Africa imbued their approach and its putative efficiencies of practice with a greater claim to moral authority and to emulation by post-colonial donors (Mawdsley, 2012). In fact, for the latter, the broad range of financial transfers and project activities, which allows tied aid, barter swaps, technical assistance and conventional investment to qualify, so long as it is deemed to be of "mutual interest" to the parties involved—which they cheerfully dub South-South cooperation—had become a crucial element of their strategy to obtain a position in Africa's rich resource sector, and became an incentive for conserving independence of action. By their robust involvement in Africa, the emerging powers have demonstrated that they can achieve "real existing development" (to paraphrase an old Soviet slogan aimed at idealized portrayals of socialism), often by ignoring the well-worn advice of Western experts on such questions as the role of the state; and inspiring an African search for a new model of development (Breslin, 2011). This has come at a crucial time for development strategy, when the discourses and policies promoted by traditional donors are being challenged as never before.

The Slow Death of the Idea of "AID"

In 2010 over US$128.7 billion was transferred worldwide by traditional OECD-DAC donors, an increase of US$119 billion over the previous year. During the same period, the leading non-DAC donors were estimated to have spent US$12 billion and private foundations US$22 billion (OneWorld, 2012). The World Bank increased its assistance in the same year, lending US$11.4 billion to build hundreds of kilometres of roads and energy projects; to establish health clinics across the African continent; and to support the budgets of several African countries (World Bank, 2010). Britain alone in 2010 provided US$1.8 billion in bilateral and multilateral aid, much of it going to fragile states, many of these in Africa (DfID, 2010). In a continent seemingly awash in ODA it is difficult to accept that the very idea of aid has been under assault for some time. Yet amongst donors and NGOs, the claim of hope that is a feature of all programmes proffering means of improving life is pockmarked with failure, recalibration and further disappointment. More troubling, the recipients themselves have gone public with scathing critiques of development aid that reflect their own experience, a far cry from the cautious optimism and support they expressed at the Gleneagles G8 Summit in 2005, where the industrialized countries pledged to double their aid and Africans agreed to instil measures for better governance (BBC, 2005). The consensus on African development reached by OECD and African government at Gleneagles, and further elaborated in the Paris Declaration that same year, now seems a distant memory.

It is no big surprise that aid should come under such withering criticism from its own beneficiaries. Betraying its missionary roots, the development industry has devoted over 60 years to a drive to exorcize Africans of various pathologies: tribalism, socialism, corruption, gender inequality inter alia—and set them on the road to a Western form of modernity. Yet despite often enthusiastic support for this strategy from major African leaders like Nkrumah, it is nowadays routinely slammed as "Euro-centric" (Williams & Young, 2013). The subsequent flurry of policy jeremiads signals imminent shifts in aid fashion of the kind that have supervened in the sector, from the dawn of "community development" in the mid-1950s and its deployment in an effort to win hearts and minds in rural populations to a robotic application of "rigorous" methods of "aid effectiveness" in recent years. In the manner of Old Testament prophets, senior practitioners periodically castigate this approach or that multilateral institution—from Michel Camdessus, former head of the IMF, on the abject failure of structural adjustment programmes, to Robert Wade, former head of the World Bank's East Asia department, on that organization's deliberate scripting-out of the state in its official account of the *East Asian Miracle*, to Joseph Stiglitz, former chief economist of the World Bank, on the misconduct of the IMF (Stiglitz, 2002; Wade, 1996).

NGOs, wary of the tendency, opaqueness and ineffectiveness of Western aid, have also joined in the offensive (Glennie, 2008). Even the Millennium Development Goals have not been spared, one architect of which declaring that the transformations they require "are seldom triggered by outsiders or caused by technical advice, let alone by loans and grants from overseas" (Vandemoortele, 2011, p. 2). A sure sign of the aid sector's loss of faith in its own shibboleths, and the concomitant fear that the austerity it has imposed on its taxpaying public will foment resistance to budgetary increases of aid, is the frenzy for technical reviews that would discover or invent more exacting ways of measuring those perennial intangibles like influence and impact.

The dependence of OECD-DAC donors on their legislatures and ultimately the taxpaying public to support their policies is an oft-forgotten aspect of policy debates on aid. Selling aid to domestic constituencies in Western democracies has always been a challenge, one that most political leaders have managed in ways not dissimilar to the mobilization of public support for the Cold War. The Manichean "othering" of Communists was necessary to secure public support for permanently high levels of defence expenditure had its parallel in the politics of foreign aid. Aid recipients were portrayed as helpless (if not—*sotto voce*—hopeless) victims of a fatal cycle of poverty, violence, natural disaster and the Past in its various forms (colonialism, tribalism, socialism). The growing discontent with aid as an instrument of national interest has led some in the aid community on a futile search for perfect altruism that reaches its extreme in non-governmental organizations' call for the renunciation of all self-interest on the part of donors, and the sacralization of the "vulnerable" as the central rationale for aid provision (Long, 2001).

This derivativeness from the fixation on "victims" did mobilize certain domestic constituencies to throw their support behind certain aid programmes, but also had the perhaps unintended consequence of reinforcing an image of Africa as a space of dysfunctional governments incapable of ministering to their own people. Running counter to this view, reflecting another facet of developed countries' domestic debate, were the neoliberals, who argued for "trade not aid" as the better route to development and claimed—based on the East Asian experience—that aid, by distorting incentives, had actually set back African enterprise. In sum, the foundations of support for aid by Western taxpaying publics have been eroding for a long time (Watson, 2014).

The rise of a more mercantilist approach from the industrializing countries of the South, with their unabashed offer of tied aid, has forced a revolution in thinking about aid by developed donors, especially the smaller ones like the Dutch, who had prided themselves on their commitment to bridging the gap between rich and poor. As one Dutch critic notes,

> In spite of a constant spate of feel-good stories intended to demonstrate that the [Dutch] money donated was used efficiently as well as effectively, the once-successful lobby of aid protagonists gradually lost ground and came to face a swelling tide of skepticism. Arguing from the donor perspective, critics at home could quote sources and voices in receiving countries denying the benign impact of Dutch largesse. And the spectacle is there for all to see: several countries that have been well endowed have not made much progress (Suriname, some African states), while other countries that received less or nothing at all (in particular China but also India which, under the BJP government decided to foreclose Dutch funding) have leapt ahead. (Breman, 2011, pp. 833–834)

Developing countries' very successes in reducing poverty have impelled Dutch politicians to refocus on relative deprivation in their own country, where one child in ten grows up poor (Breman, 2011). The resulting vigorous embrace of nationalism and enterprise has stripped away all but the thinnest veneer on the transformative discourse of the recent past.[5] The UK, too, has undergone partial refocus, although there remains a core consensus between the parties to keep aid expenditures at their record levels for the time being, whilst venturing to include a role for British commercial interests. The tabloid press's nose for weakness has yielded *exposés* of the scandal of UK aid for competitive emerging markets like China and India, which is already spilling over into the prestige media: a sure sign that the consensus will erode further in the future (Gray, 2011).

Across the Atlantic, the US aid sector was already suffering decline after the Cold War ended, the technical expertise of USAID being hollowed out in all but a few departments and superseded by "beltway bandit" subcontractors. The tawdriness of US Congressional politics produced annual cuts to the aid budget, sparing only those programmes patronized by powerful Congressmen, and confining development assistance to a limited domain (e.g. health). The rise of private foundations, the Gates Foundation chief among them, as self-styled catalysts and innovators in the development aid business has also been contributing to the refocus away from the social sector (with the notable exception of HIV-AIDS) and towards the economies of developing countries.

The changing discourse on aid amongst Western policy practitioners and publics has been echoed by some African publicists, the loudest, doughtiest of whom is Dambisa Moyo, whose headline-grabbing book *Dead Aid* seemed to draw a line under the debate. She tells us in no uncertain terms that "aid *is* the problem" (Moyo, 2010, p. 47). Yash Tandon's tome *Ending Aid Dependence* calls aid, in effect, war by other means (Tandon, 2008)! Rwandan President Paul Kagame's celebrated refusal of aid—despite Rwanda's critical dependency on donor assistance for budgetary support—chimes with the recipients' chorus of protest crying aid down. Kagame pointedly stated in a 2009 article in the *Financial Times*:

> Unfortunately, it seems that many still believe they can solve the problems of the poor with sentimentality and promises of massive infusions of aid, which often do not materialise ... Why should anyone in Rwanda feel comfortable that taxpayers in other countries are contributing money for our well-being or development? (Kagame, 2009, para. 1, 6)

These arresting sentences have contributed to the growing bewilderment of Western aid workers, as troubling as the rapid embrace of the Chinese by Africa and the concomitant search for a new development model. As a result, the effectiveness of aid itself has been challenged, a process that perhaps reaching its crescendo at the 2011 Fourth High Level Forum on Aid Effectiveness held in Busan, Korea, which yielded the Global Partnership for Effective Development. Since then, the shop talk of the development industry has been of a "post-aid world" and the redux of development as modernization at the instance of the South, with industrial-based growth being recentred back to the heart of development (Mawdsley, Savage, & Kim, 2014).

Risk, Modernity and Development

Development practitioners working to deliver humanitarian aid to conflict zones began to wrestle publicly in the 1990s with some inconvenient truths about their practice (De Waal, 1997; Macrae & Zwi, 1994; The Sphere Project, 2004). After its emancipation from the Cold War, development humanitarianism ambitiously aspired to redefine sovereignty to be conditional and to justify armed intervention on human rights grounds, yet this was dogged by controversy over such cardinal NGO operating tenets as neutrality. First, they came to realize that they were perceived by recipient communities in cruder terms than their altruistic self-image, as a significant source of wealth and power. Recipients took protestations of neutrality as disingenuous at best. Worse still, their interventions, how be it carefully weighed, were being observed to cause as many problems as they solved. Some of the unintended consequences were appalling, such as sustaining a genocidal militia in the heart of a refugee camp in central Africa. The double-bind is that "giving no assistance would also have an impact—often negative [as one report plaintively noted]" (Collaborate Learning Projects, 2004, p. 1). One prescriptive policy corrective to the various challenges of aid that captured attention was the injunction "Do no harm" (Anderson, 1999). The ICRC in a seminal 2003 document on the topic declared:

> Although aid can become part of the dynamics of the conflict and may even prolong it, humanitarian organizations must strive to "do no harm" or to minimize the harm they may be inadvertently doing simply by being present and providing assistance. (UNICEF, 2003, para. 11)

Before long, the fumigant of caution began to seep through other niches of the aid sector, especially those operating in the fragile post-conflict context where economic activity is critical to conserving any momentum away from violence (UNDP, 2008). Even nutritional programmes serving newborns were not immune: one policy maker from USAID invented a "nutritional impact assessment tool" as "a way for organizations designing or reviewing agricultural programs to mitigate any risks or potential negative effects on nutrition—in other words a 'do no harm' approach" (IRIN, 2011, para. 4).

The adaptation of medicine's iconic Hippocratic Oath—*primum non nocere*—by members of the aid community was a turning-point in the story of development aid which reflects new thinking in Western societies. Its cousin is the Precautionary Principle, which tries to foresee the remote harms to the environment and society in developing countries (Beck, 1992). This wariness of prospective threats and unintended consequences of modernization have, in the minds of Western policy-makers, begun to take precedence over the single-minded pursuit of modernity's triumph over the past—this despite notional fidelity to "ending poverty" by promoting the "[e]nlightenment objectives of democracy, global security, and the advance of science" (Sachs, 2005, p. 460). All the new values are post-industrial, if not indeed post-modern, in tenor, expressions of what Ulrich Beck (1992) calls "the risk society". Their insertion in the aid lexicon holds significant implications for the future of development; they suggest that the West is no longer capable of or committed to it.

The dilemma of Western aid today fell out of a shift in thinking about the ontology of society and its relation to modernity and to risk. The modernization process consists of a growing individuation amongst social actors in relation to social structures, which in turn induces social actors to be more reflexive about prevailing social structures, like the family, the workplace and so forth. The "social production of wealth is systematically accompanied by the social production of risk" (Beck, 1992, p. 19). In the past, the threats to humanity were challenges to survival itself, which modernity has largely resolved; increasingly, however, Western society views the process of modernization itself as containing threats which are an inherent in its attainment (Matunhu, 2011). The central question facing post-industrial societies is, "[h]ow can the risks and hazards systematically produced by modernization be prevented, minimized, dramatized or channelled?" (Beck, 1992, p. 19).

By a parallel process the West has lost touch with its own history of conceiving development aid in globalized and imperial terms. The messiness of its own road to modernity, underpinned by violent Hobbesian nation-building projects, the social upheaval of industrialization, bounded by deep corruption, is a matter of record: the emergence of the "robber barons" was as critical to the economic development of the US in the late nineteenth century (and Great Britain and Germany) as the much-criticized corruption of the *chaebol* magnates has been to the contemporary modernization of Korea (or China or India). By contrast, the belief that modernization can be achieved by alternative routes that would avoid its worst features—the "leap-frogging" that IT, for instance, was supposed to provide impoverished societies—is an expression of *post*-industrial risk aversion.

Fabian dreamers who abhor the signature events and revolutionary turmoil that enabled modernity—from capitalist enclosures and factory exploitation to socialist collectivization—for the brutalities that they wreaked upon the vulnerable—seem to have lost the nerve to unleash the genie that could change the unhappy situation of many peoples in developing countries. Rather than to instil the destructively creative policies of modernization, the Western aid industry prefers to minister to the victims of the *failure* to achieve modernity; all while offering no concrete vision of escape from the cycle of poverty. It is the West's loss of faith in modernization, reflected in its changing attitude towards risk, which risks its ability to act as a partner of any effectuality (other than as a consumer market) in the developing world's struggle for development. Christopher Coker's adaptation to the field of international relations of notions of the Risk Society, specifically the hoary problem of war, bears repeating:

> Our civilian societies are in the business of managing risks … (d)istributional conflicts over "goods" such as income, jobs and social security (the traditional agenda of modern politics) have given way to distributional conflicts over "bads"; that is, the risks created by advances in technology (chemical and nuclear), genetic research, the threat to the environment. Politics is about the control and prevention of such risks. Society is risk aversive, and the same is true of how our politicians conduct war. War is no longer used to advance "goods" (constructing a new world order, putting a new regional security system in place) but managing "bads" (nuclear proliferation, terrorism). Generals are no long asked to produce security, but to manage insecurity. War too has become *risk averse.* (Coker, 2001, p. 56)

Development policy as practised by Western governments is likewise no longer about advancing African society but offsetting the fallout of modernization—even while it has yet to take hold fully in the developing countries. As development policy becomes mired in concerns to avoid all risk, institutionally focussing on managing modernization's "bads" rather than promoting its "goods", Western governments diminish their capacity to play a constructive role in development.

Tackling the Risks

The developing countries' tough-minded realism about their situation, riding in tandem with their lack of control and daily deprivation, can entertain no such hesitancy about risk. The monumental undertakings needed to improve the lives of communities—from clean running water provision to infant mortality reduction—form a stark agenda measured in hard, quantifiable terms. Pragmatism, experimentation and adapting to circumstance are all necessary ingredients for success. One can scarcely imagine a Chinese provincial official, compelled to report annually to superiors in Beijing on progress in achieving growth targets, lasting a day in office by articulating development—much less implementing policies—on the basis of "do no harm" as prime directive. The "fetishes" of modernization—aggregate growth, infrastructure capacity, consumer demand, standard of living—are for developing countries yardsticks of success, on a path animated by an ironclad faith in the positive outcomes of modernity. What is past is past, existing in a kind of darkness in which one inquires about nothing, and must be escaped *by any means possible.* The future is, in this harsh reality, necessarily bright with promise and fulfilment.

Post-industrial talk of development that is pro-poor and minds vulnerable communities not only rings hollow in aspiring countries, it also breeds the suspicion that donor paternalism has a darker purpose. Echoing the old saw that NATO's purpose was to keep the US in [Europe], the Russians out and the Germans down, one might be forgiven for misgiving that the purpose of Western aid is to keep the donor in, the emerging powers out and the developing country down. It looks all the worse in light of the demonstrable achievements of the emerging powers, not least of which is their very acquisition of power in all its manifestations; and in light of the fact that it was acquired and achieved not by blindly following but by resolutely ignoring the faddish canons of Western development policy on issues such as the role of the state.

Conclusion: After AID or Back to the Future?

The Western way of development showed few signs of strategic planning and design in the earliest years. Rather, the West has at times been reactive, lurching from turning-point to historical watershed, from World War II to decolonization to Cold War's end and beyond, adapting to events ad hoc. Only with the advent of the OECD-DAC, a multilateral forum dedicated to harmonizing economic practices amongst the Western states, introduced an element of strategy into development assistance. But the emergence of a common strategy did not forestall (indeed it may have precipitated) the rising critique by aid recipients, who have berated the West for its conception and implementation of development assistance. It is the Western world's own loss of nerve and its fetishization of risk aversion that is chiefly to blame for the failure of its many and strenuous efforts to spark development in the non-Western world so as to "make poverty history".

Notes

1. In 1961, President Kennedy replaced the International Cooperation Administration with the US Agency for International Development. For a good historical overview see: Barry Riley, *The Political History of American Food Aid: An Uneasy Benevolence* (New York: Oxford University Press, 2017).
2. Even South Africa, an economic minnow in this landscape of emerging-power whales, felt compelled to rebrand its tariff disbursements to Lesotho and Swaziland under the Southern African Customs Union as a form of "aid", thus propelling it into the ranks of non-DAC donors.

3. The five partnership commitments are: "(1) Ownership: Partner countries exercise effective leadership over their development policies, and strategies and co-ordinate development actions. (2) Alignment: Donors base their overall support on partner countries' national development strategies, institutions and procedures. (3) Harmonisation: Donors' actions are more harmonised, transparent and collectively effective. (4) Managing for Results: Managing resources and improving decision-making for results. (5) Mutual Accountability: Donors and partners are accountable for development results".
4. The Millennium Development Goals are: "(1) Eradicate extreme poverty and hunger; (2) Achieve universal primary education; (3) Promote gender equality and empower women; (4) Reduce child mortality; (5) Improve maternal health; (6) Combat AIDS/HIV, malaria and other diseases; (7) Ensure environmental sustainability; (8) Global partnership for development". UN, "Background", news release, 2017. http://www.un.org/millenniumgoals/bkgd.shtml.
5. Dutch government officials, personal communication, May 2011.

References

Alden, C., & Sidiropoulos, E. (2012). *Busan and the Emerging Aid Architecture*. Retrieved from South African Institute of International Affairs (SAIIA) Website: http://www.saiia.org.za/opinion-analysis/special-report-busan-and-the-emerging-aid-architecture

Anderson, M. B. (1999). *Do No Harm: How Aid Can Support Peace – or War*. Boulder, CO: Lynne Rienner Publishers.

Atwood, J. B. (2012). *Creating a Global Partnership for Effective Development Cooperation*. Retrieved from Center for Global Development (CGD) Website: https://www.cgdev.org/sites/default/files/1426543_file_Atwood_Busan_FINAL_0.pdf

Bataineh, B., Bennon, M., & Fukuyama, F. (2018). *Beijing's Building Boom: How the West Surrendered Global Infrastructure Development to China*. Retrieved from Foreign Affairs Website: http://www.foreignaffairs.com/articles/china/2018-05-21/beijings-building-boom

BBC. (2005). African Head Defends G8 Agreement. *BBC News Channel*. Retrieved from http://news.bbc.co.uk/1/hi/business/4666769.stm

Beck, U. (1992). *Risk Society: Towards a New Modernity* (Vol. 19). London: Sage Publications.

Breman, J. (2011). A Change for the Better? Dutch Development Aid in Good Times and Bad Times. *Development and Change, 42*(3), 833–848.

Breslin, S. (2011). The "China Model" and the Global Crisis: from Friedrich List to a Chinese Mode of Governance? *International Affairs, 87*(6), 1323–1343.

Chin, G. (2012). Two-Way Socialization: China, the World Bank, and Hegemonic Weakening. *The Brown Journal of World Affairs, 19*(1), 211–230.

China-DAC Study Group. (2011). *Economic Transformation and Poverty Reduction: How It Happened in China, Helping It Happen in Africa*. Beijing: CFEPH.

Coker, C. (2001). *Humane Warfare*. London: Routledge.

Collaborate Learning Projects. (2004). *The Do No Harm Handbook*. Cambridge, MA: Collaborative for Development Action (CDA).

Cooper, F. (2014). *Citizenship between Empire and Nation: Remaking France and French Africa, 1945–1960*. Princeton: Princeton University Press.

De Waal, A. (1997). *Famine Crimes: Politics and the Disaster Relief Industry in Africa*. Oxford: J. Currey.

DfID. (Ed.). (2010). *Department for International Development Annual Report & Resource Accounts 2009–2010 – International Development Committee Contents*. London: House of Commons.

Ekbladh, D. (2010). *The Great American Mission: Modernization and the Construction of an American World Order*. Princeton: Princeton University Press.

El-Ojeili, C., & Hayden, P. (2006). *Critical Theories of Globalization: An Introduction*. Basingstoke, UK: Palgrave Macmillan.

Engel, J. A. (Ed.). (2016). *The Four Freedoms: Franklin D. Roosevelt and the Evolution of an American Idea*. New York, NY: Oxford University Press.

Fornes, G., & Mendez, A. (2018). *The China-Latin America Axis: Emerging Markets and the Future of Globalisation* (2nd ed.). New York: Palgrave Macmillan.

Fox, J., & Godement, F. (2009). *A Power Audit of EU-China Relations* (pp. 20–27). London: European Council on Foreign Relations.

Freedman, L. (2000). *Kennedy's Wars: Berlin, Cuba, Laos, and Vietnam*. New York: Oxford University Press.

Gilman, N. (2003). *Mandarins of the Future: Modernization Theory in Cold War America*. Baltimore: The Johns Hopkins University Press.

Glennie, J. (Ed.). (2008). *The Trouble with Aid: Why Less Could Mean More for Africa*. London: Zed Books.

Gray, R. (2011, November 27). … But Government Still Finds 1bn to Help Combat Climate Change in Africa. *The Sunday Telegraph*, p. 1. Retrieved from https://bit.ly/2rJZPx8

IRIN. (2011, September 11). Nutrition: Let Agriculture "Do No Harm". *IRIN News Report*. Retrieved from http://www.irinnews.org/news/2011/09/26/let-agriculture-do-no-harm

Kagame, P. (2009). Africa Has to Find Its Own Road to Prosperity. *Financial Times*. Retrieved from https://www.ft.com/content/0d1218c8-3b35-11de-ba91-00144feabdc0

Leimgruber, M., & Schmelzer, M. (2017). From the Marshall Plan to Global Governance: Historical Transformations of the OEEC/OECD, 1948 to Present. In M. Leimgruber & M. Schmelzer (Eds.), *The OECD and the International Political Economy Since 1948* (pp. 23–61). Cham, Switzerland and Berlin and Heidelberg: Springer.

Long, C. (2001). *Participation of the Poor in Development Initiatives: Taking Their Rightful Place*. Sterling, VA: Earthscan Publications.

Macrae, J., & Zwi, A. (Eds.). (1994). *War and Hunger: Rethinking International Responses to Complex Emergencies*. London: Zed Books.

Mahon, R. (2017). Gendering Development: The OECD's Development Assistance Committee, 1981–2000. In *The OECD and the International Political Economy Since 1948* (pp. 335–356). Cham: Palgrave Macmillan.

Matunhu, J. (2011). A Critique of Modernization and Dependency Theories in Africa: Critical Assessment. *African Journal of History and Culture, 3*(5), 65–72.

Mawdsley, E. (2012). *From Recipients to Donors: Emerging Powers and the Changing Development Landscape*. London: Zed Books.

Mawdsley, E., Savage, L., & Kim, S. M. (2014). A 'Post-aid World'? Paradigm Shift in Foreign Aid and Development Cooperation at the 2011 Busan High Level Forum. *The Geographical Journal, 180*(1), 27–38.

McCormick, T. J. (1995). *America's Half-Century: United States Foreign Policy in the Cold War and After* (2nd ed.). Baltimore: Johns Hopkins University Press.

MFAN. (2011). *Forming a Strong Partnership with Brazil* [Web Log Post]. Retrieved from http://modernizeaid.net/2011/02/usaid-impact-blog-forming-a-strong-partnership-with-brazil/

Moyo, D. (2010). *Dead Aid: Why Aid Makes Things Worse and How There Is Another Way for Africa*. London: Penguin.

Mutume, G. (2008). Africa Secures New Southern Partners. *Africa Renewal, 22*(3), 6–7.

Nolan, C. J. (1993). *Principled Diplomacy: Security and Rights in US Foreign Policy*. London: Greenwood Press.

OECD. (2005). *The Paris Declaration on Aid Effectiveness*. Retrieved from https://www.oecd.org/dac/effectiveness/34428351.pdf

OneWorld. (2012, July). *Foreign Aid Guide*. Retrieved from OneWorld Website: http://archive.li/NPk0b

Reisen, H. (2015). Will the AIIB and the NDB Help Reform Multilateral Development Banking? *Global Policy, 6*(3), 297–304.

Rostow, W. W. (1960). *The Stages of Economic Growth: A Non-communist Manifesto*. Cambridge: Cambridge University Press.

Sachs, J. (2005). *The End of Poverty: How We Can Make It Happen in Our Lifetime*. London: Penguin.

Schild, G., Woods, B., & Oaks, D. (1995). *American Economic and Political Postwar Planning in the Summer of 1944*. New York: St. Martin's Press.

Stiglitz, J. E. (2002). *Globalization and Its Discontents*. London: Allen Lane.
Taffet, J. F. (2007). *Foreign Aid as Foreign Policy: The Alliance for Progress in Latin America*. London: Routledge.
Tandon, Y. (2008). *Ending Aid Dependence*. Fahamu/Pambazuka (2nd ed.). Oxford: Fahamu.
The Sphere Project. (2004). *Humanitarian Charter and Minimum Standards in Disaster Response*. Geneva: Sphere Project.
UNDP. (2008). *Guidance Note on Early Recovery*. Geneva: Bureau for Crisis Prevention and Recovery, UNDP. Retrieved from https://bit.ly/2SWXYAK
UNICEF. (2003). *Humanitarian Principles*. In Principled Approach to Humanitarian Action (PATH Training Programme). New York: UN. Retrieved from https://uni.cf/2xIISsz
USAID. (2015). *United States and Brazil Expand Partnership to Promote Food Security in Mozambique* [Press Release]. Retrieved from https://www.usaid.gov/news-information/press-releases/jul-1-2015-united-states-and-brazil-expand-partnership-promote-food-security
USAID. (2016). *Trilateral Cooperation* [Press Release]. Retrieved from https://www.usaid.gov/brazil/our-work/trilateral-cooperation
Vandemoortele, J. (2011). The MDG Story: Intention Denied. *Development and Change, 42*(1), 1–21.
Wade, R. (1996). Japan, the World Bank, and the Art of Paradigm Maintenance: The East Asian Miracle in Political Perspective. *New Left Review, 217*, 3–36.
Wade, R. (2015). Agenda Change in Western Development Organizations: From Hard Production to Soft, Timeless, Placeless Policy. *The Lahore Journal of Economics, 20*, 1–12.
Watson, I. (2014). *Foreign Aid and Emerging Powers: Asian Perspectives on Official Development Assistance*. Abingdon, UK: Routledge.
Williams, D., & Young, T. (2013). The International Politics of Social Transformation: Trusteeship and Intervention in Historical Perspective. In M. Duffield & V. Hewitt (Eds.), *Empire Development and Colonialism: The Past in the Present. Suffolk: Boydell and Brewer Ltd*. Oxford: James Currey.
World Bank. (2007). *China Eximbank and World Bank Come Together to Sign Cooperation Memo*. Retrieved from http://www.worldbank.org/en/news/press-release/2007/05/21/china-eximbank-world-bank-come-together-sign-cooperation-memo
World Bank. (2010). *Annual Report*. Retrieved from Washington, DC: http://siteresources.worldbank.org/EXTANNREP2010/Resources/WorldBank-AnnualReport2010.pdf
Yeung, H. W. C. (Ed.). (2010). *Globalizing Regional Development in East Asia: Production Networks, Clusters, and Entrepreneurship*. Abingdon, UK: Routledge.

CHAPTER 3

The Emergence of New Development Assistance: Conceptual and Operational Frameworks

Yu Zheng

INTRODUCTION

The rising inequality among developing countries has changed the dynamics of global development and poverty reduction. The divergent development trajectories of these countries make it increasingly inappropriate to use the generic term of "developing countries" to refer to a highly heterogeneous group of countries. The income gaps between low-income countries (LICs) and middle-income countries (MICs) are larger than the gaps between upper-middle-income countries and high-income countries. MICs are a large diverse group by size, population, and economic performance. Having 73% of world's poor people, MICs are the primary recipients of international aid, but they are also the major contributors of global growth (World Bank, 2017).

A new system of international development cooperation is needed to engage emerging economies as both contributors and recipients. On the

Y. Zheng (✉)
School of International Relations and Public Affairs, Fudan University, Shanghai, China
e-mail: yzheng@fudan.edu.cn

Y. Jing et al. (eds.), *New Development Assistance*, Governing China in the 21st Century,
https://doi.org/10.1007/978-981-13-7232-2_3

one hand, the international community needs emerging economies to help support global development goals. On the other hand, emerging economies need the support of international community to achieve sustainable economic growth. This framework should strengthen, rather than replace, the existing ODA system.

Emerging economies are playing a key role in transforming the development cooperation agenda, resulting in a "silent revolution" that creates competitive pressures into the existing ODA system (Woods, 2008). It is important to ensure the participation of emerging donors be rightly measured and assessed as it is crucial to the credibility of an international framework of development cooperation and a necessary step to improve effective development cooperation. The concept of South-South Cooperation (SSC), an expression of collaboration and partnership among developing countries that emerged with the Bandung conference in 1955 and the Non-Aligned Movement, has been praised for its potential of promoting horizontal partnerships and enriching the aid effectiveness agenda. While the conventional ODA framework was structured alongside the donor-recipient dyad, the SSC advocated structural reform that could create the necessary conditions for mutual benefit and autonomous decisions on development policies in the global south (Esteves & Assunção, 2014). But the question is not only how to build connections between MICs and LICs, but also how best to derive benefits from the connections for the economy and society at large.

Debates on Aid Effectiveness

Since the 1990s, due to the disappointing economic performance in many aid-recipient countries, there was a rising concern in the developed donor community for how effective aid was used in developing countries. An extensive literature on aid effectiveness suggests that the hypothesized positive effect of aid on economic growth does not have consistent empirical support (e.g. Burnside & Dollar, 2000; Collier & Hoeffler, 2004; Easterly, 2003; Rajan & Subramanian, 2008). In the first decade of the twenty-first century, the Development Assistance Committee (DAC) attempted to conduct reforms on the existing ODA system in a series of High-Level Forums on Aid Effectiveness: Rome (2003), Paris (2005), Accra (2008), and Busan (2011). These reforms set two different, somewhat contradictory, goals for foreign aid: donors should delink aid and commercial-oriented capital or trade flows on the one hand, and connect aid with investment on the other hand.

On the one hand, the DAC criticized tied aid for its lowering aid effectiveness, urging donors to increase "alignment of aid with partner countries' priorities, systems and procedures and helping to strengthen their capacities" Organization for Economic Cooperation Development (OECD, 2005, p. 1). On the other hand, the donor community highlighted the catalytic role of aid in economic growth, encouraging donor countries to use aid to leverage private investment. The Monterrey Consensus in 2002 emphasized the need to intensify efforts to "promote the use of ODA to leverage additional financing for development, such as foreign investment, trade and domestic resources" (United Nations, 2003, p. 15). The basic idea is that many investments in developing countries are sufficiently lucrative in private sector eyes, but with some help from donors to either raise returns or mitigate risk, private investments will start flowing. The UNCTAD estimates that developing countries need an annual investment of $3.9 trillion in key sectors of sustainable development goals (SDGs). This is only partially bridged by current levels of investment amounting to $1.4 trillion (UNCTAD, 2014, pp. 14–15). The investment gap of $2.5 trillion would need to be covered by some combination of increases in public sector budgets, foreign aid, and new investments from the private sector.

Despite the tremendous demand for investment in less-developed countries' economic development, empirical evidence is largely inconclusive on the catalyst effect of aid on investment (Rodrik, 1995). On the one hand, aid can ease important bottlenecks in developing countries by financing public infrastructure and human capital investments that would not have been undertaken by private actors. On the other hand, foreign aid invested in physical capital competes directly with other types of capital (Selaya & Sunesen, 2012). Providing aid may create a positive "vanguard effect" to attract investment from the same donor country but has no effect on investment from other donor countries (Kimura & Todo, 2010).

The UNCTAD estimates that developing countries need an annual investment of $3.9 trillion in key SDG sectors. This is only partially bridged by current levels of investment amounting to $1.4 trillion. The investment gap of $2.5 trillion would need to be covered by some combination of increases in public sector budgets, foreign aid, and new investments from the private sector (UNCTAD, 2014).

Diversity of Emerging Donors

The rising presence of emerging economies in development cooperation has highlighted the differences between the traditional and emerging donors, but the group of emerging donors remains heterogeneous. It is conceptually and analytically difficult to define a model that fits all emerging economies. There are several reasons. Instead of developing institutionalized, comprehensive, and more dependable structures of aid management, emerging economies appear to prefer various ad hoc mechanisms to address specific needs and policy concerns. Emerging economies do not have an aid strategy as clearly specified and institutionalized as that of traditional donors. Nor do they face a strong domestic pressure to share more international responsibility. Moreover, emerging economies vary greatly in their motives of aid policy and patterns and distribution of their development finance.

Some recent studies have used different criteria to categorize these new actors. Manning divides non-DAC donors into four groups: countries that belong to the OECD but are not DAC members, new EU members that are not members of the OECD, Middle Eastern Arab countries, and other countries that do not fall into the previous groups (Manning, 2006). De Renzio and Seifert (2014) divide emerging donors into two groups. The first is a small group of large players that have been active in SSC for a long period, including China, India, and Brazil. The second group is a number of smaller middle-income countries whose aid programs are more recent (De Renzio & Seifert, 2014). While these grouping approaches are useful to distinguish heterogeneous emerging donors, they do not provide a systematic evaluation on emerging donors' impact on international development cooperation.

Definition and Scope of Emerging Economies

An emerging economy is broadly defined as a nation's economy that is progressing toward becoming advanced but is not as advanced as developed countries. This definition leads to various classifications of emerging economies which sometimes lumps together countries with very different development stage. In this chapter, three main aspects underline the relevance of emerging economies as key players in development cooperation: (1) the outstanding size of their economies with rising importance in the world economy; (2) regional power demanding for stronger political voice in regional and global governance; (3) active engagement in providing assistance to other developing countries.

Based on these criteria, we consider three groups of countries as emerging economies. They include *the BRICS (Brazil, Russia, India, China, and South Africa)*, *emerging economies in G20*, and *major non-DAC donors.*

BRICS: Their economic size marked them out as special group among all emerging economies. China, India, Russia, and Brazil are among the largest ten national economies in the world. They have a relatively long history in providing assistance to developing countries and generally accept the principles of the SSC.

Emerging economies in G20: As the premier forum for global economic governance since 2008, the G20 countries constitute the principal donors for both bilateral and multilateral lending agencies. The emerging economies in the G20 carry not only economic significance but regional geopolitical power. They serve as the key drivers of global growth and development cooperation.

Major non-DAC donor: This group includes other emerging economies that actively engage in development assistance to less developed countries. In particular, Gulf Cooperation Council (GCC) donors have accounted for about 75% of aid in this group from 1975 to 2008 (Minor, 2014). Arab donors such as Saudi Arabia, United Arab Emirates (UAE), Qatar, and Kuwait have more established and generous aid programs in the world. It has consistently served as an alternative model to the DAC model. Arab foreign aid tends to predominately flow to other Arab countries. Arab donors' activities are more cohesive and coordinated than those of other emerging economies. It may be a result of common cultural, religious, and linguistic ties between Arab donors.

As shown in Fig. 3.1, the three groups overlap each other. From the three groups, we choose 13 countries as the representatives of emerging economies based on their economic size, geopolitical influence, and aid activities. They are *Argentina, Brazil, China, India, Indonesia, Kuwait, Mexico, Qatar, Russia, Saudi Arabia, South Africa, Turkey,* and the *United Arab Emirates.* All these countries are at the upper-middle-income or even high-income levels and many are both providers and recipients of development assistance at the same time. We label this group of countries as *EE13*. Together, *EE13* make up half of the world's population and had a combined GDP of over $21 trillion in 2016, more than 28% of the global total (Table 3.1). The term "emerging" does not mean that all these countries are newcomers in the donor community. In fact, some countries (e.g. China, India, and Brazil) have long histories of providing aid to other developing countries whereas others embarked upon development assistance programs recently. Nevertheless, they differ significantly from traditional donors in the motives and patterns of their aid activities.

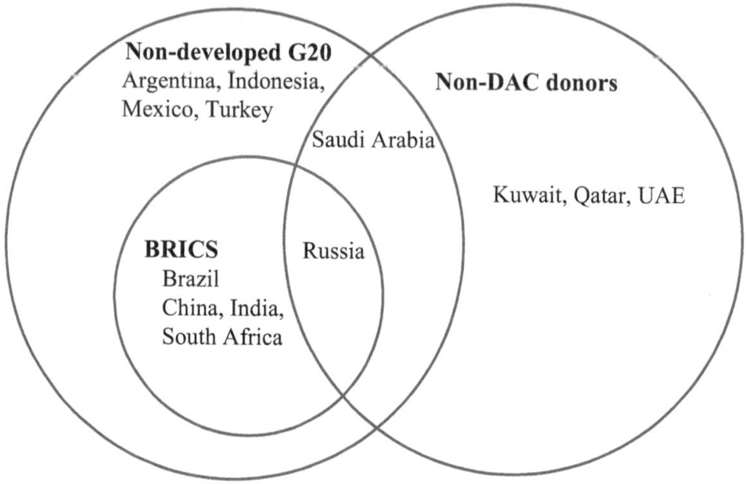

Fig. 3.1 Scope of emerging economies

Table 3.1 Non-DAC countries' contribution in ODA

	2011	*2012*	*2013*	*2014*	*2015*	*2015 (% of total)*
ODA from 28 DAC countries	135.0	126.9	134.7	137.4	131.4	84.2
ODA from 20 reporting countries beyond the DAC	8.9	6.2	16.4	24.7	17.7	11.3
Estimated development cooperation flows from ten non-reporting countries beyond the DAC	5.2	5.6	6.8	7	6.9	4.4
Subtotal flows from non-DAC providers	14.1	11.8	23.2	31.7	24.6	15.8
Estimated global total	149.1	138.7	157.9	169.1	156.0	100

Source: https://www.oecd.org/development/stats/non-dac-reporting.htm

Emerging Economies and New Development Assistance

With their growing financial wealth, some emerging economies have transformed from aid recipients to aid contributors and increased their presence in the international donor community. Emerging donors were given high priority in the discussions at Accra and Busan, but there has been much debate on their contribution to and impact on international development cooperation. Over the years, the definition of ODA has been continuously redefined to ensure the greatest possible consistency among DAC donors. These changes, however, have not adequately addressed emerging donors' positions and concerns. The current DAC system does not put emerging donors' aid into the same category with ODA. According to DAC's statistics, non-DAC donors disburse $14–25 billion of aid per year (see Table 3.1). Using a broader definition of aid that includes both ODA-like and other official flows (OOF) flows, AidData estimates that non-DAC countries' contribution could be as high as $41.7 billion per year (AidData, 2017).

In recent years, some new concepts have been proposed to broaden the scope of development cooperation beyond ODA as means necessary for sustainable development goals (SDGs). For example, Justin Yifu Li and Yan Wang use "development finance" to capture both official and private finance that are used in pursuit of development objective (Lin & Wang, 2015). In addition to ODA, it would include OOF, OOF-like loans, and investments with intention for development. They emphasize that special attention should be paid to the non-monetary development assistance provided by Southern partners, such as "turnkey projects", "real sector (barter) exchanges", and "resource financed infrastructure" (RFI).

OECD proposes the concept of total official support for sustainable development (TOSSD), aiming at creating a broad framework for inclusive measurement of sustainable development finance. Based on the similar framework, the Brookings Institute proposes the concept of International Development Contributions (IDC) (Kharas & Rogerson, 2016). TOSSD would cover all international public finance extended to developing countries and multilateral institutions in support of sustainable development, regardless of the type of instrument used and the associated terms. Specifically, it would include concessional and non-concessional bilateral and multilateral public finance from both DAC and non-DAC providers, private resources mobilized through public schemes, as well as the activities of diverse financial intermediaries, including collective investment vehicles (CIVs) and venture capital funds (OECD, 2015). A new OECD report estimates that 29 emerging providers disburse $32 billion of finance for development cooperation, accounting for 17% of total global development cooperation in 2014. If using broader scope of international cooperation, emerging economies provide $300 billion of international cooperation (Luijkx & Benn, 2017).

These proposals indicate a fundamental change on the understanding of economic development. Private capital flows have become an increasingly significant source of investment in developing countries, indicating the high degree to which developing countries have become integrated into the global economy.

Developing countries have been advised to find the best-practice solutions for economic development, but emerging economies have heterogeneous development experiences feasible to their specific situations. Therefore, emerging economies tend to hold a more open and inclusive perspective on development assistance: what matters is how aid interacts with the prevailing power relations and affects governance.

We propose the following principles for conceptualizing and measuring new development assistance (NDA). The NDA can be defined broadly to cover all flows that may have a public interest as a motivation.

Multiple sources. From a recipient's perspective, various types of financial flows, not just official flows, are important for achieving SDGs. The new framework should include not only designated government expenditure on aid, but also private finance subsidized or guaranteed by the government.

Mutual benefit. A strict application of the DAC methodology in assessing concessionality would have made many loans from emerging donors unqualified to be counted as ODA. Relaxing the restriction would encourage emerging economies to contribute more. It should include both concessional and non-concessional financing and captures all financial instruments.

Sustainable development. The new framework should cover activities that promote and enable sustainable development, including contributions to global public goods, where these are deemed relevant for development and aligned with developing countries' priorities. It means that providers themselves may have broader policy objectives than development, and do not solely focus on developing countries.

Based on these principles, we will evaluate emerging economies' role in NDA from four aspects.

- Size. How much do emerging economies give to other countries for development?

- Destination. What has been the allocation by country and/or region?
- Patterns. What sectors and types of projects is the NDA directed?
- Motivations. What are the purposes of the NDA? Is it to secure access to scarce natural resources, commercial expansion, geostrategic goals, or geopolitical competitive dynamics?

The Size of NDA

According to DAC, Total ODA contributed by 30 non-DAC countries peaked at $31.7 billion in 2014. In 2015, their contribution dropped by 30%, accounting for 15.8% of total ODA in 2015 (Table 3.1).

Table 3.2 presents the information of 12 emerging economies (Argentina's information is not available). These countries account for 90% of non-DAC aid. Arab donors—Saudi Arabia, Kuwait Qatar, and UAE—have been among the most generous in the world as they often gave more than 0.7% of GNI, the proposed aid target set in the 1960s but rarely met by DAC countries. Saudi Arabia is the largest emerging donor.

Table 3.2 Emerging economies' ODA or ODA-like flows (million $)

Country	*2011*	*2012*	*2013*	*2014*	*2015*	*As a % of GNI*
Brazil	469	411	316			0.02
China	2785	3123	2997	3401	3113	0.03
India	794	1077	1223	1398	1772	0.07
Russia	478.99	465.01	713.66	875.85	1161.4	0.09
South Africa	229	191	191	148	100	0.04
Qatar	733	543	1344			0.83
Kuwait	175.16	179.74	231.04	276.83	304.46	
Saudi Arabia	5094.9	1298.87	5683.27	13633.95	6758.22	1.02
UAE	717.8	759.15	5401.9	5080.37	4381.37	1.18
Turkey	1273.01	2533.3	3307.67	3591.08	3919.14	0.50
Mexico	99	203	526	169		
Indonesia	16	26	49	56		
BRICS	4755.99	4190.01	4217.66	4424.85	6146.4	
Arab donors	6720.86	2780.76	11316.21	18991.15	11444.05	
Total ODA-like	12864.86	9733.07	19416.54	27232.08	21509.59	

Source: OECD (2017). *Development Cooperation Report 2017: Data for Development*, Table 33 and 38.1

BRICS, despite their dominant economic size in emerging economies, provided only $6 billion of aid in 2015, accounting for a quarter of total aid provided by 30 non-DAC countries. None of these countries gave more than 0.1% of GNI as ODA, significantly lower than the average level of DAC countries (0.3% of GNI).

These figures, however, may have underestimated emerging economies' actual contribution in development finance. There are several reasons. First, emerging economies appear to be less altruistic in aid giving as they provide less budget support than DAC donors do and the concessional proportion of their assistance is lower. Second, emerging economies provide more assistance in the form of non-monetary technical assistance, which is difficult to measure quantitatively. Third, development financing from emerging economies often comes as a package, where grants and concessional and non-concessional loans are a complement to trade and investment arrangements.

OOF include transactions that do not meet ODA concessionality criteria (e.g. non-concessional loan), and transactions that are primarily export-facilitating in purpose (e.g. export credits). China's development finance, often combining aid, loan, and investment, has clear developmental intent, but it does not qualify as ODA. Similarly, much of India's development assistance is also not treated as ODA because its primary intent is to promote trade and investment in the global south. After a spike in response to the global financial crisis, OOF receded in recent years, but emerging economies continue to grow significantly. As shown in Table 3.3, non-DAC countries' OOF flows grew from $36 million in 2011 to $3533 million in 2015, or 0.6% to 47% of global total.

Moreover, South-South trade has grown faster than total world trade since the early 1990s. LICs export to BRICS grew from $15 billion in 2000 to $61 billion in 2009. Trade between Asia and Latin America has also more than doubled over the past decade. If different sources of

Table 3.3 Emerging economies' non-concessional official flows (million $)

	2011	*2012*	*2013*	*2014*	*2015*
Non-DAC OOF	36.27	117.1	−5.66	574.07	3533.23
% of global	0.6	1.6	−0.1	30.1	47.3

Source: https://www.oecd.org/development/stats/non-dac-reporting.htm

development finance are included, emerging economies' contribution to NDA would increase significantly.

As shown in Table 3.4, emerging economies' share in exports and outward FDI flows in comparison to OECD countries is still a minor one, but has been increasing rapidly, particularly after the global financial crisis. From 2001 to 2016, emerging economies' share in the global FDI outflows increased from 1.6% to 16.8%. Their exports increased from 13.4% to 22.9%. BRICS countries are the prominent investors. Their outward FDI has risen from $8 billion in 2001 to $251 billion in 2016, or from 1% to 16% of world flows.

In particular, BRICS has increasingly engaged in economic cooperation with African countries. FDI flows to Africa from India, China, and Brazil have risen from 18% of the total in 1995–1999 to 21% in 2000–2008, making them among the top investing countries in Africa. Most BRICS FDI projects in Africa are in manufacturing and service (UNCTAD, 2013).

Table 3.4 BRICS and emerging economies' roles in international development

	2001	*2006*	*2011*	*2016*
Population				
BRICS	2.7 B	2.9 B	3.0 B	3.1 B
% of global	43.8	43.2	42.6	41.8
EE13	3.2 B	3.3 B	3.5 B	3.7 B
% of global	51.0	50.5	50.0	49.3
GDP				
BRICS	$2.8 T	$6.0 T	$14.5 T	$16.8 T
% of global	8.4	11.8	19.7	22.3
EE13	$4.5 T	$8.9 T	$19.2 T	$21.4 T
% of global	13.5	17.4	26.3	28.3
Export				
BRICS	$557.9 B	$1795.1 B	$3454.5 B	$3277.7 B
% of global	7.3	12.1	15.4	15.8
EE13	$1029.4 B	$2830.6 B	$5264.6 B	$4746.0 B
% of global	13.4	19.0	23.4	22.9
FDI outflows				
BRICS	$8.3 B	$102.7 B	$143.8 B	$250.9 B
% of global	1.1	4.7	6.7	16.0
EE13	$11.7 B	$133.7 B	$196.0 B	$264.5 B
% of global	1.6	6.2	9.2	16.8

Source: Data are collected from World Development Indicators. Retrieved from www.wdi.org

From 2000 to 2011, Chinese total financial commitments to Africa reached $73 billion, significantly higher than the official figure of foreign aid of $15 billion (Strange et al., 2013). China's trade and investment to Africa have also grown exponentially. FDI inflows surged from $75 million in 2000 to $3.2 billion in 2014 (MOFCOM, 2015). With an average of 30% of annual trade growth between China and Africa in the last 15 years, China has become Africa's largest trading partner and stood at $180 billion in 2015.

Key Features of NDA

Compared with developed donors, emerging economies may find it more difficult to address two questions: how to effectively help others without compromising one's own interests, and how to ensure national interests are being met without alienating the recipient countries. While emerging economies have increased their presence in the foreign aid community, their engagement with LICs is associated with the principles of SSC, which differs from the ODA model noticeably. In particular, their development finance policies share some similar features. The comparison of key features of ODA and NDA is presented in Table 3.5.

Table 3.5 Comparison of key features of ODA and NDA

	ODA	*NDA*
Primary motivations	Mixture of strategic, political, and economic interests	Economic and commercial interests
Intercountry relationship	Donor-recipient	Development partners
Major recipients/ partners	LICs in Africa	Neighboring countries
Primary sectors	Social infrastructure (e.g. health and education)	Economic infrastructure and productive sector
Patterns	Separation of aid and investment	Integration of aid, investment, and trade
Bilateral channels	Earmarking	Unspecified
Multilateral channels	Traditional multilateral development banks (MDBs) (WB, IMF)	New MDBs (AIIB, NDB)

Aid Patterns

Emerging donors emphasize "developing country identity", indicating that their outward engagement is in tandem with their domestic development. They have less capacity to commit to a target of aid close to developed countries' targeted (0.7% of GNI) and actual level (0.3% of GNI) of delivering ODA to developing countries. In addition, emerging economies' development cooperation has been guided by the principle of "equality and mutual benefit", indicating that the interplay of aid and investment in international development cooperation is a default arrangement. Therefore, their development finance often comes as a package with a mixture of aid, loans, export credit, and investment to secure natural resources or expand overseas market for their domestic firms. For example, China pledged $60 billion in development assistance to Africa in 2015. Of the $60 billion package, only $5 billion will fit the OECD criteria of ODA as it will come as grants and interest-free loans. The rest of the flows will arrive as loans and export credits (Robertson & Benabdallah, 2016).

A distinct feature of NDA is the integration of aid, investment, and trade, representing a reversal to the historical precedent of linkage between aid and investment. With the integrated development finance as the predominant form and relatively rare outright grant, the financial flows are less concessional in nature than traditional ODA; traditional donors are concerned that the expansion of "tied aid" may result in more protectionism and low efficiency.

Intercountry Relations

Unlike the traditional hierarchical donor-recipient relations, NDA is based on a horizontal process of experience sharing and knowledge co-creation. Considering themselves as development partners, not traditional donors, emerging economies aim to foster cooperative and collaborative relationships with LICs. They often emphasize the principles of non-interference in the domestic affairs of other countries and out of respect for sovereignty and territorial integrity, part of which was drawn from the consensus reached at the Bandung Conference of 1955 attended by 29 newly independent states. They tend to not attach political conditions to economic assistance, nor do they attempt to bypass the governmental machinery in the partner country in implementing projects.

Sectoral Allocation

Emerging economies highlight their different development experiences in the allocation of NDA in recipient countries. For example, China's development cooperation is often channeled in infrastructure financing, which was a crucial factor that helped China to transform its economy through industrialization. India also uses international development cooperation to share its successful development experience. But unlike China, India emphasizes its experience in combating various diseases. In recent years, India has spent $100 million on health projects overseas, largely focused on building up local medical systems and transferring expertise. Much of Brazil's development cooperation initiatives revolve around its flagship program, termed "technical cooperation", which became a core theme of the country's overseas aid activities. Brazil's aid has a strong focus on social infrastructure. About 72% of the technical cooperation was directed to projects related to social infrastructure, higher than in any DAC donor country (Semrau & Thiele, 2017).

Distribution Channels

The channels through which emerging economies allocate NDA are less diverse and specified. China and India tend to give the majority of aid through direct bilateral channels whereas Brazil and South Africa are more open to engage with multilateral channels. The newly established multilateral development institutions such as Asian Infrastructure Development Bank (AIIB) and BRICS New Development Bank (NDB) may provide a strong platform for uniting development finance from emerging economies. For DAC countries, aid earmarking, the practice of dedicating aid to spending on specific public services in recipient countries, has been the primary way for allocating bilateral aid. Emerging economies are less specified when providing development finance to partner countries, which may give partnership countries more control on their development programs.

Geographical Distribution

Aid from emerging donors tends to be more geographically concentrated than aid from DAC donors (Dreher, Nunnenkamp, & Thiele, 2011). Emerging donors tend to focus on neighboring countries as the major partners of NDA. For example, Brazil's development cooperation is predominantly shaped by historic and cultural ties to the Lusophone world, the community of Portuguese language countries, and Latin America, accounting for a share of about 83% of total commitments. Another 11% was channeled to other African countries.

The primary recipients of Russian aid are Commonwealth of Independent States (CIS), followed by Syria, Serbia, and Guinea (OECD, 2017). Some countries in Latin America (e.g. Ecuador), Africa (e.g. Libya), and Central Asia (e.g. Kyrgyzstan) are also the major recipients of Russian aid.

India's traditional major development cooperation partners were Bangladesh, Myanmar, Nepal, and Bhutan. In recent years, particularly since 2008, Africa has emerged as a major focus of India's development cooperation partners. At the 2011 India-Africa Forum Summit, India pledged $5 billion in aid to Africa in the form of concessional loan (Bijoy, 2010).

China is probably an exception in terms of geographical distribution of development finance as Africa is the primary destination of Chinese aid. Within Africa, Chinese aid is more evenly distributed than its investment. The top 15 African recipients account for about half of the total Chinese aid projects whereas the top 15 destinations account for more than 70% of Chinese FDI projects.

South Africa's development assistance is predominantly directed to states in Southern Africa, accounting for 70% of its total development assistance. The rest of its development assistance went to other African countries emerging from periods of conflict such as South Sudan, the DRC, Burundi, Rwanda, and Somalia (Tapscott, this volume).

Motivations

Emerging donors have become wealthy enough to use their resources as a policy instrument in pursuit of geopolitical interests, but they are not ready to set aid as a priority for their foreign policy strategy. While increasing their global presence and impact is a key policy objective, their motivation is always a combination of several different goals and the relative balance of these goals may change over time. In particular, their desire to either develop or further strengthen their relationships with other Southern countries is driven primarily by their economic interests. Given the developmental problems that emerging economies continue to face domestically, they would have to emphasize their own expected benefits in order to obtain domestic support for aid programs. Therefore, emerging economies have stronger incentives to use their aid programs to promote their own trade, investment, and commercial interests.

Brazil's emergence as a key player in South-South cooperation reflects the country's desire to pursue a permanent seat on the UN Security Council and expanding overseas business activities (Troilo, 2012). In particular, technical cooperation with developing countries is an important operational instrument of Brazilian foreign policy.

The Chinese aid policy is often contested by diplomatic and commercial agendas. The diplomatic agenda regards aid as an instrument for exercising diplomatic influence on the international stage and deepening cooperation with selected countries whereas the commercial agenda views aid as a useful way of assisting domestic businesses to "go international" and expand exports and investments.

India also tries to balance the strategic and economic goals of development cooperation. As Sri argues in this volume, India's development cooperation with its neighboring countries is largely driven by political and security motivation whereas the emerging shift in focus to Africa is for long-term relationship building rather than immediately correlated with trade and investment relationships. However, commercial goals are so integrated into its development cooperation programs that researchers cannot separate the aid component from its loan programs.

Russia appears to lack a clear strategic vision for regional aid allocation: on the one hand, it follows short-term political interests; yet on the other, it feels compelled to demonstrate compliance with international commitments. And the more Russia engages bilaterally, the more important aid conditionality and proper criteria for the selection of recipients will become (Bakalova & Spanger, 2013).

South Africa's development cooperation programs are likewise motivated by its foreign policy objectives, which are geared toward the maintenance of its role as a regional hegemon (Quadir, 2013).

Conclusion

The concern on aid effectiveness has been a key driver behind the aid reform within the traditional donor community. With the emerging economies gaining prominence in providing aid to less-developed countries, international development cooperation has undergone fundamental changes. While emerging economies share some similar features noticeably different from traditional donors—members of the OECD-DAC—there is a great deal of diversity among them. In order to understand the impact of these heterogeneous emerging donors on international development cooperation, we need to adopt more analytically and conceptually diverse approaches to study these new actors.

While the OECD-DAC's aid architecture has served as an important benchmark for emerging economies to engage with traditional donors, empirical evidence suggests that the effectiveness of ODA is inconclusive regardless of the component and sectoral distribution. Despite repeated calls and action plans for aid effectiveness reform since the beginning of the twenty-first century, there is no promising solution to improve aid effectiveness. It is imperative to develop a more coherent strategy for international development cooperation, which may fit well with the missing parts of the traditional ODA norm. NDA, as an integrated platform for various sources of finance, may gain more prominence rather than fade away.

The convergences between the traditional and emerging donors on the patterns of development finance may lead them toward a middle ground that is more inclusive and development-oriented. A recent form of development cooperation that has been increasingly prominent on the global scale is Triangular Development Cooperation, where a traditional (North) and a non-traditional (South) donor work together with a beneficiary (South) to run an aid program. Since emerging economies often engage with LDCs more than just giving aid, assessing their impact on poor countries should not focus not just on their aid policies in the narrow sense but on a broad scope of development finance that combines aid, loans, and investment.

References

AidData. (2017). *Tracking Underreported Financial Flows*. Retrieved from http://aiddata.org/tracking-underreported-financial-flows

Bakalova, E., & Spanger, H. J. (2013). *Development Cooperation or Competition: Russia as a Reemerging Donor* (PRIF-Report No. 123). Frankfurt: Peace Research Institute.

Bijoy, C. R. (2010). India: Transitioning to a Global Donor. *The Reality of Aid, South-South Cooperation: A Challenge to the Aid System*. Retrieved from http://www.realityofaid.org/userfiles/roareports/roareport_3ce2522270.pdf

Burnside, C., & Dollar, D. (2000). Aid, Policies, and Growth. *American Economic Review, 90*(4), 847–868.

Collier, P., & Hoeffler, A. (2004). Aid, Policy and Growth in Post-conflict Societies. *European Economic Review, 48*(5), 1125–1145.
De Renzio, P., & Seifert, J. (2014). South–South Cooperation and the Future of Development Assistance: Mapping Actors and Options. *Third World Quarterly, 35*(10), 1860–1875.
Dreher, A., Nunnenkamp, P., & Thiele, R. (2011). Are 'New' Donors Different? Comparing the Allocation of Bilateral Aid Between Non-DAC and DAC Donor Countries. *World Development, 39*(11), 1950–1968.
Easterly, W. (2003). Can Foreign Aid Buy Growth? *Journal of Economic Perspectives, 17*(3), 23–48.
Esteves, P., & Assunção, M. (2014). South–South Cooperation and the International Development Battlefield: Between the OECD and the UN. *Third World Quarterly, 35*(10), 1775–1790.
Kharas, H., & Rogerson, A. (2016). *Why and How Might a New Measure of Development Cooperation Be Helpful? A Positive Approach to International Development Contributions (IDC)*. Brookings Institution.
Kimura, H., & Todo, Y. (2010). Is Foreign Aid a Vanguard of Foreign Direct Investment? A Gravity-Equation Approach. *World Development, 38*(4), 482–497.
Lin, J. Y., & Wang, Y. (2015). China's Contribution to Development Cooperation: Ideas, Opportunities and Finances. *Development, 119.*
Luijkx, W., & Benn, J. (2017). *Emerging Providers' International Co-operation for Development.* OECD Development Cooperation Working Paper, 33.
Manning, R. (2006). Will Emerging Donors Change the Face of International Cooperation? *Development Policy Review, 24*(4), 371–385.
Ministry of Commerce (MOFCOM). (2015). *Report on Development of China's Outward Investment and Economic Cooperation.*
Minor, A. (2014, October 28). *Measuring Development Finance from Arab Donors* [Web Log Post]. Retrieved from http://aiddata.org/blog/measuring-development-finance-from-arab-donors
OECD. (2005). *The Paris Declaration on Aid Effectiveness and the Accra Agenda for Action.* Retrieved from http://www.oecd.org/dac/effectiveness/34428351.pdf
OECD. (2015). *Measuring Total Official Support for Sustainable Development.*
OECD. (2017). *Development Cooperation Report 2017: Data for Development.*
Quadir, F. (2013). Rising Donors and the New Narrative of "South–South" Cooperation: What Prospects for Changing the Landscape of Development Assistance Programmes? *Third World Quarterly, 34*(2), 321–338.
Rajan, R. G., & Subramanian, A. (2008). Aid and Growth: What Does the Cross-Country Evidence Really Show? *The Review of Economics and Statistics, 90*(4), 643–665.
Robertson, W., & Benabdallah, L. (2016). China Pledged to Invest $60 Billion in Africa. Here's What That Means. *Washington Post.*

Rodrik, D. (1995). Why Is There Multilateral Lending? In M. Bruno & B. Pleskovic (Eds.), *Annual World Bank Conference on Development Economics*, 167–205.

Selaya, P., & Sunesen, E. R. (2012). Does Foreign Aid Increase Foreign Direct Investment? *World Development, 40*(11), 2155–2176.

Semrau, F. O., & Thiele, R. (2017). Brazil's Development Cooperation: Following in China's and India's Footsteps? *Journal of International Development, 29*(3), 287–307.

Strange, A., Park, B., Tierney, M. J., Fuchs, A., Dreher, A., & Ramachandran, V. (2013). *China's Development Finance to Africa: A Media-Based Approach to Data Collection*. Center for Global Development Working Paper, 323.

Troilo, P. (2012, July 09). *Setting Its Own Course, Brazil's Foreign Aid Expands and Evolves*. Retrieved from Devex Website: https://www.devex.com/news/setting-its-own-course-brazil-foreign-aid-expands-and-evolves-78631

UNCTAD. (2013, March 25) *The Rise of BRICS FDI and Africa*. Retrieved from http://unctad.org/en/PublicationsLibrary/webdiaeia2013d6_en.pdf

UNCTAD. (2014). *World Investment Report 2014*. Retrieved from https://unctad.org/en/PublicationsLibrary/wir2014_overview_ch.pdf

United Nations. (2003). *Financing for Development: Monterrey Consensus of the International Conference on Financing for Development*. Retrieved from http://www.un.org/en/development/desa/population/migration/generalassembly/docs/globalcompact/A_CONF.198_11.pdf

Woods, N. (2008). Whose Aid? Whose Influence? China, Emerging Donors and the Silent Revolution in Development Assistance. *International Affairs, 84*(6), 1205–1221.

World Bank. (2017). *Middle-Income Countries: An Overview*. Retrieved from http://www.worldbank.org/en/country/mic

CHAPTER 4

The Aid Management Systems in BRICS Countries

Jianzhi Zhao and Zhe Ouyang

Introduction

The distribution of foreign aid since WWII has been mostly in the form of Official Development Assistance (ODA henceforth) from the developed countries to developing countries. However, since the beginning of the twenty-first century, especially the Global Financial Crisis in 2008 which led to the accelerated shift of economic growth engine from traditional advanced countries to emerging economies, the international development has entered a new stage and the change in the players in international development area. As shown in Fig. 4.1, the share of ODA by OECD Development Assistance Committee (OECD-DAC) countries, traditional advanced economies, have shrunk from 90% in 2000 to 77% in 2014 and rebounded to 83% in 2017, whereas non-DAC countries have been increasing their share from 2% to 8% during the same period and reached a peak of 14% in 2014. The role by multilateral agencies is stable around 10%. The increase in donor countries

J. Zhao (✉) • Z. Ouyang
School of International Relations and Public Affairs, Fudan University, Shanghai, China
e-mail: ouyz16@fudan.edu.cn

Y. Jing et al. (eds.), *New Development Assistance*, Governing China in the 21st Century,
https://doi.org/10.1007/978-981-13-7232-2_4

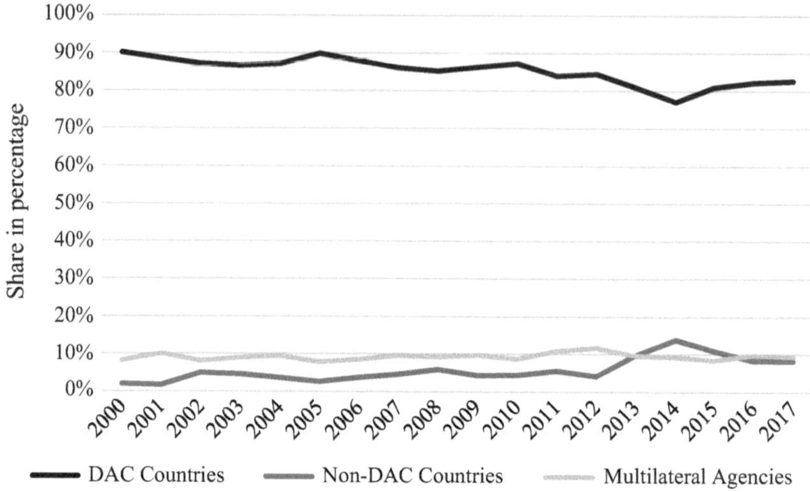

Fig. 4.1 The change of the landscape in international development society. Source: Author's calculation based on *OECD International Development Statistics* (IDS) (2018)

and total amount of aid have provided more funding and cooperation options to recipient countries but also further widened the division of international aid structure and intensified the competition among donor countries.

It is, however, worth noting that foreign aid from emerging countries has its own characteristics, different from those by OECD-DAC countries. Their main aid philosophies and practices as well as management system are derived from their own development experience and in many cases not well recognized by the traditional developed donors. Based on the framework of "South-South Cooperation" (U.N. Secretary-General, 2012), some developing countries have put forward new aid philosophies and aid practices on the basis of national sovereignty and autonomy, equality, unconditionality, non-interference and mutual benefit, making an impact on the traditional international aid structure. Among these emerging donors, the prominent emerging donors include BRICS: Brazil, South Africa, India and China. In this chapter, we will review their aid management system to better understand their challenges and strengths.

The Aid Management System of Emerging BRICS Donors

Brazil

The history of Brazilian foreign aid dates back to the 1950s. Technical cooperation in developing countries (TCDC) was initially the core part of Brazil's foreign aid. In 1959, Brazil created the National Commission for Technical Assistance (CNAT). The commission is composed of representatives from the Ministry of Foreign Affairs, the Secretariat of Planning (SEPLAN), which is responsible for determining the priorities for technical cooperation, and other ministries. In the 1960s, Brazil's multilateral and bilateral technical cooperation projects gradually increased, and the mechanism was reorganized into a technical cooperation system jointly led by the Ministry of Foreign Affairs and the SEPLAN. Two departments were set up under the two agencies to deal with the operation of technical cooperation, respectively. In the 1980s, the shortcomings of this "two-head-two-implementation-agency" mechanism became gradually noticeable where the two departments served almost the same functions with poor coordination. Finally, with the support of UNDP, Brazil merged the two departments into the Brazilian Cooperation Agency (ABC) and placed it under the leadership the Ministry of Foreign Affairs, making it the core of Brazil's foreign aid institutions (Agência Brasileira de Cooperação, 2018).

Currently, within the Brazilian aid management system (Fig. 4.2), five ministries including Ministry of Foreign Affairs (MFA), Ministry of Health (MOH), Ministry of Agriculture (MOA), Ministry of Education (MOE) and Ministry of Science and Technology (MOST), as well as other parallel ministries related to foreign aid, are responsible for the formulation and coordination of foreign aid policies. Since most of Brazil's foreign aids are centered on health (particularly HIV/AIDS), agriculture, professional education and technical assistance, MOH, MOA, MOE and MOST as well as their affiliates directly participate in the implementation of foreign aid. They are the key players in the formation and coordination of foreign aid policies because of their expertise, networks and resources.

At the center of the system is the MFA, which is responsible for interpreting the actions of other ministries in accordance with the foreign policy. The ABC, as a subsidiary of MFA, plays a central role in Brazil's foreign aid. Its main function, prescribed by law, is to coordinate, negotiate, approve, mon-

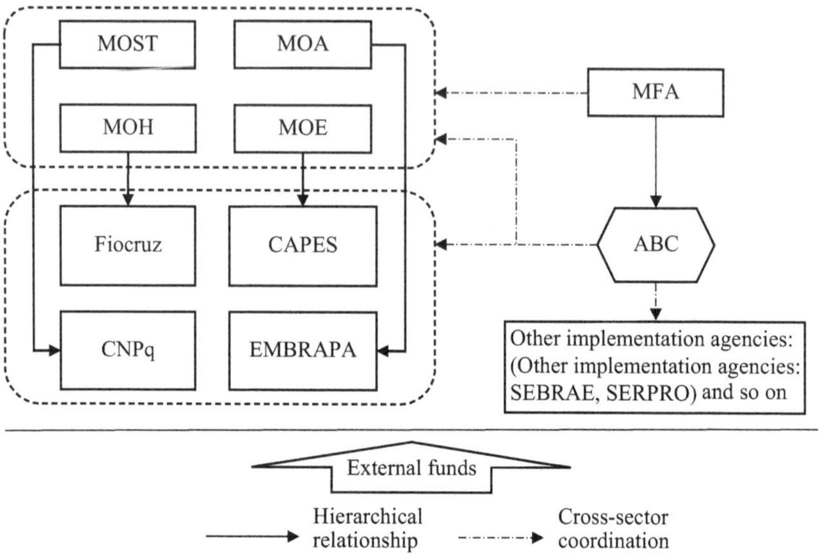

Fig. 4.2 Brazilian aid management system

itor and evaluate all Brazilian technical cooperation projects, to coordinate Brazilian technical cooperation implementation agencies and their counterparts in the recipient countries, and as auxiliary financing agency, to coordinate the funds for technical cooperation projects (Presidência da República, 2016). Other ministries usually have their own subordinates or supporting agencies to implement foreign aids, such as the Fiocruz (National Health Research Institute/Oswaldo Cruz Foundation) under MOH, EMBRAPA (Brazilian Agricultural Research Corporation) under MOA, CAPES (Coordination for the Development of Graduate Human Resources) under MOE and CNPq (National Council for Scientific and Technological Development) under MOST.

Many Brazilian aid projects are carried out in collaboration with third parties (developed countries or international aid agencies), forming tripartite partnerships between Brazil, recipient countries and third-party aid agencies. Usually, Brazil signs a Memoranda of Understanding (MOU) with partner third countries or international organizations, and either Brazil or the third party signs another cooperation agreement with the recipient country. Typically, the third party will provide financial and or technical assistance, Brazil will provide mostly technical assistance, and they will cooperate and complement with each other to help the recipient country. Japan, Germany, International Labor Organization (ILO) and UNDP are among the most important partners with which Brazil forms trilateral aid projects. In this way, Brazil's foreign aid leverages a large amount of money and other resources, and Brazil's national budget support is only a limited part of its foreign aid sources.

India

India's foreign aid system construction dates from its assistance to Nepal. In 1954, India established the Indian Aid Mission (IAM) to monitor and coordinate its aid projects in Nepal. IAM was replaced by the Indian Cooperation Mission (ICM) in 1966, indicating that India's foreign cooperation was beyond the scope of aid. ICM was replaced in 1980 by the New Economic Cooperation Wing (NCW). India also launched the Economic Cooperation Division (ECD) in 1961 under the Ministry of External Affairs (MEA) to tackle the technical assistance projects. It also established Joint Commission in 1969 for the Indian aid and cooperation in Afghanistan. Since then, with the continuous development of its foreign aid, India had set up more institutions to carry out different aid missions or projects and most of them were affiliated with MEA. The increasing complexity of Indian aid system has brought the call for India to establish a new aid agency to integrate and coordinate all Indian foreign aid projects. Even though the India Development Initiative (IDI) was launched in 2003, it was not until 2012 that the Development Partnership Administration (DPA) was finally established when this decade-long initiative culminated in a milestone achievement.

In the Indian aid management system (Fig. 4.3), MEA occupies a dominant position and controls the vast majority of foreign aid budgets. DPA, under MEA, is responsible for managing and coordinating foreign aid projects, for the purpose of "ensuring efficient execution of India's development projects through the stages of concept, launch, implementation and commissioning" (Ministry of External Affairs, 2013, p. xii). Depending on the aid projects and aid areas, DPA has three divisions to manage the foreign aid as shown in the figure. The Ministry of Finance (MOF) is another important actor in India's foreign aid. MOF is responsible for regulating Lines of Credit (LoCs) from the Export-Import Bank of India (Exim Bank), and MEA's proposal for LoCs to other countries needs to be approved by the Economic Affairs Division (EAD) of MOF. Ministry

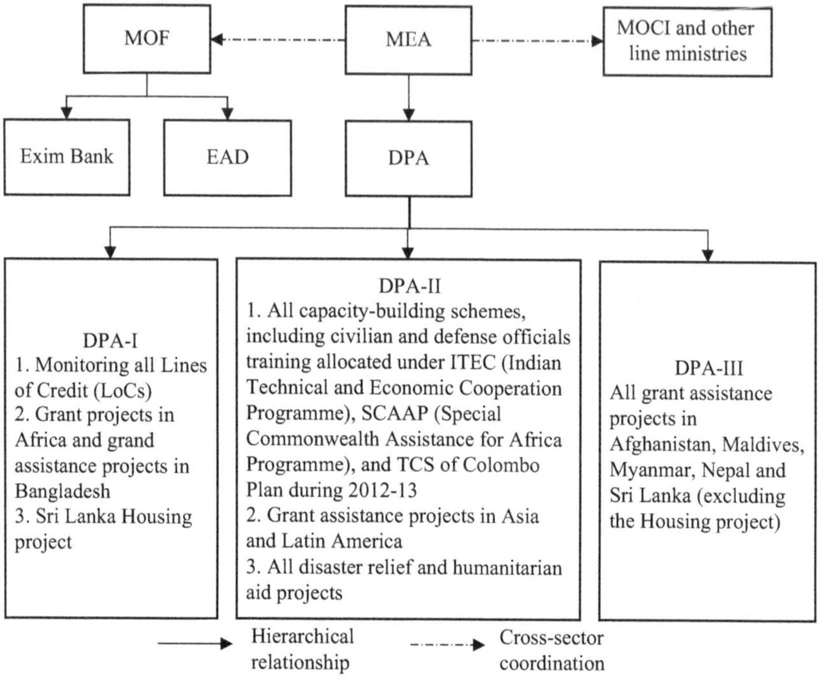

Fig. 4.3 Indian aid management system

of Commerce and Industry (MOCI) and other Indian ministries also play roles in Indian foreign aid. On deciding whether to provide LoCs to a country, MEA usually consults with MOCI on the economic relationship between the two countries. MOA, MOH and other line ministries also work closely with MEA in the implementation of the specific foreign aid tasks (Ministry of External Affairs, 2013).

South Africa

South Africa began to give foreign aid during the apartheid government since the 1950s. The aid projects were concentrated in Africa as a way to seek international support for the apartheid government. These aid projects were under the responsibility of the Ministry of Foreign Affairs and continued even after the 1994 democratic election in South Africa. At the end of 2000, these aid projects were terminated and replaced by the

African Renaissance and International Cooperation Fund (ARF), which was formally established in 2001. ARF is set up under the Department of International Relations and Cooperation (DIRCO) (previously the Ministry of Foreign Affairs), responsible for providing foreign aid of South Africa (Parliament of the Republic of South Africa, 2000). However, the foreign aid carried out by the ARF accounts for only a small part in South Africa. A large number of foreign aid projects are implemented separately through the budgets of each individual ministry. After taking into account the foreign aid activities by various government-funded agencies, semi-state-owned enterprises and other statutory bodies, the proportion of international assistance through ARF is even smaller. The fragmentation among various agencies and lack of coordination in the South Africa aid management system attracted severe criticism domestically. Along with the expansion and diversification of South Africa's development aid, the system with multiple agencies and delivery channels has greatly hindered the effectiveness for aid provision. As a response, in 2007, South Africa proposed an initiative to reconstruct and rationalize its aid management system followed by the official launch of the South African Development Partnership Agency (SADPA) in 2012.

SADPA is to be established to "assume responsibility for all South African outgoing international development cooperation and assistance, including bilateral, trilateral and multilateral partnerships with countries, development institutions, civil society and the private sector", to "coordinate policy formulation on South Africa development cooperation and ensure coherence throughout government in implementation", and to "use SADPA Fund for development cooperation initiatives" (Department of International Relations & Co-operation, 2011). However, the reality is a bit different (Fig. 4.4). SADPA only performs the function of communication and coordination; the operation of aid projects still relies on the line ministries (most active ones are the Ministry of Defense (MOD) and the MOE) with relevant expertise, competencies and networks, and ARF still plays a major role. ARF is in theory under the leadership of DIRCO and reports to DIRCO, but in reality every aid project funded by ARF should be examined and approved by the Advisory Committee of ARF jointly controlled by MOF and DIRCO, and each aid project should be jointly signed by both ministers to take effect (Parliament of the Republic of South Africa, 2000), which makes the ARF very inefficient in both funding usage and organization operation. The SADPA Fund was designed to replace ARF and address the problems aforementioned; however, the

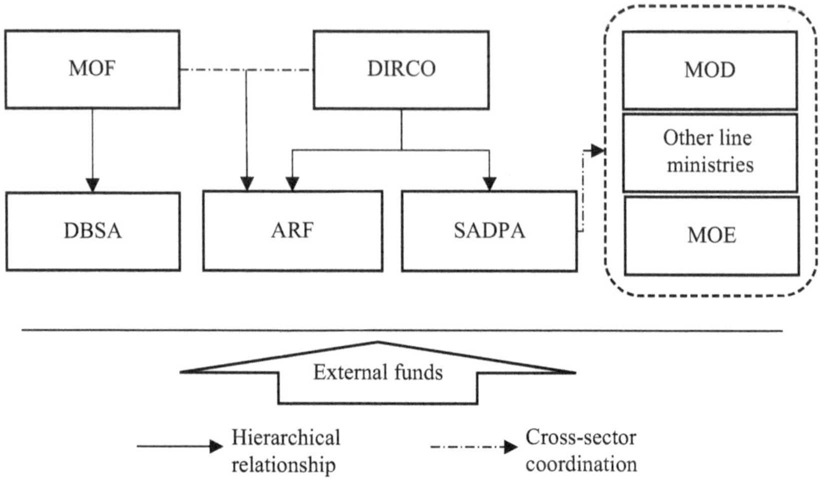

Fig. 4.4 South African aid management system

establishment of this new fund remains to be seen as a result of the failure of political consultation.

MOF is another major actor in South African foreign aid. In addition to the co-direction of ARF with DIRCO, MOF also directs a series of state-owned enterprises which play an important role in South Africa's foreign aid, the most important of which is the Development Bank of South Africa (DBSA). DBSA provides development loans or sovereign lending to other countries which is also a critical aid instrument of South Africa. In addition, MOF also represents South Africa to attend international foreign aid activities in various occasions, such as those development and aid forums of OECD-DAC and the African Development Bank.

Moreover, other ministries, such as MOD and MOE, also play an important role in foreign aid. These ministries have their own independent budgets for international assistance. For example, MOD also has a special Peacekeeping Fund to support its foreign aid activities.

Another source of foreign aid comes from third parties. During the 2000 Mozambique flood, South Africa accepted funds from other donors for its relief actions, and this made the start for trilateral partnership foreign aid model in South Africa. South Africa is a regional power and a large aid provider in Africa, and many donors are willing to cooperate with South Africa in providing aid in Africa. Individual departments prefer to use Memoranda of Understanding or treaties to formalize their cooperation with their counterpart agencies in the third parties. With the increasing number of tripartite cooperation aid projects in South Africa, these ministries can gradually obtain additional funds and resources from third-party aid agencies. Their participation is also an indispensable part of South Africa's foreign aid.

China

Shortly after the founding of People's Republic of China (PRC), China began to provide foreign aid to third-world countries, mainly in the form of in-kind donation and technical assistance. In 1952, China decided to set up the Ministry of Foreign Trade (MFT), responsible for China's in-kind donation. In 1961, Foreign Economic Liaison Administration was established, taking over the foreign aid affairs. It was replaced by Foreign Economic Liaison Committee in 1964, and after a few more institutional changes, in 1982, it was combined with MFT and several other institutions, forming Ministry of Foreign Trade and Economic Cooperation (MOFTEC), but the function of charging Chinese aid issues remained unchanged. Finally, in 2003, it was replaced by the Ministry of Commerce (MOFCOM). The history of being the central executor of foreign aid lay a strong foundation for MOFCOM's core position in Chinese aid management system. The Department of Foreign Aid (DFA) is set up under MOFCOM to manage China's international aid. Later three additional affiliates were created under MOFCOM: Agency for International Economic Cooperation (AIECO), responsible for the management of complete sets of projects and technical cooperation projects; China International Center for Economic and Technical Exchanges (CICETE), responsible for in-kind donation; and Academy for International Business Officials (AIBO), responsible for human resources development cooperation projects. These three affiliate agencies take over the specific implementation work of DFA, and DFA is therefore more focused on long-term international aid management and planning. In order to strengthen the coordination between various ministries and agencies, MOFCOM, together with MFA and MOF, established the Inter-Agency Foreign Aid Contact Mechanism in 2008 and it was formally upgraded to Inter-Agency Foreign Aid Coordination Mechanism (IAFACM) in 2011, becoming an important mechanism for the directing the overall strategy of Chinese foreign aid. In March 2018, China set up Agency for International

Development Cooperation (AIDC) to take charge of China's increasingly large and complicated foreign aid affairs, mainly taking over the foreign aid function from MOFCOM and MFA.

In the Chinese aid management system as shown in Fig. 4.5, MOFCOM, MFA and MoF are important actors, among which MOFCOM is currently playing a central role. The majority of the budgets for bilateral foreign aid are allocated to MOFCOM, although the detailed information on the breakdown among agencies remains unknown to public. DFA of MOFCOM is the core institution of China's foreign aid. DFA is responsible for drafting the aid policy, planning the budget, negotiating and signing the aid agreements, supervising and inspecting aid projects and so on (MOFCOM, 2008). MOFCOM has also set up AIECO, responsible for the management of complete sets of projects and technical cooperation projects; CICETE, responsible for in-kind donation; AIBO, responsible for human resources development cooperation projects. This specific implementation of the foreign aid project, which was originally under the auspices of the DFA, was transferred to these affiliate institutions directly under MOFCOM. The Economic and Commercial Counselor's Office (ECCO) of the Chinese Embassy in recipient countries is responsible for the direct coordination and management of foreign aid projects in the

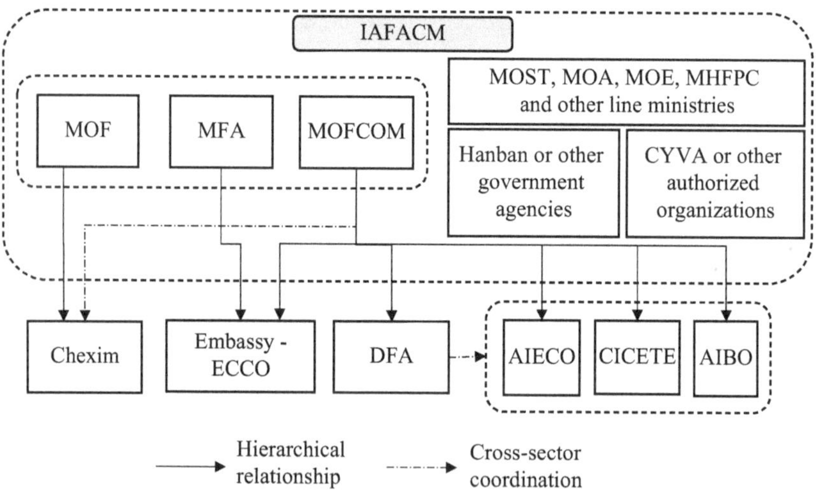

Fig. 4.5 Chinese aid management system

recipient country. MOFCOM has also cooperated closely with the Export-Import Bank of China (Chexim) on concessional loans and export buyer's credits to aid recipient countries.

MFA also plays an important role in China's foreign aid decision-making. MFA and MOFCOM often negotiate to ensure that China's foreign aid policy is in line with China's national foreign policy. MFA can also advise on the design and implementation of aid projects through the embassies overseas. MOF, as the source of funding for Chinese foreign aid, is also vital to the Chinese foreign aid. The budgets and aid programs drafted by MOFCOM are subject to the approval of MOF and incorporated into the national budget for allocating funds. MOF is also responsible for China's multilateral aid compensating for the interest rate of the concessional loans provided by the Chexim.

Other government organizations also engage in the provision of aid in specific fields. For example, MOA is responsible for cooperation with the Food and Agriculture Organization of the United Nations (FAO) and the World Food Program, including assistance to third-world countries. Hanban (Confucius Institute) provides teachers and other educational resources overseas. Chinese Young Volunteers Association (CYVA) and other authorized organizations also play a role in China's international assistance.

A Comparison of the Aid Management System

It is noticeable that all four countries keep reforming their aid management systems, which is also a manifestation that international development is an important topic for emerging economies. This part seeks to compare the aid management systems of these four emerging BRICS donors from the aspects of specialized aid agency, leadership mechanism, funds allocation and cross-sector network.

Specialized Aid Agency

All these four countries have set up specialized aid agencies. Due to the difference of historical legacy, regime and national institutions, the functions of these aid agencies are significantly different. The ABC of Brazil and the SADPA of South Africa tend to be more focused on foreign aid coordination and communication. The two agencies are all based on the condition that the domestic aid implementation actors are very fragmented, and they possess much budget and fund autonomy. Under such institutional heritage and vested sectional interests, the orientation of ABC and SADPA is not to facilitate decision-making or specific aid projects implementation, but to harmonize communication and coordination among various aid actors and agencies. In theory, ABC and SADPA have a comparative advantage in information gathering, diplomatic guidance and monitoring and evaluation. However, in reality, both ABC and SADPA cannot take full advantage to coordinate foreign aid affairs. Even though ABC is in charge of the allocation of funds for technical cooperation and SADPA has a certain influence over the ARF, a large amount of foreign aids are carried out by various ministries and departments respectively, and such a phenomenon has seriously weakened ABC and SADPA's authority to integrate the national aid management system. India's DPA and China's DFA are deeply involved in both foreign aid policy making and implementation. The three divisions under Indian DPA are directly responsible for Indian aid projects, while China's DFA has a direct operational guidance for the implementing agencies of China's aid programs. To some extent, aid policy making and implementation have been integrated for India and China, and therefore they have better performance in communication, coordination, implementation and so on.

Leadership Mechanism

A clear, stable and powerful leadership is an important guarantee for the smooth operation of aid management system. In this regard, the performance of the four countries is all not satisfactory, with India's performance slightly better. The aid leadership in Brazil, which is the coordination between MFA and other ministries, is very loose, while ABC under MFA is essentially only a coordinating agency. The leadership of Brazil is fragmented, and ABC does not have the necessary authority to fulfill its overall coordination function. The situation in South Africa is similar. The communication and coordination between DIRCO and MOF is the most important leadership mechanism. SADPA is also only a coordinating agency. In addition, as DIRCO and MOF have long been competing for the leadership position in foreign aid, and they are now responsible for different aid projects and functions of South Africa separately, the situation is even more complex. In China, MOFCOM is authorized by the State Council to take charge of China's foreign aid, but it needs to communicate with the MOF and the MFA in the actual operation. MOF has less involvement in the bilateral foreign aid, while MFA has relatively a large say. MFA and MOFCOM are quite different in the goal of foreign aid: MFA focuses on the maintenance of China's diplomatic interests, while MOFCOM is to promote China's economic interests. With both ministries posing critical influence on China's foreign aid, there is much friction and competition, especially when diplomatic interests and economic interests are not fully coordinated. India's foreign aid projects are mostly concentrated on MEA, and MEA is also responsible for leading foreign aid; hence, even though there are many ministries involved in foreign aid, in general, the leadership of MEA in India's aid management system is better recognized than in other three countries.

Funds Allocation

The allocation of funds is also an important factor affecting the decision-making and implementation of foreign aid. In this regard, China and India performed slightly better since they have more systematic controlled and coordinated funds allocation system. Most of India's foreign aid funds are allocated through MEA, and the concessionary loans provided by the Export-Import Bank of India also need to be negotiated with MEA. India's other ministries have their respective foreign aid budgets and funds but are quite small compared with that of MEA. In general, India's fiscal power is more concentrated. The situation in China is similar to that of India. MOFCOM is responsible for drawing up the draft for aid budget and obtaining the vast majority of bilateral aid funds, and the provision of concessional loans from the Export-Import Bank of China also needs be decided with MOFCOM. Whereas MOFCOM has little decision-making power on the international cooperation funds of other aligning ministries, these funds are rather small compared to that of MOFCOM. Grimm, Rank, McDonald, and Schickerling (2011) estimated that, between 2001 and 2009, 90% of the final account of the central-level public budget expenditure for foreign aid was appropriated to and implemented by MOFCOM (Grimm et al., 2011). Brazil's federal funding for technical cooperation is allocated mainly through ABC, but parallel ministries and other government agencies have their own budgets or funds for foreign aid, and they can leverage resources from third-party aid agencies through tripartite collaboration. With the fragment of aid budget and aid sources, coordination, and communication, for ABC is quite challenging. The situation in South Africa is also unsatisfactory. ARF is the main administrator for traditional aid projects in South Africa, but the foreign aid expenditure of ARF accounts for a very small proportion of South Africa's overall foreign aid expenditure. Moreover, due to the joint leadership of MOF and DIRCO, the operation of ARF is relatively inefficient. In addition, LoCs provided by DBSA and led by MOF are also a critical fund source of foreign aid. Moreover, other ministries also have large resources for foreign aid and they can get access to third-party funds. In another word, South Africa's aid fund allocation is also dispersed.

Cross-Sector Network

A well-functioning cross-sector network is also critical to the effective operation of foreign aid. From this perspective, all of the four emerging BRICS donors are not good enough compared to many counterparts in developed countries. Various ministries in Brazil and South Africa have their own large budget for international assistance in addition to receiving resources from third-party aid agencies. As such, it is rather difficult for ABC or SADPA to function properly on coordination to play a central role in international assistance practice. The competition between MOF and DIRCO makes the coordination even more difficult in South Africa. Although the DPA in India manages nominally all of India's foreign aid, there remain huge gap and interest conflicts between the three divisions within DPA. Various aid projects are still managed in a much decentralized way due to lack of sufficient cross-sector communication and coordination. Similarly, China's IAFACM is of more symbolic significance than practical significance, whose main task is to hold annual meeting, without daily coordination. Even though MOFCOM theoretically plays a dominant role in China's foreign aid projects, the competition with MFA also makes China's foreign aid management system challenging to integrate and operate in a systematic way.

Conclusion

By analyzing and comparing the aid management systems of the four BRICS emerging economies, it is suggested that all of these four countries still need to improve their systems. All of these four countries have established specialized aid agencies, with Brazil, India and South Africa integrating them into ministries of foreign affairs, while China's into Ministry of Commerce, and China has just recently separated it into an individual cabinet-level aid agency. India's DPA and China's DFA are better integrated than Brazil's ABC and South Africa's SADPA, since DPA and DFA are much more deeply involved in both decision-making and implementation of foreign aid affairs. In terms of leadership mechanism, the Ministry of External Affairs is the sole established authority in terms of foreign aid, while in other three countries, the leadership is shared among a few parallel ministries, making the leadership mechanism complicated and sometimes inefficient. In terms of funds allocation, India's DPA and China's DFA control most of their bilateral aid budgets, respectively, making their aid management system more regulated, compared with their counterparts in Brazil and South Africa, where the funds are dispersed among different ministries and aid agencies without a systematic plan and organization. In regard to cross-sector network, either the competition over decision-making power of foreign aid or the autonomy of getting aid funds of different ministries or aid agencies has made the cross-sector network not satisfactory enough in all four emerging economies.

References

Agência Brasileira de Cooperação. (2018). *Histórico da Cooperação Técnica Brasileira*. Retrieved from http://www.abc.gov.br/SobreAbc/Historico

Department of International Relations & Co-operation. (2011, August 3). *Establishment of Africa Development Partnership Agency (SADPA)* (Presentation to the NCOP Select Committee on Trade and International Relations) [PPT]. Retrieved from http://pmg-assets.s3-website-eu-west-1.amazonaws.com/docs/110803sadpa-edit.pdf

Grimm, S., Rank, R., McDonald, M., & Schickerling, E. (2011). *Transparency of Chinese Aid – An Analysis of the Published Information on Chinese External Financial Flows*. CCS Policy Briefing, November, Stellenbosch: Centre for Chinese Studies.

Ministry of Commerce of the People's Republic of China (中华人民共和国商务部). (2008, August 22). *The Structure and Personnel of Main Agencies and Responsibilities of MOFCOM* (商务部主要职责内设机构和人员编制规定). Retrieved from http://www.mofcom.gov.cn/aarticle/ae/ai/200808/20080805739577.html

Ministry of External Affairs, Government of India. (2013). *Annual Report 2012–2013*. Retrieved from http://www.mea.gov.in/Uploads/PublicationDocs/21385_Annual_Report_2012-2013_English.pdf

Organization for Economic Co-operation and Development (OECD). (2018). *OECD International Development Statistics* [Data File]. Retrieved from https://stats.oecd.org/

Parliament of the Republic of South Africa. (2000). *The African Renaissance and International Co-operation Fund Act* (Act No. 51 of 2000). Retrieved from http://saflii.org/za/legis/num_act/araicfa2000479.pdf

Presidência da República. (2016). *Decreto N° 8.817, de 21 de Junho de 2016.* Retrieved from http://www.planalto.gov.br/ccivil_03/_ato2015-2018/2016/decreto/D8817.htm

U.N. Secretary-General. (2012). *Framework of Operational Guidelines on United Nations Support to South-South and Triangular Cooperation.* Retrieved from https://www.cbd.int/financial/southsouth/un-framework2012.pdf

CHAPTER 5

Two Approaches to Institutionalizing the New Development Assistance: A Comparative Analysis of the Operational Institutions of NDB and AIIB

Jiejin Zhu

Introduction

The BRICS New Development Bank (NDB) and the Asian Infrastructure Investment Bank (AIIB) share some similar features. They are initiated and created by emerging economies and promote infrastructure investment and global governance reform as two institutional mandates. However, their operational modalities and approaches are different. NDB is a borrowing-country-led multilateral development bank (MDB); while AIIB's operation is donor-country-oriented.

On the quota allocation, NDB founding members share the quotas equally, and all the founding members are both borrowers and contributors. In contrast, AIIB's quota allocation is similar to that of existing multilateral development banks. AIIB is composed of borrowing and donor

J. Zhu (✉)
School of International Relations and Public Affairs, Fudan University, Shanghai, China
e-mail: zhujiejin@fudan.edu.cn

Y. Jing et al. (eds.), *New Development Assistance*, Governing China in the 21st Century,
https://doi.org/10.1007/978-981-13-7232-2_5

countries, in which donor countries have important influence. In the environmental and social frameworks, NDB adopts the country system principle, which is different from existing MDBs, to promote borrowing countries' capacity-building and development effectiveness; AIIB adopts the international best standards of environment and society, through co-financing with existing MDBs. On financing, NDB actively uses the local currency financing and capital market, while AIIB focuses on the international capital market and all the projects are denominated in US dollars. NDB has paid more attention to build partnership with the local financial institutions, including national development banks and commercial banks, while AIIB is eager to build partnership with the existing MDBs.

Why do NDB and AIIB differ in their operational models in institutionalizing the new development assistance? Both of them are initiated and created by emerging economies, with infrastructure investment and global governance reform being their institutional mandates. Our main finding is that different dynamics of power politics have shaped the establishment process of these two banks. On NDB, the competition between India and China for leadership emphasizes equality as the prominent feature of institutional design. All the founding members agree that the bank should be borrowing-country-led, especially by its founding members. While on AIIB, with the joining of the European founding members, China is more concerned with the international legitimacy rather than the interests of borrowing countries, so the political pressure of multilateralism from Europe and market pressure of credit rating agencies from the US are driving forces shaping the design of the bank, making it similar to existing MDBs. Although AIIB has some innovations to improve efficiency, such as non-resident board of directors and global procurement, it is still a shareholding-country-led MDB.

Since their establishments, NDB and AIIB have been popular research topics of international political economy. Most scholars have paid attention to the background, governance structure, strategic positioning, and China's role in these banks (Griffith-Jones, 2014; He, 2016; Lichtenstein, 2018; Wan, 2016; Zhu, 2015), but few studies have been done on the difference of operational models of these two banks and the reason why the difference exists.[1]

In addition, the operational models of these two new international institutions represent the different approaches that emerging economies adopt in reforming the global economic governance. The AIIB represents an incremental change approach, taking similar operational models with several small changes to increase the efficiency of the institution, while the NDB is a paradigm shift, from the donor-country-oriented to borrowing-country-oriented. In the short term, it is easier for AIIB to get higher international credit rating and reputation in international financial market. In the long term, however, the NDB can provide more institutional choices for the reform of the global economic governance in favor of developing countries.

This chapter has three parts. First, we discuss the significance of NDB and AIIB in promoting the infrastructure investment and global governance reform. Second, we analyze the operational model of NDB and explain its cause through process tracing of the establishment negotiation, especially the role of India and China. Third, we discuss how AIIB's institutional design was influenced by the political pressure of multilateralism and market pressure of credit rating agencies. In the conclusion, we briefly point out advantages and disadvantages of these two operational modes and their implications for the institutionalization of new development assistance.

Emerging Economies and the Fourth Wave of MDBs

There are four waves of MDBs, each linked with a big event of international politics (Wang, 2017). The first wave was in the 1940s, began by the end of World War II. At the Bretton Woods conference, the US proposed to establish a new multilateral development bank for the European reconstruction and named the bank as International Bank for Reconstruction. But soon after that, the Marshall Plan, also initiated by the US, took the responsibility of the European reconstruction, so the Bank transferred its attention to developing countries and was renamed as International Bank for Reconstruction and Development (IBRD).

The second wave occurred in the 1960s with the tide of decolonization. Responding to demands of many new developing countries, a lot of regional development banks were created, including Asian Development Bank (ADB), African Development Bank (AfDB), Inter-American Development Bank (IDB), Islamic Development Bank (IsDB), Development Bank of Latin America (CAF), and International Development Associate (IDA) and International Financial Corporation (IFC) affiliated with the World Bank Group (WBG). Among these MDBs, only CAF and IsDB are taking different operational modalities from the IBRD.

The third wave began in the 1990s with the end of the Cold War. When the Soviet Union collapsed and many East European countries experienced transition from socialist system to the democratic market system, West European powers proposed to establish the European Bank for Reconstruction and Development (EBRD). Meanwhile, European Investment Bank (EIB) also expanded its businesses to support the integration of East European countries.

The fourth wave was around the 2008 global financial crisis. The rise of emerging economies brings the change of world economic and political architecture. Since 2001, the GDP of BRICS countries are rising from 8% to 23%, while that of the G7 countries decreasing from 65% to 45%. To improve its voice and status in global economic governance, emerging economies initiated two new multilateral development banks: one by India at the BRICS leaders' summit in 2012 and the other by Chinese President Xi Jinping during his trip to Southeast Asian countries in 2013. The four waves of MDBs are summarized in Table 5.1.

Both NDB and AIIB are entrusted with two institutional mandates, promoting infrastructure investment in developing countries and global economic governance reform toward developing countries. There is a huge deficit in infrastructure investment in the developing world. It is also no secret that heavy investment in infrastructure was a key factor in driving sustained growth and modernization for all of the traditional economic powers, as well as the "newly industrialized countries" of Northeast Asia.

Yet there are major shortfalls in infrastructure financing for developing countries. Dr. Nagesh Kumar, former director of the UNESCAP Office (Bangkok), and the ADB, estimates that developing Asia needs to invest $800 billion per year in order to close the infrastructure gaps. The African continent has only started to put its infrastructure in place, despite the many decades of support from the Northern donors. The African Development Bank (AfDB) reports that, as early as 2011, only about a

Table 5.1 The four waves of multilateral development banks (MDBs)

Time	*Defining event*	*Establishment of MDBs*
1940s	End of World War II	IBRD
1960s	Decolonization	ADB, AfDB, IDB, IsDB, CAF, IDA, IFC
1990s	End of the Cold War	EBRD, EIB expansion
2010s	Rise of emerging economies	NDB, AIIB

third of the continent's rural population had access to roads, less than 40% of Africans had access to electricity, only 5% of agriculture was under irrigation, only 34% of the population had access to improved sanitation, and about 65% to clean water (Kaberuka, 2011). Then AfDB President Donald Kaberuka estimated that Africa would need at least $93 billion per year until 2020 to bring the continent's infrastructure on par with that of other low- and middle-income countries. But even the major emerging economies, BRICS countries, had major infrastructure investment needs. At the 2013 BRICS Summit in Durban, South African president Jacob Zuma stated that the infrastructure investment needs of the BRICS countries amounted to $4.5 trillion over the five years up to 2018 (Smith, 2013). The G-24 Secretariat, the coordinating body for a group of 24 developing countries (and China), based at IMF headquarters, estimated that around US$1–1.5 trillion in infrastructure investment per year would be needed to sustain the growth trajectory in the developing world, while the total amount actually invested was about US$800 billion (Bhattacharya & Romani, 2013). Traditional Western donors and the existing MDBs provide limited official development assistance (ODA) to finance infrastructure in developing countries, especially for greenfield projects. The traditional donors had moved away from infrastructure dramatically, and were pulling their aid from the emerging economies for the past two decades (Chin, 2012). Their aid institutions now allocate less than 10% of their resources to infrastructure projects, with most going instead to social sectors such as health and education. The World Bank and the regional development banks (the ADB is the exception) also moved away from infrastructure in the 1980s and 1990s, and channeled their resources instead toward "pro-poor poverty alleviation", and focused especially on health, education, social protection ("human development"), and agriculture, including some investment in water and sanitation ("sustainable development").

Why can't the existing MDBs contribute more to the infrastructure investment in the developing world? The main reason is obstruction by the developed countries, which dominate the decision-making process of the existing MDBs and stick to the Washington Consensus, intentionally neglecting the infrastructure investment needs of the developing countries. In this sense, NDB and AIIB are representing the new ideas and aspirations of emerging economies in the reform of global economic governance.

There are "three dilemmas" in the global governance reform. With the establishment of NDB and AIIB, emerging economies have the potential to play a bigger role in the new global economic governance and address "three dilemmas": knowledge dilemma, advanced countries' opportunistic behavior dilemma, and emerging economies' collective action dilemma.

Firstly, NDB and AIIB can help emerging economies to provide their own knowledge to global development thinking. How to go beyond the Washington Consensus is a big challenge for the current global governance reform. Liberalism and neoliberalism are the dominant thinking of international development, which universalize the development experiences of the advanced countries. In 1998, Joseph Stiglitz, the chief economist of the World Bank, made a famous speech on diversifying the development thinking. It was popular among the developing countries, but resisted by the board of directors of the WB. One year later, Stiglitz was forced to leave the World Bank. For the emerging economies, it is necessary for them to contribute new development knowledge to the mainstreaming thinking if they want to play bigger role in global development governance. Just as Zhu Xian, former WB vice president and currently NDB vice president, said that the main purpose for establishing the New Development Bank is to provide new development knowledge. NDB will focus on infrastructure investment and sustainable development and push South-South financial cooperation. The level of development is different, so the development need is different. The NDB will accumulate the different development knowledge and share it with more developing members.

Secondly, NDB and AIIB can help constrain the opportunistic behavior of advanced countries. For the existing MDBs, most of them are established by advanced countries and have provided a lot of help to developing countries in terms of development finance and technology transfer. However, they sometimes are used by advanced countries as their foreign policy tools (Li, 2016). In this sense, NDB and AIIB can be seen as the institutional balancing and partial exit strategy of the emerging economies, constraining the opportunistic behavior of the advanced countries. Albert Hirshchman's theory of voice and exit can help us understand the logic. When the members are dissatisfied with the organization, they will complain, but if their complaints are not well received by the leader of the organization, then they will exit. So if the members can complain with partial exit, then their complaints will be more effective (Hirschman, 1970).

Thirdly, NDB and AIIB can also help solve the collective action problem of emerging economies. Collective action problem is another dilemma for emerging economies to reform the global economic governance. Every emerging economy wants to improve its own voice, but does not want to pay for this. Mancur Olson's theory shows how the rationality of individuals leads to the irrationality of the collective because of the free-rider problems (Olson, 1971). For emerging economies, advanced countries may make concessions toward some developing countries, like giving the vice president positions of WB and IMF to nationalities of developing countries in 2011 and 2012. Under such circumstances, how to overcome the dilemma of individual rationality and collective rationality is important. With the creation of the NDB and AIIB, emerging economies can have long-term thinking of their national interests and integrated vision of future global economic governance.

Both NDB and AIIB are important in terms of infrastructure investment and global governance reform, but why do these two banks adopt different operational modalities?

Equal Shareholding, Country System, and Borrowing-Country-Oriented NDB

At the first G20 Summit in Washington, DC, on November 14–15, 2008, Indian Prime Minister Manmohan Singh proposed to strengthen the infrastructure investment in developing countries in his speech at the summit table, but his suggestion was almost neglected by the advanced countries and existing multilateral development banks (Singh, 2008). In March 2012, Prime Minister Singh, at the Fourth BRICS summit in New Delhi, proposed to establish a new developing-country-led multilateral development bank, which was basically agreed to by other BRICS leaders. "We have considered the possibility of setting up a new Development Bank for mobilizing resources for infrastructure and sustainable development projects in BRICS and other emerging economies and developing countries, to supplement the existing efforts of multilateral and regional financial institutions for global growth and development. We direct our Finance Ministers to examine the feasibility and viability of such an initiative, set up a joint working group for further study, and report back to us by the next Summit" ("Fourth BRICS", 2012, para. 13), said the BRICS in their summit declaration. So the BRICS New Delhi summit signified the beginning of the establishment of NDB.

In the establishment process of NDB, India and China are two key players. India is an initiating power and China is the de facto veto power because of its huge foreign exchange reserves and much experience on infrastructure investment. Although India and China have the basic consensus on establishing the bank, their concerns and preferences differ. India is more concerned with borrowing countries' interests and sees the NDB as a new source for meeting its own massive infrastructure development needs. Delhi has traditionally relied heavily on the World Bank for infrastructure financing. But India is facing the prospect of no longer being eligible for International Development Association loans. It is therefore not surprising that India has been the advocate for the NDB. However, China is more concerned with the donor countries' interests and sees the NDB as a new source for infrastructure investment. At the same time, China is trying to be a real new donor who can understand the needs of borrowing countries better, based on its own experience with WB and ADB in the past 30 years. The Chinese also take a long view on the NDB, seeing it as useful for driving sustained growth in developing countries and thereby cultivating the new market for Chinese business (Chin, 2014, pp. 366–373). Therefore, India and China are competing for the leadership and direction of this new bank.

At the same time, the change of distribution of power between India and China also has some influence on the establishment process. In 2006 when the BRICS began its cooperation, India's GDP was US$0.8 trillion, and China's GDP was US$2.6 trillion, 3.25 times of India. While in 2012 when India proposed the NDB, India's GDP was US$1.83 trillion, and China's GDP was US$8.56 trillion, 4.68 times of India. This power change has made India more cautious toward China's role in the Bank. Moreover, the bilateral distrust due to national security interests was another factor. China's growing military and diplomatic power is a security threat to India's regional aspirations. An Indian commentator, Jyoti Malhotra, suggested that Delhi worried about China's dominance in the Bank: India joined the BRICS cooperation enthusiastically several years ago, motivated by its anti-Western tradition, but China's rising global influence was making Delhi increasingly nervous (Malhotra, 2013).

Given this concern, India emphasizes the principle of equality as the feature of the new bank. The intensity to which India held this position reflects not only its frustration toward the lack of fairness in dealing with the Bretton Woods system, but also the sensitivity that its ideational leadership on the NDB initiative was threatened by China's financial clout. It is important to note that it was India, rather than China, that took the lead in exploring alternative strategies for development financing in the aftermath of the 2008 global financial crisis (Cooper, 2017, p. 3). However, China's support to this initiative is necessary given China's structural heft in infrastructure investment.

According to India's proposal, the initial capital will be US$10 billion, equally shared by five BRICS members. China didn't block this proposal, but showed hesitation especially toward this kind of quota allocation. China emphasized that this kind of political thinking may cause to undermine the efficiency of the bank. Zhu Ning, an influential scholar at Shanghai Advanced Institute of Finance, was quoted from an interview with China Central Television: "if the five BRICS countries have an equal share in the same entity, there will be coordination problem" (Cooper, 2017, pp. 275–284). The main concern remained the efficiency. Wang Jianye, the leading economist of China Exim Bank, noted, "There are only two kinds of quota allocation, one is according to GDP and financial contribution, the other is according to the political equality, one country one vote. Until now, all the international financial institutions are taking the former one. So the NDB's quota allocation modality needs to do more feasibility studies" (Cooper & Farooq, 2015, pp. 1–15).

China's hesitation, however, further strengthened India's concern that China may dominate the decision-making of the NDB. Ultimately, with the help of other members, India was able to mobilize a successful defense of the principle of equality, a condition embedded in the declaration of the NDB. Meanwhile, China also proposed three suggestions for the bank's operation in terms of improving the efficiency, and they were accepted by India and other BRICS members.

First, the headquarters of NDB should be in Shanghai, China. Although the principle of equality reflects the aspiration of BRICS countries for a new world order, it also has limited China's financial contribution to this bank. To borrow the money from local capital market by issuing bonds is an important tool to expand the NDB's capital base. For this reason, Shanghai, one of the best financial centers in the BRICS countries, is a good choice for the headquarters of NDB.

Second, the authorized capital of NDB should be expanded from US$10 billion to $100 billion. China suggested that the NDB should be more ambitious in terms of capital base. At the same time, in order not to increase financial burden for those BRICS members who have less foreign exchange reserves, the paid-in capital of NDB is still US$10 billion. It is a good balance between the US$100 billion authorized capital and the US$10 billion paid-in capital.

Third, the Bank should lend money to all the developing countries. In order to get more money from the Bank, India once proposed the Bank should be focused on BRICS members, while China took the different view that the Bank should lend globally in order to increase its influence in the developing word. In addition, in order to balance China's influence as the hosting country of the Bank, India insisted that the first president of the Bank should come from India, and it was accepted by China too. The summary of the different institutional proposals can be seen in Table 5.2.

On July 15, 2014, BRICS leaders announced the establishment of the NDB, which was useful in reducing the skepticism about BRICS' institutional capacity to produce real results. Just as the BRICS leaders mentioned in the declaration, "we are pleased to announce the signing of the Agreement establishing the New Development Bank (NDB), with the purpose of mobilizing resources for infrastructure and sustainable development projects in BRICS and other emerging and developing economies. The Bank shall have an initial authorized capital of US$100 billion. The initial subscribed capital shall be of US$50 billion (paid-in capital shall be US$10 billion), equally shared among founding members. The first chair of the Board of Governors shall be from Russia. The first chair of the Board of Directors shall be from Brazil. The first President of the Bank shall be from India. The headquarters of the Bank shall be located in

Table 5.2 Indian proposal, Chinese proposal, and BRICS proposal of NDB

	Quota allocation	*Capital base*	*Headquarter*	*President*	*Scope of lending*
Indian proposal	According to the principle of equality	US$10 billion	New Delhi	First president from India	BRICS countries
Chinese proposal	According to GDP size	US$100 billion	Shanghai	First president from China	All the developing countries
BRICS proposal	According to the principle of equality	US$10 billion as paid-in capital, and US$100 billion as authorized capital	Shanghai	First president from India	All the developing countries

Shanghai. The Africa Regional Center shall be established in South Africa concurrently with the headquarters" ("The 6th BRICS", 2014, p. 3).

In addition to the equal shareholding principle, the use of country system is another institutional innovation that favors borrowing countries. The idea of strengthening and using country systems came from many years of aid allocation experience in developing countries. Evidence shows that when donors bypass country systems and policies in favor of the donors' own policies and procedures, the sustainability of their efforts, along with the country's ability to manage their own development, is undermined. The use of country systems promises to alleviate the load on borrowing countries of having to deal with multiple policies, in particular procurement rules; make it easier for donors to co-finance operations; and in the long run reduce the transaction costs for the countries. Most importantly, it also provides a strong incentive for countries to bring their systems to an acceptable standard and thus scale up development by improving the return on all government expenditures, not just those funded by donors.

For India, country system can improve the borrowing countries' development autonomy, while for China, country system can improve NDB's influence and popularity in the developing world, so both India and China agreed on the use of country system during the negotiation. In fact, country system is not a new concept. It has been discussed extensively in the G20 and existing multilateral development financing system, but the implementation of country system is very slow. In the 2010 G20 Toronto summit, the G20 leaders made the commitment, "Existing MDBs should take specific actions for greater transparency, stronger accountability, improved institutional governance deeper country ownership, more decentralization and use of country systems where appropriate" ("The G20 Toronto", 2010, p. 24). Although the G20 built the consensus, the use of country system is still very limited.

In its reform of Environmental and Social Framework during 2012–2016, the World Bank also emphasized the use of country system, but the process proved to be controversial and slow. Anis Dani, a former senior evaluator at the bank's Internal Evaluation Group, said that World Bank's future influence lies in persuasion and capacity-building rather than enforcement. "The only way that safeguards will work is if countries take this on board, and the bank no longer has the leverage to thrust this down the throats of countries like China and India and even in Africa" (Chavkin, 2016); However, many international non-governmental organizations give their pressure on the WB's use of country system. Nadia Daar, program director at Oxfam International, bluntly criticized the idea of country system, "We are disappointed that if the World Bank use the country system. We have a high expectation towards the World Bank that it can set the highest standards in environmental and social protection, but the use of country system will shift the responsibility to borrowing countries, which is an irresponsible behavior" (Donnan, 2016).

On the contrary, NDB prefers to use the country system principle in its operations. In the NDB's first Five-Year General Strategy, NDB sees using country system as the best way to strengthen a country's own capacity and achieve long-term development results better. As such, in every project, NDB intends to verify ex ante the quality of borrowing country's environmental, social, fiduciary, and procurement systems, and use them whenever they meet NDB's requirements. In case a country's systems are not deemed acceptable, NDB will fill the gaps with additional requirements tailored to the specific needs of the project at hand. Importantly, the use of country system means encouraging clients to thoroughly apply the country's own legislation and procedures, and work together with relevant agencies to propose actions whenever compliance falls short of national and local requirements (NDB, 2017). Zhu Xian, NDB's Vice President and Chief Operations Officer, points out that every country is concerned with the environmental and social protections, but there are no unified high standards suitable for every country. World Bank, often under the pressure from some advanced counties, lifts the standards to the advanced countries' level and makes it too high for some developing countries, increasing unnecessary operational costs for some projects. If NDB uses the high standards of World Bank, the projects might be safer, but projects would succeed only when borrowing countries are in charge of their own development path, as the NDB learns from its founding members' experiences.[2]

To sum up, NDB is a new South-South multilateral development bank with equal shareholding and use of country system as two prominent institutional features. The competition between India and China is an important reason for this. The final institutional design or the multilateral proposal of the NDB, emphasizing borrowing-country-oriented and localized operational modality is mainly a concession between Indian proposal and Chinese proposal. The process of establishment of NDB reflects the spirit of BRICS, namely mutual respect and understanding, equality, solidarity, openness, inclusiveness, and mutually beneficial cooperation.

Multilateralism, Market Pressure, and Donor-Country-Oriented AIIB

In contrast, AIIB is a new multilateral development bank initiated by China. In order to increase the international legitimacy of AIIB and attract the European countries to be the founding members, China faces the political pressure of multilateralism mainly from the European countries and market pressure of credit rating mainly from the US, pushing the AIIB into taking a donor-country-oriented operational modality which is similar to that of existing MDBs.

In October 2013, Chinese President Xi Jinping proposed to establish the AIIB during his visit to Indonesia. His initiative was welcomed immediately by the developing countries from Southeast Asia, South Asia, and Central Asia, but the non-Asian countries, especially those from Europe and North America, were skeptical about it. Two main concerns were raised: one is whether the AIIB is a Chinese bank or a multilateral bank; the other is whether AIIB will lower the high standards of the existing multilateral development banks, including governance structure, environmental and social standards, transparency, and procurement policies (Harpaz, 2016). Behind these concerns, a core question is what China really wants from the initiative of AIIB.

From the geoeconomics perspective, one critique is that China wishes to use the AIIB to export its excessive industrial capacity and promote the renminbi (RMB) internationalization. The Chinese economy presently has major overcapacities in many of its industrial sectors, such as steel, energy, and construction, where domestic returns have been declining. As much of this could be put to use in infrastructure projects, several analysts argued the AIIB is in part designed to create business for Chinese heavy industrial sectors. More broadly, AIIB can create opportunities which encourage Chinese companies to "go abroad" by expanding their access to new markets (Sun, 2015). In addition, China holds massive foreign exchange reserves, much of which are used to buy the US bonds. If the Chinese government uses the AIIB to ensure the infrastructure contracts are awarded to its companies, and are RMB-denominated, it can help Chinese government to diversify its investment and also promote the internationalization of China's currency, the RMB. According to the Chinese proposal, China is the largest shareholder of the AIIB, and its headquarters will be located in Beijing, and its president will be a Chinese citizen. So some people even see AIIB as a disguised cash register for

Chinese state-owned enterprises (Roach, Daojiong, Kennedy, & Chovanec, 2015).

From the geopolitics perspective, some people doubt that AIIB will be the "Belt and Road Bank" and serve China's foreign policy. Since both AIIB and "Belt and Road Initiative" (BRI) are proposed by Chinese President Xi Jinping in 2013, and both emphasize the infrastructure investment and economic connectivity, it is suggested that China may use the AIIB to channel capital those which politically align with its BRI plan (Beeson & Li, 2016, pp. 491–499). In addition, AIIB may be used as a diplomatic tool for China to "subsidize" those countries that are friendly toward China in the escalating US-China competition in the Asia-Pacific area since the Obama administration released the strategy of "Pivot to Asia".

In fact, these critiques have produced negative influences on AIIB's international legitimacy and its membership expansion. In October 2014, 21 countries signed the Memorandum of Understanding (MoU) to establish the AIIB, including Bangladesh, Brunei, Cambodia, China, India, Kazakhstan, Kuwait, Laos, Malaysia, Mongolia, Myanmar, Nepal, Pakistan, the Philippines, Qatar, Singapore, Sri Lanka, Thailand, Uzbekistan, and Vietnam. Except China and India, most of the signatories are small developing countries in South, Southeast, and West Asia. Major economies, including Japan, Korea, Australia, and Russia, initially sat on the sidelines. Japan refused to join on several occasions, expressing its concerns on the AIIB's governance and transparency as well as its possible competition with the ADB. The US repeated its concern that AIIB may lower the international standards of WB and ADB, and also discouraged its Asian allies, including Australia and South Korea, from joining it.

On March 12, 2015, the UK became the first major Western country to seek to join the AIIB. The Chancellor of the Exchequer, George Osborne, announced that the UK intends to become a prospective founding member of the AIIB. "UK will play a key role in ensuring that the AIIB embodies the best standards in accountability, transparency and governance, which will be essential to ensuring the success of the initiative and to unlocking the potential benefits for the wider global economy" (Treasury & Osborne, 2015). However, the US government made clear its displeasure about Osborne's decision to join the AIIB. A US official told the *Financial Times*: "We are wary about a trend toward constant accommodation of China, which is not the best way to engage a rising power" (Watt, Lewis, & Branigan, 2015, para. 6). While the UK's joining has set off a flood of other membership applications, including Germany,

France, Italy, Switzerland, Russia, South Korea, Brazil, Turkey, and so on, Germany, France, and Italy mentioned in their joint declaration to establish the AIIB that follows the best standards and practices in terms of governance, safeguards, and debt and procurement policies (AIIB, 2015). Zhao (2015), a Chinese scholar specializing in European studies, argues that it is a new engagementalism that the main players of the existing MDBs join the AIIB to guarantee the high standards. Doris Fischer, a China expert in Germany, points out that it is a good division of labor for European countries to join the AIIB while the US keeps outside, because Europeans have higher standards than the US in terms of human rights and sustainable development (Fischer, 2015).

By the deadline of March 31, 2015, 57 countries signed up as the founding members, including 37 Asian and 20 non-Asian countries. The number was much higher than expected and widely seen as a victory for China. Jin Liqun, director of the Interim Secretariat, points out that the Chinese government's original expectation was around 20 countries, mainly Southeast, South, and West Asian developing countries. The unexpected growing membership, especially with the admission of the European powers, poses a dilemma for AIIB: whether it should be a bank dominated by Asian developing economies and China-controlled or an internationally legitimate bank similar to the existing MDBs in which China's influence is limited. If it was dominated by Asian developing countries, and China in particular, the AIIB will be more concerned with developing countries' needs and national circumstances, but its international influence and legitimacy will be more limited. If it was more broadly represented, especially with the participation of European powers, the AIIB will still be a donor-country-oriented bank like the World Bank and ADB, but it will be more influential and legitimate. During the negotiation process, Chinese negotiators chose the latter (Ikenberry & Lim, 2017; Kaya & Woo, 2018).

After the participation of European powers, the interim secretariat organized three important conferences to negotiate the AIIB's Articles of Agreement (AOA) and operational policies (OP). Generally, although China and European powers have the basic consensus on establishing the bank, there are also some differences of their concerns and preferences. China hopes the AIIB can contribute more to Asian infrastructure investment and to export its own infrastructure industrial capacity. At the same time, China also wants to be a new donor who can understand borrowing countries' needs better and take some innovative measures to improve the efficiency of MDBs. However, for European countries, besides making profits and material interests for their domestic infrastructure companies in Asian infrastructure investment, they are more concerned with AIIB's high standards, avoiding its possible negative effects on the international best practices of environment and social protection, including environmental and social safeguards and procurement policies.

In order to analyze the detailed differences among the key players of the establishment negotiation, we can first take the MoU of AIIB in October 2014 as the Chinese proposal, because at that time, most prospective founding members were small and middle-sized Asian developing countries, and Chinese institutional thinking and argument are basically reflected in the MoU. Then we can take the European suggestions to "polish" the Chinese proposal as the European proposal which mainly happened after March 2015 (Wilson, 2017). Finally, we can take the AOA and Operational Policy of the AIIB as the multilateral proposal, which is a compromise between China and the European Powers. The difference between the Chinese proposal, the European proposal, and the final multilateral proposal can be seen in Table 5.3.

On shareholding allocation, China would hold more than 50% of share in its original proposal. From China's perspective, holding the majority share would guarantee the Bank to be established and well functioned. With the joining of more countries, especially non-regional countries, Chinese shareholding will naturally be diluted but China still holds the largest share. From the European perspective, however, Chinese veto power concession was made to secure the involvement of European countries, who from the outset had made this as a condition for their participation (Wilson, 2017). Finally, both sides make compromise: Europe agrees that China will have the veto power in the initial period of the AIIB's operation in order to play a leadership role; China agrees to give up the veto power when more countries join the bank.

On governance structure, the Chinese proposal is to combine the advantages of MDBs and the private sectors which usually delegate more power to the management team, while the existing MDBs have big problems of labor of division between the management team and Board of Directors, but from the European perspective, it is important to supervise the management team and the operation of the Bank on a regular basis. The bank should be a real multilateral and transparent bank rather than a China-controlled or Chinese-style bank. Finally, both sides make concessions: on one hand, European countries agree that the board of directors will be non-resident and delegate the project approval power to the

Table 5.3 Chinese proposal, European proposal, and multilateral proposal

	Shareholding allocation	*Governance structure*	*Environmental and social framework*	*Procurement policy*
Chinese proposal	More than 50%	Strengthen the power and efficiency of the management team and reduce the interference of board of directors	Environmental and social safeguards should be different according to different levels of development	Procurement policy should be tailored to different countries' circumstances and respect the borrowing countries' development strategy
European proposal	Chinese veto power should be avoided	Strengthen the oversight mechanism by the board of directors in line with the principles of transparency and accountability	High environmental and social standards similar to existing MDBs	Avoid the AIIB to be the tool of Chinese export of its overcapacity
Multilateral proposal	Chinese share is 30.34%, but with new members joining, Chinese veto power will be diluted.	Board of Directors is non-resident, but it will supervise the management team on a regular basis including on audit, evaluation, fraud and corruption, project complaints, and staff grievances, and reflect the Bank's character as a multilateral financial institution	International best environmental and social standards similar to existing MDBs	The bank shall place no restriction upon the procurement of goods and services from any country and pursue commercially oriented procurement goals, which emphasize value for money and transparency

management team; on the other hand, China agrees that the board of directors will establish an oversight mechanism to supervise the management team, in line with the principle of transparency, openness, independence, and accountability. The oversight mechanism will address such areas as audit, evaluation, fraud and corruption, project complaints, and staff grievances, reflecting the Bank's character as a multilateral development bank focused on infrastructure investment.

On environmental and social policies, Chinese proposal is to simplify the existing MDBs' environmental and social high safeguards to improve the development ownership of borrowing countries and reduce the lending cost. From the European perspective, MDBs, including the AIIB, should bear the responsibility to promote environmental and social high standards in developing countries. Finally, the multilateral proposal mentions that "Representatives emphasized that the operational policies would be subject to approval by the board of directors and should be based on international best practices. These policies, among others, would include environmental and social frameworks, disclosure, and debt sustainability".[3]

On procurement policy, the Chinese proposal is that procurement policy should be differentiated and diversified according to the different development stages and national circumstances of the borrowing countries. From the European perspective, in order to avoid the AIIB to be a policy tool for China to export its industrial overcapacity and serve China's interests of Belt and Road Initiative, AIIB should adopt a market-based approach to procurement policy and pay due regard to the desirability of avoiding a disproportionate amount of its resources being used for the benefit of one country. Finally, the multilateral proposal mentions that "the AIIB procurement policy should be based on international best practices. The bank shall place no restriction upon the procurement of goods and services from any country from the proceeds of any financing undertaken in the ordinary or special operations of the bank".[4]

To sum up, after a series of multilateral negotiations, AIIB became a new donor-country-oriented multilateral development bank with international best standards similar to WB and ADB. Of course, AIIB has some institutional innovations compared to the existing MDBs, such as focus on the infrastructure investment, non-resident board of directors, global procurement, and global recruitment. However, from the perspective of the relationship between borrowing countries and donor countries, AIIB is still a traditional donor-country-oriented bank or the North-South cooperation bank, which is the biggest difference between the AIIB and NDB.

In addition to the political pressure of multilateralism from European countries, market pressure from the US big three credit rating agencies also played a role in shaping AIIB's operational modality. Like the World Bank and Asian Development Bank, the AIIB is not funding its projects mainly by the paid-in capital of its founding members, but rather the funding comes mainly from the capital raised in the international financial markets. In order to reduce the borrowing costs, it is important for the AIIB to take similar standards from the existing MDBs. In AIIB's first series of projects, three of the four projects are co-financed with the WB, ADB, and EBRD, and apply to similar environmental and social standards, which is a deliberate strategy to allow the AIIB to build up a portfolio of low-risk projects and positive reputation in financial markets. The structural feature of relying on international capital markets to fund multilateral development loans inherently pushes the AIIB to take the operational modality similar to WB and ADB (Ikenberry & Lim, 2017). Just as Jin Liqun pointed out, international credit rating is very important for AIIB, and we need to take all these factors related to credit rating into account, including governance structure, quota allocation, institution building, and so on. AIIB will gradually be welcomed by the Western powers, because it is really operated with international high standards (Liu, Han, & Yu, 2018).

Conclusion

From a historical institutionalism perspective, this chapter has explored the difference between NDB and AIIB in their operational modalities, focusing on the political interactions among the key players during the establishment processes. In the NDB case, India is the initiator, while China is the veto player. The competition between India and China for the leadership of the Bank resulted in equal shareholding and the use of country system as two prominent institutional features, and it finally leads to a borrowing-country-oriented or South-South cooperation-style bank; in the AIIB case, China is the initiator, while European countries are the major veto players in terms of the success of the new bank. After the joining of European powers, China is more concerned with the international legitimacy of the bank rather than the needs of borrowing countries, leading AIIB to be a donor-country-oriented bank which is similar to existing MDBs.

As emerging economies, BRICS countries, especially China, have the willingness and capabilities to create new multilateral development banks. Varieties of operational modality reflect different approaches of emerging economies participating in the global economic governance. The borrowing-country-oriented model, such as what the NDB has used, reflects developing countries' thinking on international development. The donor-country-oriented model with international best practices, such as what the AIIB has used, is similar to existing MDBs. Each strategy has its own strengths and weaknesses.

On the one hand, it would be easier for the AIIB to get higher credit rating and lower borrowing costs in the international capital market. On the other hand, NDB might be more able to provide institutional choices and ideas based on its practice of equal shareholding governance and use of country system. NDB is the first multilateral development bank of global scope set up exclusively by developing countries with no participation of advanced countries in the initial stage, which is a testament to creating a truly transformative development finance institution.

Beyond the study of operational modalities of NDB and AIIB, this chapter has implications for the post-crisis global development governance reform. For the new development assistance, NDB represents a new type of South-South cooperation approach, and the AIIB represents a new type of "old" North-South cooperation approach. Multilateral development bank is one of the few areas that global governance has transitioned from the one dominated by advanced countries to the one co-led by advanced and emerging economies, but several factors still affect emerging countries' participation in global economic governance. One is the relationship among the emerging economies, especially the lack of mutual trust and confidence; another is the structural power of the advanced countries, whether it is in the form of legitimacy of the new international institution or in the form of market pressure like credit rating. Only when the emerging economies can play a greater role in solving these problems, global governance can be really "Global" governance rather than the "Western" governance.

Notes

1. There are a lot of misjudgments about these two banks; most of them think AIIB is more effective than the NDB. In the first two years, AIIB now has 84 members, projects worth 4.2 billion dollars, and AAA credit ratings from the big three international credit rating agencies, while NDB has only five members, projects worth 3 billion dollars, and AAA credit ratings from the big three China domestic credit rating agencies. From different operational modalities perspective, both AIIB and NDB have their advantages and disadvantages.
2. See: http://www.nsd.pku.edu.cn/meetings/gezheng/JB/2016/0530/26526.html

3. "Report on the Articles of Agreement of the Asian Infrastructure Investment Bank", Explanatory Notes, Article 13, Paragraph 4.
4. "Articles of Agreement of the Asian Infrastructure Investment Bank", Article 13, Paragraph 8.

References

Asian Infrastructure Investment Bank (AIIB). (2015, March 17). *Federal Ministry of Finance (Germany)*. Retrieved from http://www.bundesfinanzministerium.de/Content/DE/Pressemitteilungen/Finanzpolitik/2015/03/2015-03-17-PM12.html

Beeson, M., & Li, F. (2016). China's Place in Regional and Global Governance: A New World Comes into View. *Global Policy, 7*(4), 491–499.

Bhattacharya, A., & Romani, M. (2013, March). Meeting the Infrastructure Challenge: The Case for a New Development Bank. In *Prepared for the G-24 Technical Group Meeting*.

Chavkin, S. (2016, August 3). Debate Surrounds World Bank's Proposed New Safeguards Rules. *International Consortium of Investigative Journalists*. Retrieved from https://www.icij.org/blog/2016/08/debate-surrounds-world-banks-proposed-new-safeguards-rules/

Chin, G. T. (2012). China as a 'Net Donor': Tracking Dollars and Sense. *Cambridge Review of International Affairs, 25*(4), 579–603.

Chin, G. T. (2014). The BRICS-Led Development Bank: Purpose and Politics Beyond the G20. *Global Policy, 5*(3), 366–373.

Cooper, A. F. (2017). The BRICS' New Development Bank: Shifting from Material Leverage to Innovative Capacity. *Global Policy, 8*(3), 275–284.

Cooper, A. F., & Farooq, A. (2015). Testing the Club Dynamics of the BRICS: The New Development Bank from Conception to Establishment. *International Organizations Research Journal, 10*(2), 39–58.

Donnan, S. (2016, August 5). World Bank Draws Ire with Rule Changes. *Financial Times*. Retrieved from http://www.ftchinese.com/story/001068790?archive

Fischer, D. (2015, March 18). *Is AIIB Splitting the West?* Retrieved from https://www.dw.com/zh/亚投行成功分裂西方/a-18321859

Fourth BRICS Summit: Delhi Declaration. (2012, March 29). *New Delhi*. Retrieved from http://www.brics.utoronto.ca/docs/120329-delhi-declaration.html

Griffith-Jones, S. (2014). *A BRICS Development Bank: A Dream Coming True?* (No. 215). United Nations Conference on Trade and Development.

Harpaz, M. (2016). China's Coherence in International Economic Governance. *Journal of Chinese Political Science, 21*(2), 123–147.

He, A. (2016). *China in the International Financial System: A Study of the NDB and the AIIB* (No. 106). Center for International Governance Innovation.

Hirschman, A. (1970). *Exit, Voice, and Loyalty: Responses to Decline in Firms, Organizations, and States.* Cambridge, MA: Harvard University Press.

Ikenberry, G. J., & Lim, D. J. (2017). *China's Emerging Institutional Statecraft: The Asian Infrastructure Investment Bank and the Prospects for Counter-Hegemony.* Washington, DC: Brookings Institution. Retrieved from https://www.brookings.edu/wpcontent/uploads/2017/04/chinas-emerging-institutional-statecraft.pdf

Kaberuka, D. (2011). Boosting Infrastructure Investments in Africa. *World Economics, 12*(2), 7–24.

Kaya, A., & Woo, B. (2018, February). *China and the Asian Infrastructure Investment Bank: The Influence-Legitimacy Tradeoff.* Paper presented at the 11th Annual Conference on the Political Economy of International Organizations. Retrieved from http://wp.peio.me/the-11th-annual-conference-2

Li, W. (2016). International Order Transition and Realistic Institutionalism. *Foreign Affairs Review, 33*(1), 31–59.

Lichtenstein, N. (2018). *A Comparative Guide to the Asian Infrastructure Investment Bank.* Oxford: Oxford University Press.

Liu, H., Han, J., & Yu, Q. (2018, January 16). Always Take a Good Long March of AIIB. *Xinhua News.* Retrieved from http://www.xinhuanet.com/fortune/2018-01/16/c_129792362.htm

Malhotra, J. (2013, April 1). Second Thoughts on BRICS Development Bank. *Business Standard.* Retrieved from http://www.business-standard.com/article/international/second-thoughts-on-brics-development-bank-113040100035_1.html

NDB. (2017, July). *NDB's General Strategy: 2017–2021.* New Development Bank. Retrieved from https://www.ndb.int/wp-content/uploads/2017/07/NDB-Strategy-Final.pdf

Olson, M. (1971). *The Logic of Collective Action: Public Goods and the Theory of Groups.* Cambridge, MA: Harvard University Press.

Roach, S. S., Daojiong, Z., Kennedy, S., & Chovanec, P. (2015). Washington's Big China Screw-Up. *Foreign Policy, 26.* Retrieved from http://foreignpolicy.com/2015/03/26/washingtons-big-china-screw-up-aiib-asia-infrastructure-investment-bank-china-containment-chinafile/

Singh, M. (2008, November 15). *Statement by the Prime Minister of India, Dr. Manmohan Singh, at the Summit of the Heads of State or Governments of the G-20 Countries on Financial Markets and the World Economy.* Embassy of India, Washington, DC. Retrieved from https://www.indianembassy.org/archives_details.php?nid=955

Smith, D. (2013). BRICS Eye Infrastructure Funding Through New Development Bank. *The Guardian, 28.* Retrieved from http://www.guardian.co.uk/global-development/2013/mar/28/brics-countries-infrastructure-spending-development-bank

Sun, Y. (2015). China and the Evolving Asian Infrastructure Investment Bank. In D. Bob (Ed.), *Asian Infrastructure Investment Bank: China as Responsible Stakeholder*. Washington, DC: Sasakawa Peace Foundation.

The 6th BRICS Summit: Fortaleza Declaration. (2014, July 15). *BRICS Information Centre*. Retrieved from http://www.brics.utoronto.ca/docs/140715-leaders.html

The G20 Toronto Summit Declaration. (2010, June 27). *G20 Information Centre*. Retrieved from http://www.g20.utoronto.ca/2010/to-communique.html

Treasury, H. M., & Osborne, G. (2015, March 12). UK Announces Plans to Join Asian Infrastructure Investment Bank. *U.K. Government News Release*. Retrieved from https://www.gov.uk/government/news/uk-announces-plans-to-join-asian-infrastructure-investment-bank

Wan, M. (2016). *The Asian Infrastructure Investment Bank: The Construction of Power and the Struggle for the East Asian International Order*. New York: Palgrave Macmillan.

Wang, H. (2017). New Multilateral Development Banks: Opportunities and Challenges for Global Governance. *Global Policy, 8*(1), 113–118.

Watt, N., Lewis, P., & Branigan, T. (2015, March). US Anger at Britain Joining Chinese-Led Investment Bank AIIB. *The Guardian*. Retrieved from https://www.theguardian.com/us-news/2015/mar/13/white-house-pointedly-asks-uk-to-use-its-voice-as-part-of-chinese-led-bank

Wilson, J. D. (2017). The Evolution of China's Asian Infrastructure Investment Bank: From a Revisionist to a Status-Seeking Agenda. *International Relations of the Asia-Pacific*. Retrieved from https://academic.oup.com/irap/advance-article/doi/10.1093/irap/lcx015/4211033

Zhao, K. (2015). The New Engagementalism of European Countries Towards Asia-Pacific. *European Studies, 33*(2), 16–28.

Zhu, J. (2015). The Strategic Role and Institutional Design of the NDB. *Social Science*, (6), 24–34.

CHAPTER 6

Is Development Assistance Getting Better Due to the Widening Role of Emerging Economies?

Neil Renwick and Jing Gu

Introduction

There is a seismic shift emerging in the way that the international development assistance regime is conceived, managed and run. It has two primary causes: *Firstly*, the weaknesses and limitations of the existing system, as grounded in the hegemonic and exclusionary power and influence of the West. *Secondly*, the arrival of the "emerging economies" with globalization, which are challenging the structural institutional architecture, central principles and underlying values of the old system, along with its managerial system and effectiveness of delivery. A central and critical aim of these emerging states is the fundamental and irreversible reform of the existing system and, even more radical, a fundamental change in the way

N. Renwick (✉)
School of Humanities & Institute of Confucius, Coventry University, Coventry, UK
e-mail: aa2458@coventry.ac.uk

J. Gu
Institute of Development Studies, University of Sussex, Brighton, UK
e-mail: J.Gu@ids.ac.uk

Y. Jing et al. (eds.), *New Development Assistance*, Governing China in the 21st Century,
https://doi.org/10.1007/978-981-13-7232-2_6

international development assistance is understood. The new development assistance (NDA) practiced by these states reflects many influences, the most important of which are their historical experiences as colonized or semi-colonized countries and their long, often bitter paths to independence, reform and renaissance, and their experiences as recipients of international development assistance. Within this shared generic experience, each brings their own distinctive history, understanding and practices of development to NDA. At the center of NDA is the complex relationship between the traditional system and its counter-point, an intricate diachronic process. In this process, the agencies of NDA engage with the principles, structures, processes and practices of the OECD-DAC (Development Assistance Committee) system. In this respect, NDA is selectively learning from the "traditional" system whilst simultaneously stepping away from it to establish a "new" institutional architecture predicated on distinct principles and practices that deviate from that system.

This paper examines the current impact and future implications of the ever more central role played by "emerging economies" in international development assistance, in light of the wide-ranging challenges to the currently prevailing development system and the search for innovative responses. As the Introduction to the present volume has explained, the system of development assistance that has evolved since the end of the Second World War has come under increasing criticism arising from a powerful combination of economic and political transformations in the global system. The emergence of critical voices from the so-called Global South has encouraged robust, concerted pressure for changes in the way the existing system operates. Structures, processes and institutional agencies at the core of the development assistance system have been interrogated on a wide range of failings rooted in the underlying distribution of international economic, political, socio-cultural and discursive power exercised by the Western states since the conclusion of the Second World War. The domination of these states in the international development assistance system they established has long been a source of tension with the independent states of Africa, Asia and Latin America that achieved their formal political freedom from the West in the post-war era. Despite a decades-long process whereby the post-independence states have painstakingly constructed a sense of collective identity, aims and objectives, they never did find the capacity to achieve that "critical mass" of countervailing power requisite for systemic change. This is attributable to the structural power and institutional influence of the Western states: the prolonged Cold War ideological and geo-strategic competition for influence and control in the post-independence states, inciting divisions between and within them; Western sovereign and corporate economic power constraining the opportunity structure and building-in debilitating economic dependencies, political destabilization and social fragmentation in post-independence states; and the history of instability and conflict within many developing states and across developing regions. Along with prolonged criticism of the traditional international development assistance regime's exclusionary practices, operational culture and institutional bias, pressure for change has grown steadily in the post-Cold War era and attained an additional impetus with the arrival of the "emerging economies". This is a label frequently used interchangeably with "emerging market economies", "emerging powers", "rising powers", and it designates those states which have been making a critical contribution to NDA by driving new reformist processes via their strengthening economic capacity and influence, but also through soft power means such as collective dialogue, consensus-building, agreed agendas for change and the creation of new institutions.

Part of the scholarly and policy challenge lies in defining clearly just "what" and indeed "who" constitutes an "emerging power"? This taxonomical challenge reaches back to the 1990s: as far back as 2004 one reviewer's online Internet search recovered six definitions (Mody, 2004). The definition has become much more problematic as the evolution of the international system has brought forward new groupings and new waves of emerging economies, prompting new acronyms but classificatory opaqueness, analytical complexity and policy uncertainty. Witness, for example, the acronymic birth in 2001 of Jim O'Neill's first-wave grouping of Brazil, Russia, India and China as BRIC (Harvey, 1991, 2007), and his later second-wave grouping of emerging economies, the so-called MINT countries, namely Mexico, Indonesia, Nigeria and Turkey, as emerging economic powerhouses ("The Mint Countries", 2014). A key characteristic of some of them has been their widening role in the international development assistance system, bringing with them a distinctive experience as former colonized and semi-colonized economies, a number of them simultaneously recipients and new donors of assistance with their own approach grounded on a *narrative* of principles of equity, reciprocity and partnership. These principles and the practices that follow from them provide the basis for a broad contextual consensus across the diversity of the emerging scene. This narrative is also a counter-narrative or oppositional discourse to the verticality and linearity of the existing system and its founding principles embedded in the Western narrative of humanism and progress, itself embedded in a meta-narrative of modernity, industrialization and economic growth (Landes, 1969).

The present study considers the emerging economies' developing relationships with the existing system and assesses the character and quality of the value they add to it. This study addresses two questions. *Firstly*, how is the widening role of the emerging economies impacting the development assistance system? *Secondly*, does this widened role mean that development assistance is "getting better"? A central consideration is the degree of synchronization with the existing system and what potential turbulence may have arisen? Analysis focuses specifically on the changes effected by the BRICS economies, a choice reflecting their rising individual and collective economic capacity; the group's strengthening institutionalization; the recognition and importance accorded to the role in development assistance of China, India and South Africa in particular, and now of the group as a collective entity; the distinctiveness of their approach to development and development assistance; and, lastly, the availability of an established body of evidence enabling us to examine the relation between the traditional system and the new one.

This study of emerging economies' engagement with the OECD-DAC-centered system is informed by a perspective on knowledge, discourse and power influenced by the concepts of meta-narrative, narrative and counter-narrative encountered in Jean-François Lyotard's critique of postmodern knowledge (Lyotard, 1979). Meta-narrative is an overarching abstract idea understood to provide comprehensive explanation of historical experience or knowledge. Meta-narrative both contextualizes and infuses narratives pertaining to specific domains of knowledge. These narratives form powerful discursive organizing mechanisms that shape knowledge formation, privileging particular ideas, values and understanding of knowledge over subordinated, oppositional counter-narratives. Critically, a meta-narrative is reified in behavioral practice. This concept helps explain the dynamics of the complex relationships at the heart of the present study of the international development assistance system. Firstly, the system is grounded in a narrative of development that privileges a specific reading of history, economics, industrialization, growth and development, itself embedded in a foundational meta-narrative of knowledge originating in Western modernity and progress. As the emergence of a BRICS collective narrative encapsulated in the construction of a BRICS Spirit demonstrates, one facet of the emerging economies as interlocutors with the traditional system is as originators and proselytizers of a hitherto subordinated counter-narrative of development, presenting a diverging reading of development knowledge and giving rise to a critical "challenge-convergence" tension at the heart of the issue of synchronization.

This counter-narrative elucidates "development" in a more holistic and problematized way than has been allowed for in the traditional approach embodied in the OECD-DAC system. This discursive counter-point, framed as "all-dimensional and multilayered cooperation", challenges a series of foundational binary opposites in the development grand narrative, notably donor/recipient and North/South and the system's paternalistic ethos. By inference, in foregrounding the BRICS aim to overcome continuing structural inequalities to achieve a "just, equitable, fair, democratic and representative international political and economic order", it presents a juxtaposition to an system held to be inherently unjust, unfair, undemocratic and unrepresentative international political and economic order; an order upon which the principles, rules and norms of behavior, structures, processes and agencies of the traditional international development assistance system have been predicated. The critical challenge is, therefore, to the way that the mutually reinforcing dominant meta- and grand narratives work to position economies and define their functionality. In this narrative, the emphasis is upon principles of equity, reciprocity and partnership, a horizontal reading of the processes of development cooperation with roots in the 1955 Banding Conference and Non-Aligned Movement, the 1978 Buenos Aires Action Plan on Technical Cooperation between Developing Countries and the creation of the Global Partnership for Effective Development Cooperation (GPEDC) at the Fourth High-Level Forum on Aid Effectiveness held in Busan, South Korea, in 2011 (Mawdsley, 2012; OECD, 2011; UN, 1978; UNDP, 1994). This alternative reading problematizes the hierarchical reading and forms a reformist challenge to institutional exclusivity to better reflect the interests and growing influence of the emerging economies. This is a conception of development entwined with the historical remembering in these economies of anti-hegemonic resistance and overcoming, stories of reform and development resonating with other developing economies. This understanding of development identifies a central role for the state and prioritizes the wide spectrum of infrastructure needs of developing countries, knowledge exchange and technical cooperation set within a holistic approach to economic development that mainstreams the importance of trade and investment, the symbiotic components of sustainable development and international development assistance. The impact of this alternative reading has been to widen and deepen simultaneously the understanding and practices of development. In so doing, the condition of the international development system has become more congested and turbulent, its guiding precepts less certain, viscous and contested.

This study argues that while there is potential for friction in the process of change, the transition to the new development assistance will be more of a "peaceful rise". The emerging economies have generated substantial debate over their aims, conception of development practices and impact upon the traditional development assistance system and community, dividing academic and policy opinion. There are a range of concerns about their impact, including implications for understanding development assistance itself; consensus-building and application of rules, norms and expectations of right conduct over the coming decades; and the principles, values and culture of development assistance underlying the system; question marks hovering over the conception of "donors" and "recipients". Critiques also focus on the efficiency, coverage, challenges for local communities, sustainability, risks and prospects for global governance and inter-institutional effectiveness. The emerging economies have given rise to these issues insofar as they have expressed concerns over the way the current system works, its quality of governance and effectiveness. Groups like BRICS stress the need for greater inclusivity, innovation and structural and procedural reforms in the institutions of the global development assistance architecture. For some, this has spurred debate over whether development assistance has entered a "post-aid" era, the character of which is being driven increasingly by emerging economies. These challenges for development assistance are set against the dramatically changing geopolitical, economic and strategic topography of renascent protectionism, global value chain conundrums, migration, terror used as an instrument of politics by new organizations, the political turbulence generated by the Trump administration, questions over the future of the European integration project following the "Brexit" referendum outcome, uncertainties over the US-China relationship and the heightened tensions over North Korea. The complex, often contradictory, forces of globalization produce development challenges that require coordinated multilateral efforts for improvement. Most notable is the growing importance of South-South cooperation (SSC), including technical cooperation (TC), and, of both iconic and practical significance, the 2030 Sustainable Development Agenda and Goals (SDGs).

It remains to be seen what becomes of the international development assistance system in future, whether, and to what extent, the emerging economies, and the structures and institutional architecture, processes and agencies they create and promote will reform, revolutionize or, ultimately, reinforce the status quo. It is argued that they are already demonstrating that the status quo is not a credible outcome, in the fact that they have become a major force for systemic change in perspective, policy and practice. The debate is over the degree, direction and qualitative impact of that change. It is argued that in the beginning it will be reformist, but will prove revolutionary in the longer term, in the sense of upending the concepts and practices of development assistance—if only as the outcome of incremental systemic influence accumulating over time. It is further argued that while there is certainly a potential for friction in the process of change, the transition will be more of a "peaceful revolution".

Perhaps the most challenging question posed is whether the growing involvement of the emerging economies is making development assistance better? Any such evaluation requires a definition of what "better" means to development assistance. A multidimensional approach is adopted: (1) better understanding of the very concepts of "development" and the "assistance" supporting it; (2) NDA thinking; (3) better practices in the delivery of development assistance; that is, innovative ways of implementing NDA, benchmarked for greater effectiveness in achieving agreed outcomes; (4) better in terms of human development, the "lived experience" of recipients on the ground; that is, improved wellbeing and life chances. It is argued that a widening role for the emerging economies, particularly the BRICS, does offer opportunities for development assistance to get better, but for this potential to be fully realized will require a closer understanding of NDA and watchful systemic management.

Emerging Economies, NDA and Their Impact on the Global Development Community

The comprehensive analyses of the changing landscape of global development assistance provision presented in the opening chapters of this volume explain the key facets of NDA, identifying and tracing the role of the emerging economies in this transformational process. The aggregate market capacity of the emerging economies has or ought to have increased their collective influence in the economic, political and strategic systems of global governance, given that their input has become critical to global economic growth.

The emerging economies have generated substantial attention and debate; however, in the initial burst of interest lay a tendency to lump them together into one homogeneous mass: the emerging economies, having indistinguishable interests, needs and objectives. Current understanding reflects a more sophisticated reading of the differential economic trajectories underlying the high levels of GDP growth being recorded, and a more cautious estimate of the resilience of these markets and of the persistent risks they face and vulnerabilities they are exposed to in the globalizing economy. As the country studies in subsequent chapters of this volume demonstrate, the extent to which the emerging economies are seeking systemic regime change has almost certainly been exaggerated; judging not only by their declaratory statements, but quite simply in terms of the power resources and political capacity of most of these economies to effect such a power-shift, and of the significant differences between them over which ideas and practices should replace the existing system. If the emerging economies' growth and impact on the global economic, financial and development assistance systems prove durable, then of course *adaptive* change is highly probable.

The evidence of emerging economies' pressure for systemic change—respecting development assistance, in particular—so far indicates a diachronic dynamic that has been termed "challenge-convergence" (Gu, Shankland, & Chenoy, 2016). Processes of change are complex and non-linear, involving gains for some and losses for others. This is visible, for example, in the prolonged resistance of the US Congress to ratifying the 2010 reforms of the International Monetary Fund's (IMF) Executive Board representation and the review of quotas. That said, the emerging economies are not best understood as challengers to the system, but rather challengers within the system, revising it the better to reflect, recognize and respond to their needs, interests and shared understandings of sustainable development assistance. The revision involves an important element of synchronization with existing practices of the community, working within them to adapt while avoiding turbulence. This is illustrated by the BRICS group, whose experience we turn now to examine.

The BRICS

Emerging and developing economies account for an ever-greater share of global output and growth. In the five-year period 2010–2015, they were responsible for 56% of global output (in Purchasing Power Parity (PPP) terms) and 79% of global growth. Given such a shift, seeking to understand and explain the globalizing economy through the prism of advanced or developed economies has ever less currency, and for some observers is outmoded. It is against this backdrop that BRICS as a coalition is playing a substantial role in global governance and, increasingly, in the global development community. BRICS countries, as individual states, are centrally engaged in development assistance already. Their respective national policies mandate that this continue and intensify. What is new is that as a group BRICS is scaling up its development approach and programmatic components, evident in the declarations of recent BRICS Summits since 2015, especially in Ufa, Russia (seventh); Goa, India (eighth); and Xiamen, China (ninth), and in the actions and institutional initiatives resulting from these meetings and in the various ongoing BRICS consultative, deliberative and policy implementation processes: the BRICS Summit 2017; New Development Bank; Asian Infrastructure Investment Bank, and the One Belt, One Road (OBOR) Initiative; the Johannesburg Action Plan of the Forum for China-Africa Cooperation (FOCAC); and the cooperation agreement between China and the Community of Latin American and Caribbean States setting up the China-CELAC Forum. It is impossible to assess the contribution of BRICS to development assistance without a more exact understanding of the national histories, political systems and development trajectories of each of its members—factors giving distinctive hues to their perspectives and strategies. Bearing this important caveat in mind, a more unitary BRICS approach to development assistance is gradually emerging within the context of NDA and the framing of a shared and particular reading of the way the international economic and political system operates. The consensus features a diffusion of power via a multipolar structural re-ordering of that system characterized by a declaratory commitment to principles of global equity, inclusivity, the primacy of international law, and by reformed global financial, economic and political institutions. Clearly, statements of intent and the realities of trying to put these into practice are far from unproblematic. The discussion so far has flagged up the importance of recognizing factors of economic, political and societal difference across the BRICS. Whilst the BRICS economics are partners, they are also economic competitors and political rivals for influence in developing countries and there are, for example, considerations of commercial advantage and corporate confidentiality as well as differing approaches to financing, knowledge-sharing, corporate social responsibility, environmental risk assessment and local governance.

The BRICS in Principle

The epistemology of emerging economies is driven by a vision that they offer something distinctly different in the realm of development assistance with power to change the development community and its culture. The BRICS group is held to epitomize this vision; if it represents anything new on the development assistance scene, this should be evident through an interrogation of the guiding rules, norms and expectations of right conduct—the very language and tone of BRICS discourse; the extent to which words are translated into innovative action, and such action might be deemed more effective than the traditional practice.

Since the institutionalization of the BRIC (Brazil, Russia, India and China) group just over a decade ago in 2006, a substantial "BRICS discourse" has emerged in the corpus of declarations, speeches, *communiqués*, agreements, memoranda and actions plans. This body of official documents defines and by usage establishes key words and phrases the reiterative weight of which, accumulating over the past decade, constitutes a collective identity, a semiotic differentiation of the BRICS members from non-members and an inside/outside demarcation of their values. At the heart of this socially constructed identity lies a common core around which the group and its work program can cohere: a self-styled "BRICS Spirit" prioritizing "mutual respect and understanding, equality, solidarity, openness, inclusiveness and mutually beneficial cooperation" (BRICS Xiamen, 2017, p. 1). The notion of a *spirit* is important in both discursive and political terms for this paper's assessment of South-South cooperation. Discursively, it triggers meaningful "active remembering", releasing warm sentiments of common historical experiences of exploitation, marginalization, the struggle for freedom, independence and post-independence mutuality, embodied in the 1955 Bandung Declaration and enduring "Bandung Spirit"; a spirit celebrating its 50th anniversary on the eve of the BRICS group's own inauguration. Politically, the BRICS Spirit situates the group in a long historical trajectory of "otherness"—a Third World, an intermediate zone, a developing world, a global South positioning, juxtaposed against the First World of advanced industrialized states and the global infrastructure of financial, economic, political, strategic institutions they created in their own image to serve their collective self-interest. Accordingly, the stated aim of BRICS is to work together for "a more just, equitable, fair, democratic and representative international political and economic order" (BRICS Xiamen, 2017, p. 3).

In seeking to realize this vision of a "better" world order, the BRICS discourse puts great emphasis on the concept of "partnership". While this idea pervades the work of the BRICS as a group, it has taken on added resonance as the group has evolved a "development" pathway. The Declaration of the 7th BRICS Summit held in Ufa, Russia, in 2015 committed BRICS "to strengthen partnerships for advancing international development cooperation and to begin interaction through dialogue, cooperation and exchange of experience in advancing international development cooperation" (BRICS Ufa, 2015, p. 40). BRICS criticism of traditional development assistance portrays it as paternalistic, condescending and, above all, ill fitted to the needs of developing countries. The contrasting spirit of partnership is held to be the requirement sine qua non for achieving the SDGs and fulfilling the 2030 Agenda. As Quadir (2013) has argued, grounding an approach to development in these principles challenges the established system to move away from its perceived vertical structure, processes and culture to a more horizontal culture of reciprocity, mutual respect and equality. By the 9th BRICS Summit in Xiamen, China, in September 2017, the group had committed itself to being a voice for change, advocating "equitable, open, all-round, innovation-driven and inclusive development, to achieve sustainable development in its three dimensions—economic, social and environmental—in a balanced and integrated manner" (BRICS Xiamen, 2017, p. 9).

Integral to this challenge to the established order is BRICS' united call for reform of the post-war institutions of Bretton Woods: the United Nations (UN), the International Monetary Fund (IMF) and the World Bank Group (WBG). The 2005 World Summit Outcome became a fountainhead for arguing for "a comprehensive reform of the UN, including its Security Council, with a view to making it more representative, effective and efficient, and to increase the representation of the developing countries so that it can adequately respond to global challenges" (BRICS Goa, 2016, p. 3). The stress on reform was reiterated at the 2017 Xiamen Summit: "We support the important role of the United Nations, including the High Level Political Forum on Sustainable Development (HLPF), in coordinating and reviewing global implementation of the 2030 Agenda, and support the need to reform the UN Development System with a view to enhancing its capability in supporting Member States in implementing the 2030 Agenda" (BRICS Xiamen, 2017, p. 9). Accordingly, China and Russia, the permanent members of the UN Security Council which are members of BRICS, are supporting the aspirations of Brazil, India and South Africa for a higher profile in the UN and the wider global system (BRICS Goa, 2016). The change agenda also targets the IMF. With the 14th General Review of Quotas in 2010 initiating reforms finally ratified by the US Senate at the end of 2015, China and India received more voting rights, while the US and European economies gave up rights. China has become the third largest member of the IMF, and four BRICS economies rank among its ten largest shareholders (IMF, 2017). Implementation issues remain nonetheless. The BRICS Goa Summit, for example, reminded the Europeans that they agreed to relinquish two IMF Executive Board representatives as part of the reform process, and called on them to fulfill this commitment. The 2010 IMF governance agreement had stipulated that this should be completed "at the latest by the time of the first election after the quota reform takes effect" (IMF, 2010). The justification put forward for this was that reform "should strengthen the voice and representation of the poorest members of the IMF" (BRICS Goa, 2016, p. 7). However, deep frustration followed on the electoral round held at the October 2012 Annual Meeting of the IMF in Tokyo. Paulo Nogueira Batista, the outspoken IMF Executive Director for Brazil, along with several other Latin American and Caribbean countries, claimed that "this so-called reduction in the number of European chairs has petered out into a reshuffling that is largely cosmetic in nature" (Biron, 2012).

Actions Speak Louder than Words

What does BRICS want to do that is different and how does it want to do it differently? The short answer is that the agenda today is wide-ranging and technically focused on practical initiatives that stress effective implementation of BRICS programs and aims. The Xiamen Summit divided these core aims, policies and programs into four categories: (1) practical economic cooperation, which builds on the Strategy for BRICS Economic Partnership; (2) global economic governance, the aim of which is to "foster a global economic governance architecture that is more effective and reflective of current global economic landscape, increasing the voice and representation of emerging markets and developing economies"; (3) international peace and security. In a comprehensive approach detailed at the Xiamen Summit, the BRICS have committed themselves to the framework of international law and institutions embedded in "a fair and equitable international order". The group reaffirms its belief in the central importance of the UN, the UN Charter whilst reiterating their support for United Nations Security Council reform, and "respect for international law, promoting democracy and the rule of law in international relations, and making joint efforts to address common traditional and non-traditional security challenges"; (4) people-to-people exchanges. Here BRICS takes its discursive and policy point of departure from established Chinese political discourse, policy and practice. The stated aim of this distinctive category of action is "to garner more popular support for BRICS cooperation through deepened traditional friendships". This strand of the BRICS program of action reflects a need to avoid criticism of being too state-centric, concerned, in an exclusive or exclusionary way only with government-to-government relations with civil society of marginal importance. The approach is intended to reaffirm the group's distinctive understanding of development partnership as an inclusive, multilayered process, nested within the 2030 Agenda's commitment of the global partnership, intended to widen societal participation in BRICS cooperation, strengthen mutual learning, communication and understanding between their cultures and peoples, deepening traditional ties in order to make the BRICS partnership "closer to our people's hearts".

Much of the discussion of the contribution of BRICS to traditional development assistance and the character of their own assistance has centered on the two major collective initiatives of the group: the New Development Bank (NDB), and the Contingent Reserve Arrangement (CRA). The NDB was announced at the 6th BRICS Summit in Fortaleza, Brazil in July 2014 and opened its doors in Shanghai in July 2015. Article 1 of the NDB's Articles of Agreement sets out the Bank's purpose, to "mobilize resources for infrastructure and sustainable development projects in BRICS and other emerging economies and developing countries, complementing the existing efforts of multilateral and regional financial institutions for global growth and development" (NDB, 2015). The bank approved its first series of loans worth US$811 million in April 2016. Currently, four of its loan projects are in China. By the start of the Xiamen Summit, it had approved funding for 11 projects worth up to US$3 billion. It opened its first regional center in Johannesburg, South Africa, in

October 2017. The bank's strategic remit is to base its funding for infrastructure projects in developing countries on a different culture of institutional governance to that of the IMF and WBG, to whose financing the NDB's is supplementary. The estimated annual global infrastructure investment demand is about US$3.7 trillion—of which only about US$2.7 trillion is currently met (World Economic Forum, 2013). A McKinsey Global Institute Report finds that globally there is a need to invest an average of US$3.3 trillion annually in economic infrastructure in order to support currently expected rates of growth through to 2030. Emerging economies are projected to account for some 60% of that need. The report concluded that if the current pace of underinvestment continues, world infrastructure will fall short by roughly 11%, or US$350 billion a year. The size of the gap triples if the additional investment required to meet the UN's SDGs is factored in (Woetzel, Garemo, Mischke, Hjerpe, & Palter, 2016). BRICS leaders argue that existing institutions are unable or unwilling to meet the need, and that the NDB represents a necessary new mechanism to fill the gap. While this may indeed be the primary motivating rationale for the NDB, it is also an important signal to the stand-pat First World that the emerging economies, BRICS economies above all, are not willing to wait for change to be implemented from above, but are willing and able to act on their own collectively and effectively.

Delivering NDA? BRICS in Performance

Other studies in this series examine specific instances of development assistance originating from BRICS economies. One specific issue in this study is how much the BRICS group's engagement with the establishment is causing systemic turbulence. The first point to note is that while there is clear evidence of a declaratory collective commitment to development assistance and a degree of consensus on the principles associated with this, and even an institutionalization of them in initiatives like the NDB, the overall process of formulating and implementing systematic BRICS development assistance is still in its early stages. How much BRICS fit in with the existing system is in no small part determined by how well they manage the complexities of their respective differences, interests and needs. One might point to their divergent approaches to political rule and conception of political culture; for example, while China joins with four partners to make BRICS, three of the five make part of India, Brazil and South Africa (IBSA), a separate group which puts a premium on the principle of multiparty representative democracy. The structural imbalance across these economies is also an important caveat. The transitioning of the Chinese economy to a lower annual consumption-led, sustainable GDP growth rate of "around" 6.7% has had appreciably adverse knock-on effects on the income generation of commodity-exporting economies. African states, including South Africa, have warned of the structural imbalances in trade, the so-called resources curse, and the difficulties of accessing the higher value-added rungs of the value chains of large globalizing enterprises; and expressed concerns over land grabs, issues of corporate social responsibility, and limited knowledge and skills transfers to the home economy. Respecting BRICS cohesion, the reader should note that its members are competitors as well as collaborators, not only in trade and investment, but in terms of the scales, formats and operationalization of development assistance, most conspicuously perhaps in Africa.

These are important factors, indeed; however, perhaps the central consideration is the relationship between China and India. In 2017 China was the second-largest economy in the world; India, the sixth largest. Predictions are for China to become the top global economy by 2030, pushing the US into second place, with India moving up to third. Each has deep roots in the story of the developing world and has established its own development assistance programs. Long-running debates have queried whether and how these two states might work together in Africa, the presumed basis for which is their shared historical experience as colonial societies, their fight for independence, recovery and reform. They each have success stories to share with other developing countries on promoting high-level economic growth, generating higher incomes and lifting millions into the middle classes. Yet they continue to struggle against persistent poverty and widening inequalities. The two countries cooperate in multilateral fora: BRICS, NDB, Asian Infrastructure Investment Bank (AIIB). In addition, both have well-established roles working with and speaking up on behalf of the developing countries of Africa through the G-77. Their case, however, highlights the extent to which extra-BRICS factors act as constraints on the Sino-Indian relationship providing a firm platform for catalyzing development assistance cooperation. There are, clearly, a range of challenges in their relationship, from their different understandings and practices regarding political systems, economic development models and trajectories, to the scale and character of their engagement in Africa. Beneath these factors lie deeper problems in the relationship, from ongoing territorial disputes to popular nationalism. Tensions arise from India's seemingly lukewarm, even averse response to China's flagship OBOR project; Indian concern over what it sees as China's expansionist strategic ambitions in the Indian Ocean; the rejection of India's July 2016 application to join the Nuclear Suppliers Group (NSG), attributed to China's opposition; and Indian references to a Chinese strategy of "containment" of India. India did not attend the May 2017 OBOR Conference in Beijing, though Prime Minister Modi did attend the September BRICS Summit; heightened border conflict having supervened between the two events. All these are factors that have had a bearing on the character of their development assistance cooperation within BRICS, and more widely.

Conclusions: Toward "Better" Development Assistance?

This paper asked the question of whether the rising influence of the emerging economies is helping to improve development assistance. "Better" was defined in a multidimensional way as innovative thinking, improved delivery and effective outcomes. This study concludes that the evidence from BRICS' experience implies that emerging economies have on balance been contributing positively to "better" development assistance in three ways.

Firstly, they have asserted and prioritized key ideas and messages to the development assistance community about what sustainable development means to developing countries (viz., the discourse of partnership, equity, mutuality, respect and reciprocity), offering an alternative development discourse that is steadily being mainstreamed into the traditional system. The discussion of this discourse emphasizes the power of language in the construction of thought and practice, as reified in the BRICS' evolving approach to development.

Secondly, NDA rests on a consensus on practical delivery aiming for inclusivity and innovation. Multilateralized institutionalism, grounded like the NDB in an alternative culture and practice of governance, is one strand; another is a holistic approach to development that combines trade, investment, state-owned and private enterprise, development assistance and humanitarian support, an approach with potential to deliver improved assistance. However, issues of Corporate Social Responsibility (CSR) and corporate practice, non-interference and human rights, uneven knowledge and skills transfers, employment and labor rights offer mixed experiences in terms of making development assistance "better".

Thirdly, the NDA emphasizes the importance of investment in infrastructure—not least social and public infrastructure: improvements in communication, transport, health and educational capacity, the growing utility of development assistance as a factor of industrial development in African states through production-capacity building. It is evident in the establishment of industrial parks and construction of public buildings, from conference and sports centers to parliament houses, that a demonstrably substantial back-catalogue of achievement is on exhibit in developing countries.

This paper has tried to assess how BRICS are engaging with the existing development assistance system and community. The evidence indicates a strong and deliberate element of challenge involved in the principles and practices of NDA; it also indicates, however, that the BRICS' challenge is one of reform within rather than revolutionary overthrow of the existing institutional configuration; new institutions, agencies, structures and processes so far finding place within the status quo. To date there has been no evidence that BRICS or the broader cohort of emerging states is driven by any intent to sweep away the Bretton Woods institutions wholesale and reconstitute the system.

This chapter has illustrated the way in which the emerging economies of the BRICS group have evolved an approach to international development assistance as a response to the problems of traditional development assistance, responding to an incremental shift in the center of economic gravity of the global economy and system of states. Examination of the BRICS engagement with the principles and practices of the traditional system also indicate the importance of the evolution of a BRICS spirit embedded in their particular experiences, histories, economic conditions and political systems, generating a diachronic process of challenge and convergence, association and dissociation with the precepts and practices of the OECD-DAC centered system.

References

BBC. (2014). The Mint Countries: Next Economic Giants? *BBC News Magazine*. Retrieved from https://www.bbc.com/news/magazine-25548060

Biron, C. L. (2012, October 19). Brazil Frustrated with European "Backtracking" on IMF Reforms. *IPS News*. Retrieved from http://www.ipsnews.net/2012/10/brazil-frustrated-with-european-backtracking-on-imf-reforms/

BRICS Goa. (2016). *8th BRICS Summit: Goa Declaration*. Toronto: BRICS Information Centre, University of Toronto. Retrieved from http://brics.utoronto.ca/docs/161016-goa.pdf

BRICS Ufa. (2015). *VII BRICS Summit: 2015 Ufa Declaration*. Toronto: BRICS Information Centre, University of Toronto. Retrieved from http://brics.utoronto.ca/docs/150709-ufa-declaration_en.pdf

BRICS Xiamen. (2017). *BRICS Leaders Xiamen Declaration*. Toronto: BRICS Information Centre, University of Toronto. Retrieved from http://brics.utoronto.ca/docs/170904-xiamen.pdf

Gu, J., Shankland, A., & Chenoy, A. (Eds.). (2016). *The BRICS in International Development*. London: Palgrave Macmillan.

Harvey, D. (1991). *The Condition of Postmodernity: An Enquiry into the Origins of Cultural Change*. London: Wiley-Blackwell.

Harvey, D. (2007). *A Brief History of Neoliberalism*. New York: Oxford University Press.

International Monetary Fund. (2010). *IMF Executive Board Approves Major Overhaul of Quotas and Governance*. Washington, DC: International Monetary Fund. Retrieved from http://www.imf.org/en/News/Articles/2015/09/14/01/49/pr10418

International Monetary Fund. (2017). *Factsheet: IMF Quotas*. Washington, DC: International Monetary Fund. Retrieved from http://www.imf.org/en/About/Factsheets/Sheets/2016/07/14/12/21/IMF-Quotas

Landes, D. S. (1969). *The Unbound Prometheus: Technological Change and Industrial Development in Western Europe from 1750 to the Present*. Cambridge: Cambridge University Press.

Lyotard, J. F. (1979). *The Postmodern Condition: A Report on Knowledge*. Manchester: University of Manchester Press.

Mawdsley, E. (2012). *From Recipients to Donors: Emerging Powers and the Changing Development Landscape*. London: Zed Books.

Mody, A. (2004). *What Is an Emerging Market?* (WP/04/177). Washington, DC: IMF Research Department. Retrieved from https://www.imf.org/external/pubs/ft/wp/2004/wp04177.pdf

New Development Bank. (2015). *Agreement on the New Development Bank – Fortaleza*. Shanghai: New Development Bank. Retrieved from https://www.ndb.int/wp-content/themes/ndb/pdf/Agreement-on-the-New-Development-Bank.pdf

OECD. (2011). *Busan Partnership for Effective Development Co-operation. Fourth High Level Forum on Aid Effectiveness*. Paris: OECD. Retrieved from http://www.oecd.org/dac/effectiveness/49650173.pdf

Quadir, F. (2013). Rising Donors and the New Narrative of 'South-South' Cooperation: What Prospects for Changing the Landscape of Development Assistance Programmes? *Third World Quarterly, 34*(2), 321–338.

UN. (1978). *Report of the United Nations Conference on Technical Cooperation Among Developing Countries: Buenos Aires 30 August to 12 September 1978* (A/CONF.79/13/Rev.1). New York: UN.

UNDP. (1994). *The Buenos Aires Plan of Action.* Washington, DC: UNDP, Special Unit for TCDC.

Woetzel, J., Garemo, N., Mischke, J., Hjerpe, M., & Palter, R. (2016). *Bridging Global Infrastructure Gaps.* New York: McKinsey Institute. Retrieved from http://www.mckinsey.com/industries/capital-projects-and-infrastructure/our-insights/bridging-global-infrastructure-gaps

World Economic Forum. (2013). *Strategic Infrastructure: Steps to Prepare and Accelerate Public-Private Partnerships.* Geneva: World Economic Forum. Retrieved from https://www.weforum.org/reports/strategic-infrastructure-steps-prepare-and-accelerate-public-private-partnerships

CHAPTER 7

International Development Assistance: A Case Study of Brazil

Rogerio F. Pinto

Introduction

Transformations of the global economic and geo-political orders brought on at the dawn of the twenty-first century have affected development assistance (DA). Many emerging economies (EEs), among them those of the BRICS, have come to aspire to global recognition. By becoming players in the development assistance marketplace, they assert themselves as emerging nations in their own right and leaders in their regions, both sources of soft power.[1] While some countries assert their identity on nationalistic grounds, enhanced by DA on a bilateral basis, others seek to harness the dividends of globalization as a vehicle to assist lagging countries by bringing them into the global community and marketplace. Established rules of international relations among nation states drive the approach to DA by the former, whereas the latter are driven by the emerging and still imperfect global governance (Kumar & Messner, 2010, pp. 8–9).

In the wake of global economic and geo-political shifts, international development assistance has radically changed in character and scope. Critics describe today's aid architecture as fragmented, overly complex,

R. F. Pinto (✉)
World Bank, Sao Paulo, Brazil

Y. Jing et al. (eds.), *New Development Assistance*, Governing China in the 21st Century,
https://doi.org/10.1007/978-981-13-7232-2_7

inefficient and ineffective. The increasing numbers of EEs becoming donors, with their own goals and mechanisms, have created an operational challenge increasingly difficult to manage. As DA goes from functional collective action to dysfunctional hyper-collective action, costs rise, efficiencies are lost and intended benefits diminish overall.[2] An important contribution to resolving this complexity, alleviating its adverse effects, would be to profile the DA landscape, by better grasping the roles, styles and performance of these new donors.

As this increment adds to the complexity of the development assistance landscape, it will be crucial for the BRICS to invest more in the rational design and management of inflows and outflows of DA and their governance. Most importantly, this design must be specifically consistent with the nature of the public goods now being transacted in international DA. In the current international geo-political setting, and given the nature of threats and challenges to the international order and welfare, there is a premium on international public goods, which compete with national public goods in the international assistance marketplace (Pinto & De Oliveira, 2011).[3] Some observers, however, might argue that the increased focus on critical global public goods may displace the focus on lagging countries which attach a higher priority to their national public goods, hence creating a dilemma for DA which is increasingly concerned with the former.[4]

Despite these challenges, emerging countries, such as the BRICS, have gained prominence in the DA environment, adding to its diversity and innovativeness.[5] They are part of a larger group of countries that share certain key features: middle income, large territory and relatively large populations, representing a significant share of global GNP, and most importantly, influential in their respective regions. None are members of OECD, while being members of the G20.[6] These countries have become more active as both recipients and donors in bilateral DA transactions, and have brought pressure to bear on the governing boards of multilateral aid organizations. Brazil in particular has favored its role in multilateral organizations, the destination of a large share of its official development assistance resources.

Brazil has also become a key player in South-South DA by way of technical cooperation among developing countries (TCDC). This brief case study seeks to elicit this emerging country's experience by examining the evolution of its DA, its current trends and the role of its lead agency, the ABC (*Agência Brasileira de Cooperação*). By highlighting its comparative advantages and weaknesses, it provides a basis for a comparison with other country cases. It is hoped that the Brazilian experience may also inform other emerging donors as they shape their own policies and institutional arrangements as donors and/or recipients of DA and partners in TCDC. Furthermore, the study seeks to inspire them on how to navigate the increasing complexity of the DA environment.

Context and Motivation of Brazilian TCDC

Following the end of WWII, Brazil, a member of the Allied forces, became a privileged recipient of the US aid, initially in the form of military cooperation and donation of military equipment, and later infrastructure and industrial development assistance. Brazil was then seen as a potential bastion against the encroachment of Communism in the region, hence the favored nation treatment by the US. As a regional power, Brazil has had foreign relations with a broad range of countries worldwide and a correspondingly far-reaching network of embassies and consular offices. In regard to its international assistance, it does favor those with which it shares a historical, linguistic, cultural and ethnic heritage. These factors in the background, added to the breadth and depth of the knowledge and expertise of numerous national scientific, educational and research entities, emboldened Brazil as a provider of assistance to this constellation of countries and beyond. It has chosen to channel its assistance through the modality of TCDC. In doing so it shows a keen awareness and respect for the sovereignty and self-determination of those countries that it assists as "partners", not recipients of aid. By staying clear of N/S donors, developing countries such as Brazil are foregoing an important source of international assistance for its pressing needs. On the other hand, by embracing TCDC these countries have gained development partners and strengthened their solidarity ties. Apparently, Brazil has been treading both paths while advocating TCDC, which an official source claims is not "a form of aid but a feature of its foreign policy".

As Brazil has developed over recent years and gained in geo-political standing, it has become a provider of DA while continuing to receive it on a more cooperative basis from larger donors, or partners—especially, multilateral organizations. In 2015 Brazil received US$998 million in net ODA.[7] In 2009 alone it received an estimated US$200 million in bilateral aid, of which 40% was for the protection of the Amazon forest, a global asset; 22% was for agriculture; 12% for health; 10% for industry; 10% for the social sectors; and 6% for public administration.

As a staunch supporter of TCDC, Brazil has resisted the Principles on Aid Effectiveness laid out in the Paris Declaration of 2006.[8] Brazilian TCDC experience and strategy also lead it to distance itself from the N/S model of international assistance. The reason given for this position is that Brazil is not a donor country in the OECD sense. An official source affirms that Brazil's practice of TCDC coexists with its role as a recipient because it is still a developing country and continues to rely on N/S assistance: "They operate on different tracks".[9] TCDC executing agencies have a vested interest in such activities, as they are given an opportunity to advance their scientific and educational goals.

The rejection of the Paris Declaration principles by some emerging countries was driven not by objections to the intrinsic properties of these principles, but seemingly by the same geo-political drive to non-alignment with donor countries of the North. The case of Brazil likewise suggests that the objections are not directed at the principles themselves but their prescriptive tone, which an official spokesperson averred "do not apply to developing countries engaged in TCDC", based on horizontal relations between equals rather than vertical ones between donors and recipients.

The evolution of Brazil's experience with international assistance and its alignment with the bloc of countries ambivalent toward N/S assistance, which do not see themselves as donors, has to a certain extent defined its motivation to engage in TCDC. This stance would become ambiguous were Brazil to join the ranks of "new donors" that may agree on principles and rules incompatible with those that Brazil advocates. Reconciliation between being a new donor and engaging mostly in TCDC cooperation becomes problematic, as the latter would constrain its scope of action. Consequently, in today's international context—quite different from that prevailing in 1978, the era of the Buenos Aires UN Conference on Development Cooperation—a clear role definition is required; especially should Brazil eventually join the ranks of the associated new emerging economies, subscribing to the new development assistance (NDA) modality. In the current environment it may become untenable to be a donor, a recipient, a partner *as well as* an associate of the NDA at the same time. Among the many reasons why it is so difficult is the increasing challenge for emerging countries' DA institutions of navigating the complex development assistance landscape still lacking an overall rule framework.

The role and impact of TCDC on Brazil's foreign policy is an issue about which authors disagree. The official documents state that development cooperation plays an important role in policy; some interview respondents, however, argue that this has not been the case over the years. Yet Brazilian foreign policy has clearly shifted from one administration to the next, depending on the assessment by each of the global geo-political environment and their policy choices on how to insert Brazil into it. Development cooperation strategies have tended to reflect such views. Travel diplomacy, a practice based on presidential foreign travels to peripheral countries accompanied by his Minister of Foreign Affairs, is a feature of Brazil's recent foreign policy. These trips and the associated offers of technical and financial assistance, mostly for civil works by Brazilian construction companies, played an important role in Brazil's DA. The corrupt practices associated with these construction contracts later became a major political and legal issue.

The recent populist left-leaning governments of the Workers' Party (PT) have used development cooperation and development finance to strengthen ties with Angola, Cuba and Venezuela among others. In fact, a substantial portion of Brazil DA in the broad sense was enabled under PT governments through concessional loans by the National Social and Economic Development Bank (BNDES) to governments of "partner" countries that shared the PT's ideological leanings. Under this policy BNDES was mobilized to subsidize financing for infrastructure projects in these countries, on the condition that they procured civil works from large Brazilian contractors—a venture which, along with other reprehensible features, facilitated endemic corruption and the eventual unraveling of the Workers' Party itself. This practice also ran counter to the officially sanctioned principle that Brazil's development assistance seeks no commercial advantage. These loans were, at the time of this writing, under scrutiny by Brazilian investigative bodies and the courts, on the grounds of massive systemic corruption.

It is argued by some observers that a foreign policy of travel diplomacy and cooperation, such as that engaged-in by the recent government of President Lula da Silva of PT, fits in better with development cooperation. For example, the populist social policy of direct payments to very low-income families with children, known as "Bolsa Família",[10] became an attractive area for social development cooperation. A similar effect was caused by the success of Brazil's campaign to fight HIV/AIDS, which became another much-sought area for Brazil's cooperation with countries that were also struggling with HIV/AIDS.

By the same token, the PT supported Brazil's alignment with the resistance to the OECD-DAC countries on development cooperation. The more liberal government of Brazil's Social Democratic Party (PSDB) steered its technical cooperation back to the precepts of traditional diplomacy as practiced by Itamaraty, the somewhat independent and steady Ministry of Foreign Affairs, which pursues foreign policy on grounds of raison d'état[11] without necessarily conforming to the whims of changing governments. Consequently, it did not target countries for TCDC on the basis of ideological affinity. Few disagree, however, that Brazil's engagement in development cooperation has benefited its own development, in addition to promoting the county's image as a generous, progressive and reliable partner.[12]

Current Trends of DA in Brazil

Economic deceleration and chronic political instability over the last few governments have dampened the growth and innovation of Brazil's DA activities. Budgets have been curtailed significantly, and additionally a general retraction of international assistance has ensued. Current practices have therefore been driven by inertia and by the autonomy of the many government agencies and ministries relying on decentralized institutional arrangements, absent any organizing policy framework for DA. This case study could not detect any evidence that Brazilian DA agencies are seeking inspiration in emerging donors and their practices. This is explainable by the official position of ABC[13]: that Brazil, while an emerging economy, is not an emerging donor, and that it would rather chart its own DA path forward.

ABC is nominally a focal point for DA; however, given the fragmented and decentralized DA regime now prevailing in Brazil, decisions are by and large driven by bilateral agreements known as *convenios*, similar to Memorandums of Understanding (MoUs) engaging executing agencies, along with government commitments to international organizations. No comprehensive organizing policy framework driving these agreements could be discerned. The national DA multiyear plans common in the 1980s are no longer being prepared, and the network of international advisors staffing cabinet offices with diplomats has been, by and large, abolished. While ABC plays an important role in the renewal of such *convenios*, their execution depends significantly on the actual availability of resources, and on the discretion of executing agencies and ministries.[14] The prevailing decentralization enables these ministries and agencies to pursue their own institutional interests as they engage in DA. It appears that their main motive and drive are not altruistic unilateral assistance, but rather mutually beneficial exchange. This is especially true of the agencies engaged in scientific research and technological innovation. To this should be added the financial subsidies offered by ABC for international travel by their staffs.

In 1996 a system was set up to coordinate the activities of ministries and agencies engaged in DA, but it is no longer operational. In its heyday it was centered in SUBIN (Subsecretaria Internacional), the International Secretariat of the Ministry of Planning, which had broad budgetary oversight, hence a measure of influence on DA. With the 1987 transfer of DA from SUBIN to the newly created ABC (an agency inside the Ministry of Foreign Affairs), oversight was considerably weakened. What is today left is a collection of ministries and agencies which, over the years, have developed their own DA agendas, established their own claim on resources for it, in pursuit of their diverse interests, yet not subject to any policy framework other than the procedural guidelines laid out by ABC.

Brazil engages in and funds mutually beneficial TCDC projects, making substantial contributions to international organizations pursuant to its commitments, which take up 56% of its DA budget. Yet Brazil's official position is that it is not an "emerging donor" as defined by OECD, as it holds onto its condition of recipient of ODA (COBRADI, 2011–2013, p. 16). Accordingly, it is one of the non-DAC emerging countries that provide no data to OECD on its DA budgets and expenditures.[15] Political and economic turmoil of late has discouraged innovation in DA; current practices are driven by inertia and the autonomy of government agencies in the absence of any organizing policy framework. The seven pillars on which current Brazilian DA rests reflect the interests of the TCDC executing government agencies and ministries. The seven pillars are:

1. *Technical cooperation*, for transferring and sharing of knowledge and experience by federal ministries and agencies, funded in the government budget, as mandated by prior agreements or MoUs with partner countries. Between 2005 and 2013 Brazil spent US$294,898,677

on technical cooperation, and between 2011 and 2013 R211,606,564 (an estimated US$70,535,000), or 7% of its DA budget.[16] ABC manages these allocations by assessing supply and demand for DA, preparing, negotiating and supervising projects within the framework of existing agreements and MoUs on technical assistance. It spends 71.4% of allocations on technical cooperation while the 25 executing agencies use the remaining 28.4% to defray the costs of their experts' time dedicated to these projects. Six themes are normally covered in Brazil's technical cooperation: social development and mitigation of hunger, urban development and banking inclusion, human rights, agricultural research, applied economic research and public health.

2. *Educational cooperation*, covering essentially fellowships and tuition fees of foreign attendees at Brazilian schools and universities. Between 2005 and 2013 Brazil spent US$241,042,917 on educational cooperation.[17]
3. *Scientific and technological cooperation*, to advance knowledge and promote synergies of innovation for development. Assorted research projects are funded, mostly in agriculture, stock breeding and space research. Between 2005 and 2013 Brazil spent US$222,375,648 on scientific and technological cooperation.[18]
4. *Humanitarian cooperation*, to protect, promote and ensure fundamental and universal human rights in view of assorted disasters and institutional breakdowns compromising such rights, which require international assistance. Between 2005 and 2013 Brazil spent US$444,491,870 on humanitarian cooperation.[19]
5. *Protection and support to refugees*, as per international agreements, mainly the Geneva Convention of 1951 and subsequent agreements. Between 2005 and 2013 Brazil spent US$11,243,273 on protection and support of refugees.[20]
6. *Peacekeeping*, as per the United Nations Security Council peace maintenance missions. Between 2005 and 2013 Brazil spent US$701,559,543 on peacekeeping missions.[21]
7. *Contributions to international organizations* consistent with Brazil's commitments to such organizations, both regular (41.8%) and to development funds (56.7%). Between 2005 and 2013 Brazil spent US$2,230,926,490 on Contributions to International Organizations and Development Funds.[22]

Funding for DA

Brazil is a South-South cooperation provider. The most recent available figures on its development cooperation program are for 2013 (COBRADI, 2011–2013, p. 16), and were published in 2016. The 2013 figure—US$397 million—included activities that are usually not, or not entirely, included as development cooperation in DAC statistics (but may also exclude development activities that DAC would count in its statistics). The OECD estimates that Brazil's development cooperation amounted to US$397 million in 2013, down from US$411 million in 2012, varying from official data (see below) (Luijkx & Benn, 2016).[23] Of these, 66% has been channeled through multilateral organizations. More recent estimates by the OECD suggest that Brazil in 2015 channeled US$96 million through multilateral organizations (as derived from the multilateral organizations' own websites), confirming the decreasing trend. Variations between OECD estimates and official data suggest the latter's unreliability (Table 7.1).

As seen in Table 7.2, by far the largest item of expenditure is Brazil's contributions to international organizations. These contributions, though monitored, are not channeled by ABC; leading to the conclusion that, while ABC plays a focal role in DA, its leadership is effectively dispersed among the many agencies that provide DA services.[24]

Table 7.1 Overall expenditures with international development assistance, in US$

Modalities/ Years	*2009*	*2010*	*2011*	*2012*	*2013*
Technical cooperation	48,872,380	57,770,553	45,617,071	33,970,749	31,846,055
Educational cooperation	22,236,954	35,544,099	20,689,408	22,251,006	23,809,864
Scientific/tech. cooperation	n/a	24,009,084	73,106,869	72,085,370	53,174,326
Humanitarian cooperation	43,521,166	161,469,749	72,418,476	109,828,325	21,667,913
Refugee assistance	n/a	590,469	4,710,229	4,122,857	1,819,718
Peace maintenance	62,704,500	332,422,426	40,167,190	20,654,923	10,330,872
Total	177,335,000	559,806,380	256,709,843	262,913,230	142,648,748

Table 7.2 Contributions to international organizations, in US$ thousands

2005	*2006*	*2007*	*2008*	*2009*	*2010*	*2011*	*2012*	*2013*
123,105	233,731	228,421	249,863	247,579	311,569	331,642	250,857	254,157

The Ministry of External Relations (MRE) oversees Brazil's development cooperation at large, while the Brazilian Cooperation Agency oversees technical cooperation on its behalf. Apart from technical cooperation, bilateral cooperation includes humanitarian assistance, scientific and technological cooperation, scholarships and student aid, refugee intake and peacekeeping missions. Brazil is also engaged in triangular cooperation, partnering with several international organizations; for example, the United Nations Development Program (UNDP); the UN Food and Agriculture Organization; the World Food Program; the International Labor Organization; the UN Office on Drugs and Crime; the UN Educational, Scientific and Cultural Organization (UNESCO), and DAC members (e.g., Germany, Japan, Spain and the US). These programs support developing countries (e.g., South American countries, Lusophone African countries, Haiti and Timor Leste) in areas such as agriculture, food security and health, and public administration. Brazil's development cooperation with multilateral organizations in 2015 was channeled mainly via the UN (57%) and the Inter-American Development Bank (IDB) (43%). Being a key partner of the OECD, Brazil was a participant in 2016 in the DAC senior-level and high-level meetings, as well as those of the DAC subsidiary bodies: the Advisory Group on Investment and Development and the Working Party on Development Finance Statistics.

Contributions from international organizations and/or other countries associated with bilateral or trilateral programs also fund ABC Cooperation projects. Still, the figures in these budgets do not go far in funding TCDC operations[25]; moreover, ABC projects require an unusually high number of international missions of medium duration. Between 2003 and 2014 a total of 663 prospective and monitoring and evaluation (M&E) missions were carried out. This presumably excludes actual delivery of the planned technical cooperation, as execution is carried out by specialized ministries and agencies. While no figures on these mission costs were made available to this study, it was assumed that they take up a substantial portion of ABC funds. The sharp decline from the peak of 2010 to 2014 is evident and explicable as a consequence of overall budgetary reductions across the Brazilian federal government.[26]

Funding during the decade of 1995–2005 went 33.7% for Central America and Caribbean, 31.2% each for South America and Africa and the remaining 3.9% for other regions.[27] In terms of areas of focus, 23.4% went to agriculture and livestock[28]; 16.5% to health; 11.1% to environment; 9.2% to education; 7.7% to public administration; 6.1% to social development; 4.2% to energy and bio-fuels; 4.2% to professional training; 3.1% to industry; 2.3% to transport; 1.9% to mining; 1.5% to labor relations; 1.5% to entrepreneurial development; 1.5% to rural development; 0.8% to information technology; and 5.0% to others.[29]

ABC, the Lead DA Agency in Brazil

By the mid-1980s the existing institutional configuration of Brazil's international assistance was showing signs of fatigue and decreasing internal support. Consequently, the SUBIN of the Ministry of Planning and the DCOPTD (Department of Development Cooperation) of the Ministry of Foreign Affairs were abolished early in 1987, and later in the same year, ABC was created. The clear drawback of such a move was that development cooperation could no longer enjoy the interministerial cross-cutting coordination only possible from a ministry with the scope and coverage of the Ministry of Planning. Furthermore, the Ministry of Planning also had technical command of development matters. Yet international assistance was brought within the germane scope of foreign policy and international relations, the mandate of the Ministry of Foreign Affairs.

At the outset, ABC was organizationally subsumed under MRE,[30] specifically its Undersecretariat for Cooperation and Commercial Promotion, as part of a public foundation. Its statutory mandate was to "coordinate, negotiate, approve, monitor and evaluate development cooperation—with national scope—in all areas of knowledge received from other countries and international organizations, and that between Brazil and other developing countries".[31] This mandate assigns double responsibility to ABC: over *outgoing and incoming* international assistance—clearly an overload for the agency.[32] While incoming bilateral assistance has little in common with TCDC assistance, the Brazilian case brings out no major issues. Official documentation is silent on this aspect, mostly because projects and activities under outgoing TCDC are more voluminous than incoming bilateral assistance. Aside from sharing staff and systems between projects which have a few factors in common, no other advantage is envisioned. An official respondent argued for keeping both N/S and TCDC in one agency, mostly on grounds of managerial resources economy and cross-fertilization between two modalities under the same roof.

Aid agency autonomy has the obvious advantage of flexibility, such as the ability to set one's own legal and regulatory framework, operational procedures, and staffing standards and practices. In the case of the Brazilian

ABC, lack of such flexibility has been cited as the source of some of its most serious constraints. On the other hand, among the disadvantages is the loss of empowerment and prestige which comes with being embedded in a big ministry such as Foreign Affairs.

Though labeled an "agency" at inception, ABC's director was effectively the director of the Department of Technical and Scientific Cooperation, part of the top management of the Ministry of Foreign Affairs. As such it did not enjoy the autonomy that the agency model would imply. In 2004 ABC became part of the Sub-Secretariat General of Cooperation and Brazilian Communities Abroad (SGEC), and currently ABC's director does not share executive functions with any other MRE unit. ABC's organizational design partially fits model 2 (Agency within Ministry of Foreign Affairs, with policy and implementation) of the organizational typology proposed by Gulrajani (2015, p. 157). Model 2 does not fully fit the case of ABC, to the extent that project implementation has actually been shifted to the agencies executing the technical assistance.

The design of the key features of an ideal organizational architecture for an aid agency raises a central issue: whether it should be organized geographically or topically. Given the role of TCDC projects in foreign policy, it is important that their design and implementation process draw on host country knowledge and be informed by the staff of the Ministry of Foreign Affairs, who have greater exposure to and influence over these factors. Thus, these links ought to be preserved, but not at the cost of full insertion of incoming and outgoing assistance operations into this Ministry. Autonomy can and should be reconciled with free access to sources of foreign affairs knowledge and skills. Thematic expertise needs not be available in-house. In the case of Brazil, it is provided by TCDC-implementing agencies and assisted by the multiple specialized bodies in the Ministry of Foreign Affairs.

ABC has no authority to supervise all DA activities. In addition to centralizing oversight of Brazil's substantial contributions to international organizations, mostly of the UN family, it manages technical cooperation projects with very limited resources. These are seen as appendages of Brazilian foreign policy; hence the organizational placement of ABC. TCDC undertakings are more germane to exchange and joint study programs, wherein all benefit, than to concerted efforts to meet specific demands of recipient countries. Brazil draws from its technical cooperation numerous benefits to its own development, as is the case in N/S--TCDC projects and programs. No results-evaluations of ABC were available for this study, essential to assessing the direct costs and benefits of DA. Equally important, however, is to assess the indirect transaction costs to donors and recipients of DA, and to ensure that these costs are offset by the benefits ultimately accruing to recipients. Given the load on recipient countries caused by the sharp increase of donor and partner countries with multiple missions and demands, it becomes critical to give preference to those modalities likely to be least onerous to the former.

Despite the debate, TCDC has enjoyed some pre-eminence in Brazilian foreign policy. Ever since it began promoting development cooperation with development partners in financial, technical, technological, educational, cultural and humanitarian matters, Brazil has drawn numerous benefits to itself. As it has consolidated its diplomatic ties in Africa and Latin America after several decades of being primarily a recipient of international assistance, it has taken up the role of lead partner within the policy framework of S/S cooperation.[33] At the time, no commercial dividends of such cooperation were sought, hence no conditionality. It is also noteworthy that the TCDC activities coordinated by ABC and implemented by the host of specialized agencies and ministries are mostly win-win mutual exchanges. Despite ABC's official position that Brazilian cooperation is essentially demand-driven by beneficiaries, it is acknowledged that its projects are critically dependent on the specialties and operational capacities of the specialized agencies made available to recipient countries in what is an essentially supply-driven approach.

The legal-regulatory framework of Brazil's international assistance is determined by the institutional foundations of ABC and its statutory instruments. First is the Ministerial Executive Order that sets up the organizational structure of the Ministry of Foreign Affairs, in which ABC is one of 15 departments and dozens of divisions.[34] Second is the *Manual de Gestão da Cooperação Técnica Sul/Sul* (Manual of South/South Cooperation Management) (2013). Third is *Diretrizes para o Desenvolvimento da Cooperação Técnica Internacional Multilateral e Bilateral* (Directives for the Development of Multilateral and Bilateral International Technical Cooperation) (2014). Notwithstanding all such institutional/organizational instruments many Brazilian critics argue that ABC is institutionally weak, as it lacks a dedicated law on technical cooperation or one on DA. Such a law would only make sense if it were to selectively consolidate and replace the multiplicity of interrelated legal and regulatory instruments which render the framework dense and difficult to comply with.[35] Furthermore, no policy statements on DA could be identified.

As ABC is embedded in a set of very dense regulatory and operational instruments applying mostly to the Ministry of Foreign Affairs, with areas of ambiguity, Brazil would probably benefit from a dedicated law addressing all essential elements of its international development assistance regime. However, care should be taken to ensure that it supersedes the legal instruments it would make redundant, not merely accrete to the existing framework. Moreover, such a law should also provide for an enhanced concept of DA that goes beyond TCDC. Some ABC officials have advocated for just such a dedicated law. That said, it is unrealistic to expect it to pass, so long as ABC remains within the bailiwick of the MRE, as it would clash with the latter's statutes and regulations. One official respondent indicated that such a legal framework must include policy, governance, regulatory instruments and funding (Senior Official of ABC, interview, 2017). Yet no reference was made to the crucial broader DA concept of total official support for sustained development (TOSSD).

At first, and for some 12 years, ABC relied on UNDP as a vehicle for hiring "consultants" via a procedure allowed only to international agencies operating in Brazil. This bypassing of local rules to induct civil servants was finally brought under scrutiny and in 2002 terminated through legal action against ABC and UNDP. This, however, did not stop UNDP from continuing to play a role in supporting ABC over the years (currently for a 5% annual fee). This includes making its offices around the world available to support ABC operations abroad despite Brazil's extensive network of embassies and consular offices around the world. Operationally, a significant portion of ABC's workload is tied to the prospective (upstream/pre-investment) tasks undertaken by ABC staff with occasional consultants through field missions. Attendance at assorted gatherings and conferences also takes up considerable time and travel. Resources consumed in setting up projects, and in this part of ABC's workload, seem to outweigh ABC's expenditures on actually delivering assistance operations. This pattern should raise red flags regarding the agency's efficiency, which would be exposed in any credible evaluation exercise.

In the general absence of results-evaluation,[36] certain cooperation projects are "assessed" as having positive impacts, such as those relating to the environment and especially the development and application of bio-fuels, which have commercial potential. ABC documents also indicate that no significant project failures have ever been reported. Project shortfalls are usually attributed to recipients' failure to raise matching funds as per contractual stipulations. Discontinuity of recipient governments and generally low absorptive capacity are also blamed for shortfalls in certain cases. It is also admitted that certain executing agencies attach low priority to cooperation activities and fall behind on their implementation responsibilities.[37] On the whole, there are plenty of reasons justifying a more robust (preferably independent) evaluation effort on the part of ABC.

The Brazil case shows that capacity at the delivery end of TCDC, while necessary, is not sufficient. Absorptive capacity at the receiving end is equally critical, especially the integrity of systems and staff at both ends of assistance operations. Another respondent from ABC made the point that sovereignty includes the capacity to take responsibility for properly managing cooperation partnerships for development (Senior ABC official, interview, 2017). He claims that ABC has offered capacity-building interventions addressed to the management of development cooperation.

The ideal way to chart a path for an entity like ABC, going forward, is to base it on the results of evaluative efforts. As noted above, ABC has a low propensity to engage in results-based evaluation, so it effectively does not know how it is performing, except for subjective statements that applaud its successes. A senior officer of ABC argues the difficulty of monetizing the costs and results of South-South cooperation on the grounds that most technical inputs are provided by civil servants and results are somewhat subjective, amenable only to qualitative assessment (Corrêa, 2017). This is valid mostly inasmuch as ABC does not rigorously "projectize" its operations with quantified inputs, outputs and results. Under such circumstances, ABC's short- as well as long-term prospects probably depend on favorable future governments, their respective foreign policies and the extent to which they are willing to make room for development cooperation on the Ministry of Foreign Affairs' agenda. It was reported to the author that plans for evaluation policies are in the works.

ABC's annual budgetary expenditure reflects its contributions to execution of its entire portfolio for a given year (Table 7.3). Budget allocations, which include project funding and part of ABC's overhead, are estimated at 20%.[38] Personnel costs of project-executing agencies are covered by the agencies themselves, while travel costs are covered by ABC. In 2014 it was only US$7.1 million and in 2013 US$13.9 million, a mere 9.8% of Brazil's total expenditure in that year on international development, suggesting a minor financial role for ABC.[39] Given that financial information is disclosed in a schedule of running expenditures in ABC's portfolio, it is not possible to assess its share of overall DA expenditures,

Table 7.3 Number of ongoing projects by year and average annual expenditures by project

2004	*2005*	*2006*	*2007*	*2008*	*2009*	*2010*	*2011*	*2012*	*2013*	*2014*
67	87	179	246	375	555	737	783	736	472	385
\$10.776	\$10.410	\$29.656	\$14.880	\$18.670	\$34.925	\$51.315	\$34.487	\$26.919	\$29.538	\$18.439

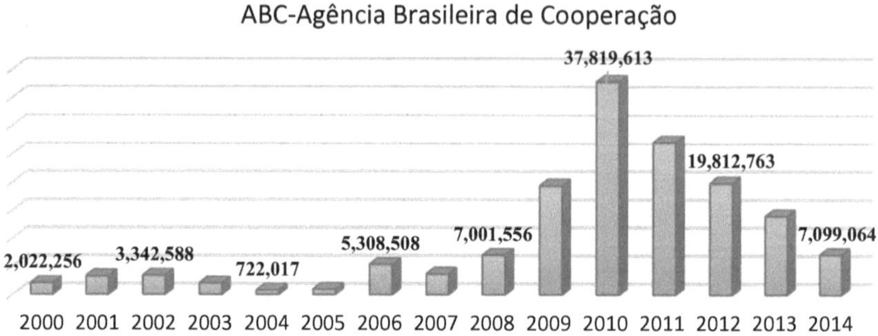

Fig. 7.1 ABC Budget 2000–2014 in US$[40]

except annually. It is assumed that project execution includes the cost of ABC's operations and overhead, including personnel. Unfortunately, ABC could not provide an administrative budget for the totality of its overhead and personnel costs, as it comes from different sources in a complex budgeting system. The figures in this budget would have given us a measure of the agency's efficiency (Fig. 7.1).

Considering that 68% of projects are an average of 1–3 years in duration, these figures suggest an average cost of approximately $50,000 per project.

In the current environment of new donors, one may question whether these countries can or should remain tied to the principles of TCDC, S/S cooperation, or aspire to become more like the N/S model of OECD-DAC by selectively adopting some of their standards and practices. While the Brazilian case shows its affinity on geo-political grounds with the TCDC, S/S model, new donors should not lock themselves into any particular mode on grounds other than maximum effectiveness of the development assistance provided. The clustering of donors under one or another mobilizing principle or movement may lead to a certain conformity with given standards and practices; however, individual countries should put *assistance effectiveness* higher on their agenda. To the extent that TCDC better assimilates to the foreign policies of the engaged partners, new donors should seek a reasonable level of harmonization among these policies, to avoid inconsistencies among members of the group. Furthermore, unless there are policies, operational or managerial restrictions associated with the principles of the Paris Declaration, which did not transpire in the Brazilian case, emerging donors should reconsider them on the basis of their intrinsic merit, not on their geo-political antics.

Development cooperation as practiced by Brazil is not equivalent to N/S development assistance, in the sense that it is not focused on the transfer of technical and financial resources to countries in need of them, accompanied by governance reforms inter alia. Instead, because of its embedding in the Ministry of Foreign Affairs, ABC plays a role of accessory to foreign policy by emphasizing the numerous missions consisting of diplomatic staff, focusing on *rapprochement* and exchanges of information and experiences around topics of common interest—a "para-diplomatic" mandate. Because of the frequency, size and duration of these missions, they represent a potential overload or even deviation of recipient countries' human resources. They stretch their scarce professional staffs who would otherwise be dedicated to their domestic development tasks. David Phillips[41] describes the impact that such activity has on the public services of recipient countries. In some instances, counterpart civil servants use such missions as occasions to pursue opportunities for personal advantage in the form of fellowships and study tours to the donor countries. In other instances, donors set up project management units which cannibalize the more qualified civil service staff, depriving other services of valuable resources and creating dependence on external institutional resources. Though none of these features came up specifically in this study, it is a real risk that can only be detrimental to the ultimate objectives of DA.

In sum, this brief case study raises a number of issues that imply lessons relevant to other BRICS members as they perfect their DA systems; viz., (a) no integrating legal/regulatory framework and no policy framework discerned; (b) significant difficulty in assessing the real financial magnitude of DA; (c) lack of a culture of evaluation to take stock of input costs, outputs and efficiency and effectiveness in terms of results/impact and (d) no effective focal point with total coverage of TOSSD. Finally, while the large collection of DA-executing agencies across government is indeed a real asset to build upon, these issues must be addressed before Brazil will be able to join any network of EEs in a concerted DA effort. Perhaps a role for NDA should be to assist potential BRICS members to address such issues.

Notes

1. In addition to being an active member of the BRICS club, Brazil had earlier sought—under a separate cluster—an association with India and South Africa, known as IBAS, covering a menu of topics for cooperation among them, which suits their shared technological and scientific aspirations (Iglesias, 2010).
2. Phillips (2013) compiles illustrations of the shortcomings of Official Development Assistance (ODA). David A. Philips (Eds.). *Development without aid: the decline of development aid and the rise of the diaspora.* London: Anthem Press/Wimbledon Publishing Co., 2013.
3. These refer to health, security, climate change, poverty, refugees and immigration, among others.
4. On the case for public goods, see for example, World Bank Development Committee (2007).
5. Also known as "rising states", "emerging powers" or "great peripheral countries". Together they represented in 2009 6.4% of total ODA. While none of the BRICS are members of the OECD, Brazil has recently (May 30, 2017) applied to accede. OECD estimates that in 2014 EEs contributed 17% of total global DA or approximately US$32 billion. Although heavily weighted by contributions of the United Arab Emirates and Saudi Arabia, if a broader concept of contribution to DA is used, this figure might grow tenfold.
6. Not included in the BRICS, yet meeting some of the emerging donor criteria are Turkey, Mexico, Chile and South Korea (OECD/non-DAC). Non-OECD and falling in no other categories are Thailand, Indonesia and Malaysia.
7. Source: data.worldbank.org/indicators/DT.ODA.ALLD.CD.
8. The principles are ownership, alignment, harmonization, management for results and mutual accountability.
9. Interview with ABC senior official in 2017.
10. A program of welfare payments to very-low-income families.
11. In the country's interest, not of a given administration's.
12. Policy domains with the largest number of technical assistance projects are agriculture, health, education, environment and public administration, availed of by over 100 countries, mostly in Africa, Latin America and the Caribbean, but also including Asia and the Middle East, with which Brazil has been cooperating. Of late, favored areas are bio-fuels and energy. The availability of specialized technical units within the Ministry of Foreign Affairs has facilitated this topical diversity.
13. Agência Brasileira de Cooperação (Brazilian Cooperation Agency).
14. In the 1980s, prior to the creation of ABC, Brazil had multiyear DA plans.

15. A number of significant providers of development cooperation do not report their development finance flows to the OECD. OECD conservatively estimates that total gross concessional development finance by non-reporting countries, including two OECD members (Chile and Mexico), two OECD accession candidates (Colombia and Costa Rica), and OECD key partners Brazil, China, India, Indonesia and South Africa, amounted to US$6.9 billion in 2015.
16. COBRADI, *op.cit.*
17. Between 2011 and 2013 Brazil funded a total of R129,588,409 of educational cooperation projects, or 5% of its DA budget, COBRADI, *op.cit.*
18. Between 2011 and 2013 Brazil funded a total of R378,234,793 worth of scientific and technological cooperation projects, or 13% of its DA budget, COBRADI, *op.cit.*
19. Between 2011 and 2013 Brazil funded a total of R382,799,884 of humanitarian cooperation projects, or 13% of its DA budget, COBRADI, *op. cit.*
20. Between 2011 and 2013 Brazil funded a total of R3,931,500 worth of refugee protection projects, or 1% of its DA budget, COBRADI, *op.cit.*
21. Between 2011 and 2013 Brazil funded a total of R129,964,200 worth of peace maintenance missions, or 5% of its DA budget, COBRADI, *op. cit.*
22. Between 2011 and 2013 Brazil funded a total of R1,594,901,097 (an estimated US$531,633,699) in contributions, or 56% of its DA budget, COBRADI, *op.cit.*
23. William Luijkx and Julia Benn "Emerging Providers" report that among EEs, Brazil's contribution to DA in 2013 (when data available) amounted to US$316 million (varying from official data), less than Kuwait, Mexico, Qatar, Russia, Saudi Arabia, United Arab Emirates, all oil exporters, China, India and Turkey. Among the BRICS Brazil ranked only below China in contributions to UN funds and specialized agencies. In regards to contributions to regional development banks and the World Bank, Brazil ranks third after China and Russia.
24. These figures suggest that ABC delivers only a fraction of what Brazil spends on all these categories, and that the bulk is carried out via contributions to international organizations.
25. Interview by telephone with ABC official in March 2016.
26. According to the ABC site, Project expenditures for 2016 were US$6,553,052.37.
27. Focal countries in South America have been Bolivia, Peru, Ecuador, Venezuela and Colombia. In the Caribbean and Central America: Cuba, El Salvador, Costa Rica and Guatemala. In Africa: Angola, Mozambique, São Tome and Principe, Cape Verde, Guinea-Bissau and Namibia.
28. EMBRAPA, the Brazilian Company for Agricultural Research, is by far the most active project implementer, representing 5.5% of all expenditures on

TCDC between 2011 and 2013, with R11.6 million spent on staff time. Lately, it implemented some 12 projects in Africa and Latin America with a total budget of approximately US$78 million. The Cotton-4 project in Togo is by far the largest one.

29. *The Economist* stated on July 5, 2010, that "the value of all Brazilian development aid broadly defined could reach $4 billion a year. That is less than China, but similar to generous donors such as Sweden and Canada". A table in that article clarified that only US$1.2 billion is "direct aid"; the rest consists of commercial loans from BNDES. However, even the US$1.2 billion is well above the figure published by the Brazilian government itself of US$923 million, not to mention the OECD estimates that indicate that US$500 million out of the US$923 million would be eligible for reporting as ODA.
30. Ministério das Relações Exteriores.
31. With the caveat that outgoing assistance is in the form of development cooperation on the model of TCDC.
32. This brief case study did not delve into DA incoming to Brazil.
33. Because of its strong official advocacy of the TCDC modality of DA, official respondents do not see Brazil as a "donor" and resent this designation. Furthermore, donor countries bring substantially more resources to the table than Brazil has. TCDC is a way to do DA economically for the donor. However, as TCDC involves numerous missions, it only adds to the costs of recipient countries, as they have to entertain such missions, tying up valuable local government and partner staff resources that could have been dedicated to other, more productive activities.
34. ABC Portaria 212 of 2008 (ABC, *op.cit.*).
35. While this brief case study cannot assess the consistency and effectiveness of such elaborate institutional and legal frameworks, they appear to be potentially redundant and cumbersome in application.
36. Only large projects are subject to independent evaluation, while small ones are evaluated internally.
37. The distribution of implementation time for projects was: <1 year, 17.2%; 1–2 years, 34.9%; 2–3 years, 33.3%; 3–4 years, 8.8%; >4 years, 5.7%.
38. From 1995–2005 budgets averaged approximately 1.27 million US$ yearly. ABC's budget for 2016 was US$6,553,052.37.
39. In 2015 ABC spent approximately US$10 million on project execution, equivalent to 2.4% of the budget of the Ministry of Foreign Affairs; in 2016 approximately US$10 million; and in 2017 approximately US$6 million. In 1995–2005 expenditure averaged approximately US$1.27 million yearly.
40. Contributions made to international organizations, programs and salaries of staff of technical entities and other government agencies and ministries mobilized for ABC projects, absorbed by these agencies were not included.
41. Phillips, *op.cit.*

References

COBRADI. (2011–2013). *Cooperação Brasileira de Assistencia Assistência ao Desenvolvimento Internacional*. Brasília: IPEA.

Corrêa, M. L. (2017). Quantification of South-South Cooperation and Its Implications to the Foreign Policy of Developing Countries. *Policy Brief, 41*.

Gulrajani, N. (2015). Dilemmas in Donor Design: Organisational Reform and the Future of Foreign Aid Agencies. *Public Administration and Development, 35*(2), 152–164.

Iglesias Puente, Carlos Alfonso. (2010). *A Cooperação Técnica Horizontal Brasileira como Instrumento da Politica Externa: a evolução da cooperação técnica com países em desenvolvimento-CTPD- no período 1995–2005*. Brasilia: FUNAG.

Kumar, A., & Messner, D. (Eds.). (2010). *Power Shifts and Global Governance: Challenges from South and North*. London: Anthem Press.

Luijkx, W., & Benn, J. (2016). *Emerging Providers – International Cooperation for Development* (No. 33). OECD Development Cooperation Working Paper.

Phillips, D. A. (2013). *Development Without Aid: The Decline of Development Aid and the Rise of the Diaspora*. London: Anthem Press.

Pinto, R. F., & De Oliveira, J. A. P. (2011). Institutional and Policy Implementation of International Public Goods: The Case of Global Commons. In A. Kumar & D. Messner (Eds.), *Power Shifts and Global Governance: Challenges from South and North*. London: Anthem Press.

World Bank. *Net Official Development Assistance and Official Aid (Current US$)* [Data file]. Retrieved August 12, 2017, from http://data.worldbank.org/indicator/DT.ODA.ALLD.CD

World Bank Development Committee. (2007). *Global Public Goods: A Framework for the Role of the World Bank*. Washington, DC: IMF and World Bank.

CHAPTER 8

Russia's Contribution to International Development Assistance

Elena Dobrolyubova

Introduction

For the past two decades, the role of Russia in international development assistance has changed dramatically. While in late 1990s to early 2000s Russia was among the largest borrowers from international financial institutions, currently the country is in transition to becoming a donor. Since 2005 the total amount of Russia's official development assistance has grown 12 times and reached US$1.2 billion a year. The country has clearly defined a state policy in supporting international development which is broadly followed in practice.

Russia has tried various formats for providing international development assistance over the past decade, but in the last few years, two key trends have emerged. The first trend is a switch from "traditional" multilateral support mechanisms like cooperation with the World Bank, United Nations Development Program (UNDP), and so on to support new South-South international development instruments, namely the institutes established in cooperation with other BRICS countries (BRICS stands for large emerging economies: Brazil, Russia, India, China, and

E. Dobrolyubova (✉)
Center for Public Administration Technologies, Russian Presidential Academy for National Economy and Public Administration (RANEPA), Moscow, Russia

Y. Jing et al. (eds.), *New Development Assistance*, Governing China in the 21st Century,
https://doi.org/10.1007/978-981-13-7232-2_8

South Africa). The second trend is the increase of the share of bilateral assistance in the total of international development assistance. While both trends are likely to be long term, the effectiveness of Russia's contribution to international development assistance, especially in bilateral programs, still largely depends on improving interagency coordination and building capacity in managing international aid inside the government.

The Concept: A Strategic Approach to Development Assistance

While in the 1990s and early 2000s Russia was a net recipient of international development aid, both economic and political factors in mid-2000s urged the country to increase its engagement as an aid provider. The political factors behind this included Russia's presidency of the G8 in 2006, active participation in international fora such as the Asia-Pacific Economic Cooperation (APEC), G20, and BRICS, as well as the need to promote its national interests and support its integration ambitions, especially, but not exclusively within the Commonwealth of Independent States (CIS). From an economic perspective, the high annual rates of economic growth and a federal budget surplus in 2000–2007 provided the resources which could be used for scaling up official development assistance.

The first Russian strategic document in the way of international development assistance ("Concept for Russia's Participation in International Development Assistance") was approved in June 2007 by the President of the Russian Federation. The Concept established the key objectives for the country's assistance program based on the principles of ownership and alignment, predictability and transparency, accountability and monitoring, and achievement of Millennium Development Goals (MDGs) established by the Development Assistance Committee of the Organization for Economic Cooperation and Development (OECD-DAC). The basic principles and priorities of the Russian Federation's policy of international development assistance set out in this first Concept are still relevant. These are a commitment to the priorities of sustainable socio-economic development of the recipient countries, a focus on strengthening equality and the democratization of the system of international relations, and interaction with third countries and coordination of joint activities in development assistance.

In April 2014 a new "Concept of Russian Federation's State Policy in the Area of International Development Assistance (IDA)" was approved by the President of the Russian Federation by Decree No. 259 dated April 20, 2014 (hereinafter the *Concept*). It is a logical development of the 2007

Concept and reflects the lessons learnt from the experience of rendering official development assistance in 2007–2014, but builds on some new priorities of the country's foreign policy.

According to the *Concept*, the key objectives of Russia's state policy of international development assistance include the following:

At the Global Level

1. Eliminating poverty and supporting sustainable social/economic development of partner states, including post-conflict states;
2. Influencing world processes and supporting a stable and equitable world system which is based on universally accepted norms of international law and comity between states;
3. Overcoming the consequences of natural disasters, technological catastrophes, and other emergencies;
4. Supporting initiatives on improving the transparency, quality, and efficiency of international development assistance, including active participation in developing common approaches to implementing agreed decisions in this domain; and
5. Projecting a positive image of Russia and its cultural and humanitarian influence worldwide.

At the Regional Level

1. Promoting neighborly relationships with bordering states, supporting elimination of existing and potential sources of tension and conflict, the illegal drug trade, terrorism and organized crime, especially in the regions bordering Russia;
2. Furthering integration processes in the Commonwealth of Independent States;
3. Facilitating effective public administration based on the rule of law and respect for human rights in countries which are aid recipients; and
4. Developing trade and economic cooperation.

Overall, the new *Concept* focuses on targeted bilateral assistance programs. While supporting the time-tested formats of international cooperation and participation in multilateral projects, it is planned to lay a foundation and expand institutional capacity for a gradual increase of bilateral aid. The *Concept* provides for the following forms of bilateral aid:

- Giving earmarked grants or delivering free goods and/or services to recipient states;
- Subsidizing credits funding delivery of industrial and agricultural products and/or implementing investment projects in the territory of recipient states;
- Providing technical assistance by transferring knowledge and experience to recipient states to aid institutional and human development in the policy domains of health care, education, environmental protection, natural disaster relief, fighting terrorism, and so on;
- Restructuring debt, including the "exchanging debt for aid" scheme, on condition that the recipient commits to using the freed-up resources for social and economic development purposes;
- Granting tariff and other preferences to enable access to the Russian market by goods and services produced in developing countries;
- Supporting the active participation of partner states in international trade; and
- Earmarking funds for implementing international programs by using the capacity of international institutions, and providing other support, on condition that Russia reserves the right to decide on the aid recipient(s) and the nature of the aid provided, and to stipulate that Russians be employed to render specialist technical assistance and to provide goods and services.

The *Concept* identifies the following four groups of countries as potential recipients of Russian international development assistance:

- Members of the CIS, plus the Republic of Abkhazia, Republic of South Ossetia, and other states which implement the policy of good-neighbor relations or alliance with Russia as well as states which participate with Russia in international unions and organizations in Eurasia;
- States which have historically close and friendly relations with Russia;
- States which participate in implementing joint economic and social projects of mutual interest;
- Developing states, cooperating with which responds to the national interests of the Russian Federation.

The above list demonstrates that the neighboring countries, especially the CIS states, continue to be the main priority of the Russian Federation. The *Concept* also emphasizes the aspect of enhancing the information-technological support of international development assistance programs.

The Current Situation of Russia's International Development Assistance

Priority areas of international development assistance for the Russian Federation are: improving the functioning of public administration; improving the trade and investment environment; providing access to essential sources of livelihood, primarily water and electricity; facilitating assurance of food security and agricultural development; strengthening national health and social protection systems; enhancing the quality and availability of education; adopting measures to protect the environmental and resolve trans-border environmental problems; fostering economic activity; setting up or improving national systems for combating organized crime and international terrorism; supporting post-conflict peace building; and facilitating regional economic integration.

The available data on Russian international development assistance confirms that the priorities set by the *Concept* are actually being implemented. First, the overall amount of official development assistance (ODA) has been rapidly increasing: in 2004 the Russian contribution to international development assistance was US$100 million, whereas by 2015 this had increased 12 times (see Table 8.1). The increase correlates both with Russian participation in new international development initiatives like the Eurasian Fund for Stabilization and Development or the New Development Bank, and with expanded bilateral assistance.

It should be noted that neither the initial *Concept* supporting international development assistance adopted in 2007 nor the revised *Concept* of 2014 contains any explicit definition of "international development assistance" or "official development assistance" (ODA). Definition is also lacking in other legal documents. Analysis of priorities for assistance and some examples provided below, however, demonstrate that the Russian concept of ODA is, at least to some extent, broader than the one used by OECD-DAC. For instance, Russia counts its contributions to the new international development initiatives noted above in its development assistance

Table 8.1 Russia's official development assistance in 2004–2015

	2004	*2005*	*2006*	*2007*	*2008*	*2009*	*2010*	*2011*	*2012*	*2013*	*2014*	*2015*
Total ODA, US$ million	100	101	102	211	220	785	472	479	465	714[a]	876	1200
Bilateral ODA, % of total	–	–	–	–	–	–	64	50	46	51	75	78

Sources: For 2004–2009, World Bank (2013); for 2010–2014, data published by Ministry of Finance; for 2015, OECD (2017). No data for bilateral ODA in 2004–2009 was published

[a]This figure does not include some direct budget support operations, such as credits worth US$3 billion provided to the Ukraine in 2013

total, despite both organizations not making the OECD-DAC list of ODA-eligible international organizations.

Secondly, in line with the current *Concept*, the share of bilateral assistance in total ODA provided by Russia has grown from 46% in 2012 to 78% in 2015. A broad menu of instruments is used for such bilateral aid; some interesting examples include:

- Special purpose funds, for example, the *Russian-Kyrgyz Development Fund* (*RKDF*) set up in 2014 to promote economic cooperation between the Kyrgyz Republic and the Russian Federation, Kyrgyz economic modernization and development, and the efficient use of the opportunities arising from both countries' participation in Eurasian economic integration. As of May 2017, the RKDF's project portfolio totaled US$226 million approved for over 700 projects; most approved projects are intended for supporting agricultural sector, transport and logistics, and trade infrastructure.[1]
- Initiatives supporting delivery of machinery to developing countries, such as *KAMAZ delivery for the implementation of humanitarian operations in remote areas.* KAMAZ cars and refuelers were delivered to Afghanistan (31 units), Uganda (14 units), Ghana (31 units), and Southern Sudan (52 units) in 2014. Warranty cards and training of specialists for maintenance and management of vehicles were provided in addition.

- Supportive social projects like *creating sustainable school food systems in Armenia, Tajikistan, and Kyrgyzstan*. The implementation of sustainable school lunch programs in Armenia, Tajikistan, and Kyrgyzstan included access to the Russian food supply and school canteen equipment (mostly Russian or local), and technical assistance in the development of the national school feeding program. Actions included training of authorities of different levels involved in the development and management of the national program, training of schools and local authorities in all aspects of school feeding, interactive games on nutrition and health for school children, and others. The program beneficiaries were mainly children from remote rural areas: 60,000 children in Armenia, 57,000 children in Kyrgyzstan, and 360,000 children in Tajikistan.

Thirdly, the geographical allocation of Russian ODA is in line with the country's strategic priorities. About 40% of the total (both bilateral and multilateral) is donated to countries in Europe and Central Asia, from CIS states to Serbia. The second largest priority region is Latin America (about 30% of aid being donated to the countries in this region).

While the overall ODA policy of Russia is developed by the Ministry of Foreign Affairs and the Ministry of Finance, implementing ODA programs and projects, given their multisectoral nature, involves quite a number of other ministries. Projects and programs of 2014 are listed by agency in Table 8.2.

The many Russian ministries involved in international development assistance does not merely reflect the multifaceted types of programs undertaken, the arrangements also challenge ministries to intensively coordinate specific interagency activities. One option is to combine these activities into one specific state program coordinated by a single ministry (viz., Ministry of Foreign Affairs, Ministry of Finance, Ministry of Economic Development). Some experts point out, however, such a general program of aid consolidation is unlikely to develop in the near future given the relatively low priority of support to ODA compared to other issues on the ministerial agendas (Larionova et al., 2014). Creating a new central agency for managing ODA, including consolidation of the sectoral functions, is another option, especially if the trend continues for increasing international development assistance in terms of scope and types of support.

Lack of a strong Russian national agency in charge of international development assistance was one of the factors driving its engagement in

Table 8.2 ODA programs and projects, implemented by the federal executive authorities in 2014

Federal executive body	*ODA programs and projects implemented in 2014*
Ministry of Finance of the Russian Federation	• "Exchanging debt for aid" • Russian-Kyrgyz development fund (RKDF) • Direct budget support to foreign countries
Ministry of Foreign Affairs of the Russian Federation	• Internships of foreign countries' diplomatic staff in the Diplomatic Academy of the Ministry of Foreign Affairs of the Russian Federation • Humanitarian aid to foreign countries
Ministry of Civil Defense, Emergencies and Disaster Relief of the Russian Federation	• Humanitarian and emergency assistance, humanitarian supplies delivery, assistance in rebuilding infrastructure after emergencies • Capacity-building for emergency situations prevention and appropriate choice of technical equipment • Supplying the truck fleet of international organizations delivering food aid to remote areas of Africa and Central Asia
Ministry of Agriculture of the Russian Federation	• Food delivery (wheat) to North Korea and Nicaragua
Ministry of Healthcare of the Russian Federation	• Scientific and practical training seminars in the field of child and maternal health at training centers under the *Research Center for Obstetrics, Gynecology and Perinatology* (a federally funded institution under the Ministry of Health Care of the Russian Federation); training of representatives of foreign governments on reducing child mortality through the Scientific Center of Children's Health of the Russian Academy of Sciences; seminars on child and maternal health through the Scientific Research Institute of Children's Infections of the Federal Medical and Biological Agency • Promoting foreign countries' health systems in order to prevent and control non-communicable diseases
Ministry of Industry and Trade of the Russian Federation	• Agricultural machinery delivery to Nicaragua
Ministry of the Interior of the Russian Federation	• Training foreign states' officials in the training institutes of the Ministry of the Interior of the Russian Federation

(*continued*)

Table 8.2 (continued)

Federal executive body	*ODA programs and projects implemented in 2014*
Federal Service for the Oversight of Consumer Protection and Welfare	• Implementation of comprehensive capacity-building programs in Eastern Europe and Central Asia in the field of prevention, control and surveillance of HIV/AIDS and other infectious diseases • The program to enhance CIS countries' capacity to fight measles and rubella • Practical and advisory assistance to the Republic of Guinea in preventing the outbreak and spread of Ebola, including the mobile laboratory of the Federal Service for the Oversight of Consumer Protection and Welfare
Federal Service for Drug Control	• Assistance to foreign governments in the field of drug traffic control to increase their capacity
Rosatom State Nuclear Energy Corporation	• Training CIS countries' medical technicians in the field of radiation oncology
Federal Customs Service	• Technical support in the field of customs control
Federal Financial Monitoring Service	• Technical assistance and capacity-building in the partner countries for combating illicit money laundering and terrorist financing

Source: Ministry of Finance (2014)

multilateral assistance organizations. This approach both uses the capacity of existing international institutions such as the World Bank Group and UN agencies, and builds the capacity of other multilateral development mechanisms (Zaytsev, 2014). The latter include Eurasian Development Bank, Eurasian Fund for Stabilization and Development, Asian Infrastructure Investment Bank, and New Development Bank.

World Bank Group (WBG), comprising the International Development Association (IDA) as well as the International Bank for Reconstruction and Development (IBRD), receives over a half of Russia's multilateral assistance. Its total contribution in 2005–2014 amounted to US$1 billion, of which 39% was earmarked for Financial Intermediary Funds, 35% for IDA contributions, and 26% for IBRD/IDA trust funds. To date, Russia has set up 21 IBRD/IDA trust funds, 15 of which are currently active. Russia's IBRD-administered trust funds are focused on the themes of infectious disease control, quality of basic education, energy access, food crisis response, and social support. Pledges to these programs have reached a total of almost US$261 million. Russia also supports some programmatic trust funds in the Europe and Central Asia (ECA) region, such as:

- *Programmatic Public Financial Management (PFM) Trust Fund*, supporting research and analysis, training, institutional development, and capacity-building programs in countries across the ECA, to strengthen their PFM systems;
- *The ECA Capacity Development Multi-Donor Trust Fund*, financing projects in low-income countries of the ECA region with a view to improving the quality and speed of their emergency management systems;
- *The ECA Statistical Capacity Development Multi-Donor Trust Fund*, addressing capacity challenges and financial constraints faced by the statistical systems of countries in Eastern Europe and the CIS region—with emphasis on IDA borrowing countries.

In its multilateral programs Russia is giving ever more attention to new development mechanisms based on regional approaches and South-South cooperation. The key regional development organizations which Russia is a party to are briefly described here.

The *Eurasian Development Bank* (*or EDB*) was founded in 2006 by Russia and Kazakhstan as a regional developmental agency. To date, several countries, including Armenia, Belarus, the Kyrgyz Republic, and Tajikistan have joined. Russia's contribution to its capital amounted to US$1 billion, or two-thirds of the total. The total investment portfolio of the EDB, as of June 30, 2017, stood at US$5.6 billion. Priorities include projects for developing transport, energy, telecommunications, and municipal infrastructure; assisting high value-added industries and energy efficiency programs. The bank supports projects in all participating countries, including Russia (about 35% of the total investment portfolio) and Kazakhstan (about 45%).[2]

During the 2008–2009 global financial crisis, when aid budgets across the developed world were being cut back, Russia's development aid contributions mounted to US$785 million. Also during this period, Russia initiated an innovative crisis response cooperation mechanism: the *Eurasian Fund for Stabilization and Development* (*EFSD*), with Russia's pledge totaling US$7.5 billion. To date, nine EFSD projects in four countries (Belarus, Armenia, the Kyrgyz Republic, and Tajikistan) have been approved, totaling US$5.3 billion.[3]

Russia has a 50% share in the *International Investment Bank* (*IIB*)—an international organization established in 1970 with the membership of Bulgaria, Hungary, Vietnam, Cuba, Mongolia, Russia, Romania, Slovakia, and the Czech Republic. The IIB is headquartered in Moscow, and its European regional office was opened in Bratislava, Slovakia in 2015. The IIB's funds amounted to €374 million. Its paid-in capital amounted to €313 million as of March 9, 2016.[4] The Bank's mission is to promote social and economic development, prosperity, and economic cooperation between member states. Priority domains of support include small and medium-sized enterprises; innovation and new technologies; trade and economic cooperation; and resources conservation, energy efficiency, and clean technologies.

Russia also has a 20% share of the *New Development Bank* established by BRICS countries in 2014 and a 6.2% share of the *Asian Infrastructure Investment Bank*.

General Trends

Overall, the above analysis demonstrates the following general trends in development of Russian ODA. First, the sum of Russian contributions to international development assistance has been growing significantly for the past decade. While there is still no clear legal definition of ODA in Russian legislation, analysis of the *Concept of Russian Federation's State Policy in the Area of International Development Assistance* and the *Concept*'s implementation practice suggest that at least some of the aid donated by Russia does not fit the OECD-DAC definition of ODA (viz., contributions to the new South-South development support mechanisms).

Secondly, there is a general trend of increasing bilateral in contrast to multilateral aid. This allows for implementing national strategic priorities and supporting national interests in tandem. But this trend is also, at least to some extent, a reaction to the restrictions imposed on Russia by certain international organizations (e.g., World Bank) in 2014.[5] Bilateral assistance calls for improved coordination of such assistance and institutional capacity-building for managing international aid.

Finally, there is a trend to favor novel development mechanisms over "traditional" multilateral aid operators, such as the WBG or the UN agencies. This trend is still weak, but it reflects the need for more transparency in ODA and the greater influence on ODA-related decision-making which Russia as an emerging donor now possesses.

Notes

1. Российско-Кыргызский Фонд Развития—О Нас [Russian-Kyrgyz Development Fund—about us]. Accessed August 15, 2017. Available at: http://www.rkdf.org/ru/o_nas.
2. Евразийский банк развития—Главная: О банке: Цифры и факты [Eurasian Development Bank—Main page: About the Bank: Facts and Figures]. Accessed August 10, 2017. Available at: https://eabr.org/about/facts-and-figures/.
3. Евразийский банк развития—Главная: Проекты [Eurasian Development Bank—Main page: Projects]. Accessed August 10, 2017. Available at: https://eabr.org/projects/efsr/?FUND=on.
4. International Investment Bank—General Information. Accessed August 10, 2017. Available at: https://www.iib.int/en/about.
5. In 2014, after the Crimea referendum and reunion with Russia, the WB suspended its lending program to Russia. Not a single new WB loan to Russia has been approved since the spring of 2014.

References

Larionova, M., Rakhmangulov, M., & Berenson, M. (2014). *The Russian Federation's International Development Assistance Programme: A State of the Debate Report* (No. 88). Institute of Development Studies. Retrieved from https://bit.ly/2QAXovE

Ministry of Finance. (2014). *Russian Contribution to the International Development Assistance in 2014*. Retrieved from https://bit.ly/2AdPHBB

OECD. (2017). *The Russian Federation's Official Development Assistance (ODA)*. Retrieved August 15, 2017, from http://www.oecd.org/russia/russias-official-development-assistance.htm

World Bank. (2013). *Russia as a Donor*. Retrieved February 1, 2018, from http://www.worldbank.org/content/dam/Worldbank/Highlights%20&%20Features/eca/russia/russia-donor-ig-eng-full.jpg

Zaytsev, Y. (2014). International Multilateral Assistance for Socio-Economic Development of the Poorest Countries of South-East Asia. *Journal of International Development, 29*(2), 249–258. https://doi.org/10.1002/jid.2999

CHAPTER 9

India as an Emerging Donor: Political and Economic Determinants

Eswaran Sridharan

Introduction

Historically, India's assistance to fellow developing countries began in 1949 with scholarships and humanitarian assistance in cases of famine.[1] The Colombo Plan was the main channel for scholarships although India's own Indian Technical and Economic Cooperation (ITEC) program started in 1964 for training and transfer of expertise. Nepal and Bhutan were the earliest recipients of Indian assistance and from 1959 India has been giving program-based assistance as annual grants to these countries, worked into their and India's five-year plans.

Indian assistance has traditionally been coordinated by two ministries, the Ministry of External Affairs (MEA) and the Ministry of Finance's Department of Economic Affairs (DEA) (see Agrawal, 2007; Chanana, 2009; Chaturvedi, 2012a, 2012b; Kragelund, 2010; Mullen, 2012; Naidu, 2008; Price, 2005, for accounts of India's emerging assistance policies). The MEA concentrates on neighbors like Nepal, Bhutan and other South Asian countries, and gave mainly grants and lines of credit

E. Sridharan (✉)
University of Pennsylvania Institute for the Advanced Study of India,
New Delhi, India

Y. Jing et al. (eds.), *New Development Assistance*, Governing China in the 21st Century,
https://doi.org/10.1007/978-981-13-7232-2_9

(LOCs) (through the Exim Bank since 2004–05), and also assistance through the ITEC program.

ITEC, which came into existence in 1964, operates through four modalities: training in India, project assistance, study trips and humanitarian assistance. The DEA (in the Ministry of Finance) gave lines of credit to a range of developing countries especially South Asian neighbors.

Exim Bank Lines of Credit

There was a basic policy shift in 2003–04 from government-to-government credit lines to government-supported lines of credit through the Exim Bank of India. As the Ministry of Finance put it:

> Policy on Lines of Credit: For about four decades, Department of Economic Affairs on behalf of Government of India had been extending Lines of Credit (LOCs) to friendly developing foreign countries. These LOCs were essentially "Government to Government" (G to G) credit lines as the credit agreements were signed between GOI and the Government of the recipient country. Till 2003–04, the LOCs were from Government to Government. Accordingly, the full amount covered by the LOCs used to be provided in the Budget. Since 2003–04, this system has been substituted by extending GOI supported Lines of Credit through Exim Bank of India.[2]

To address a question that can be raised, at the outset, namely why should lines of credit be considered foreign assistance and not commercial activity? The answer is that it is government-subsidized and below market rates of interest:

Further, the Ministry of Finance continues:

> "Q. What is the interest rate the overseas importer of Indian goods has to pay?
>
> A. The overseas importer of Indian goods has to approach the overseas borrower financial institution/recipient of Exim Bank's LOC, for approval of his proposal for import of Indian goods on deferred credit terms. The interest rate that the importer will need to pay to the recipient of Exim Bank's LOC, will depend on various factors such as the cost of fund, the currency of credit, tenure of credit, security offered by the importer, the risk perception of the importer and the interest rate structure prevalent in the country. It may however be mentioned that Exim Bank's interest rates on LOCs being competitive, the importer would normally have to pay interest rate lower than what he would otherwise pay to his Bank on similar credits."[3]

The last sentence indicates that the LOCs of the Exim Bank may be considered subsidized credit and hence foreign assistance. The interest subsidy on the Exim Bank's LOCs is given in the IDEAS line item in Statement 11 of the annual Expenditure Budget. While India does not call its development cooperation aid and therefore does not compare its criteria to Development Assistance Committee's (DAC's) Official Development Assistance (ODA) criteria, the basic principle remains that of below-market-rate concessional loans and grants.

Between 2003–04 and May 2015, India provided $11,634 million in 193 operative Exim Bank LOCs with another $1384 million in the pipeline to be operationalized, totaling 214 LOCs of $13,017 million (Table 9.1). The average worth of an operative LOC was $61 million.

Region-wise and country-wise (Table 9.2), 139 LOCs (of 193 operational) worth $6770 million went to sub-Saharan Africa (henceforth, Africa refers to sub-Saharan, that is, non-Arab Africa, plus Sudan and Djibouti, and including the island states of Madagascar, Mauritius and Seychelles), 10 LOCs worth $3256 million to South Asian countries, 9 LOCs worth $601 million to Myanmar, 14 LOCs worth $536 million to Southeast Asia and Pacific (other than Myanmar), 4 LOCs worth $167 million to the (non-oil) Middle East and Central Asia, and 15 LOCs worth $148 million to Latin America and the Caribbean. Thus, 72 percent of the number of LOCs went to Africa and 5 percent to South Asia, 5 percent to Myanmar, and 7 percent to Southeast Asia and Pacific. By value, 58 percent went to Africa and 28 percent to South Asia, these two regions getting 86 percent of the total amount loaned.

Table 9.1 Operating Exim Bank lines of credit as on May 2015

Level of utilization of LOC	*No. of LOCs*	*Amount ($ million)*
Operating	193	11,633.60
Pipeline	21	1383.63
Total	214	13,017.23
Of the operating		
Fully used[a]	119	4700.91
Partly used[b]	35	4299.37
Totally unused[c]	39	2633.32

Source: *Exim Bank*—http://www.eximbankindia.in/lines-of-credit, accessed on 17 September 2015

[a]Assuming amount left for utilization is zero, where such data is missing in relevant columns

[b]Of partly used, the amount left for utilization is $2414.52 million

[c]"To be made effective" are clubbed under this

Table 9.2 Region-wise (operating) lines of credit as on May 2015

Country/Region	*No. of LOCs*	*Amount ($ million)*
Africa	139	6769.69
Eurasia	2	155.60
LAC	15	147.65
Middle East and Central Asia	4	166.80
Myanmar	9	601.39
South Asia	10	3256.16
South East Asia and Pacific	14	536.31
Total	193	11,633.60

Source: *Exim Bank of India*—http://www.eximbankindia.in/lines-of-credit, accessed on 17 September 2015

Table 9.3 Purpose-wise (operating) lines of credit as on May 2015

Purpose	*No. of LOCs*	*Amount ($ million)*	*Amount left for utilization ($ million)*
General	13	326.00	190.75
Agricultural	26	961.31	456.10
Cement	6	157.13	70.13
Rural electrification	23	1841.86	1220.85
Power	25	1760.35	747.51
Sugar industry	10	880.32	24.29
Railway	11	1620.22	562.36
Non-bilateral	3	500.00	233.28
Miscellaneous	76	3586.41	1550.97
Total	193	11,633.60	5056.2322

Source: *Exim Bank*—http://www.eximbankindia.in/lines-of-credit, accessed on 17 September 2015

By major purpose (Table 9.3), the largest single chunk was 76 (of 193 operational) LOCs, 39 percent of the total number, covering a wide range of miscellaneous purposes to diverse to slot into sectors, worth $3586 million, or 31 percent of the total amount of credit extended. By identifiable purpose, the loans show a focus on power and electrification, railways, agriculture and sugar, or more generally, electricity, transport and agriculture. The largest amounts loaned by major sector were in power projects ($1760 million in 25 LOCs) and the related area of rural electrification ($1842 million in 23 LOCs), the latter two between them $3602 million or 31 percent of the total amount equaling the Miscellaneous category.

There was also a significant category of general purpose LOCs which the recipient could use for any purpose ($326 in 13 LOCs).

Grants and Loans Other Than Through the Exim Bank

Other than the LOCs extended by the Exim Bank, and subsidized by the government, since 2004–05, India provided a grand total of $11,070 million in grants and loans over the period from 1984–2015, of which $9404 million was over 1997–2015 (Table 9.4), particularly since

Table 9.4 India's bilateral aid, excluding Exim Bank LOCs, 1997–2016 ($ million)[a]

Year	*Plan*			*Non-plan*			*Total*
	Grant	*Loan*	*Total*	*Grant*	*Loan*	*Total*	
1997–98	10	6	16	91	43	134	150
1998–99	44	27	71	100	30	131	202
1999–00	57	36	92	88	33	121	213
2000–01	76	44	120	88	38	127	247
2001–02	50	34	84	110	34	144	228
2002–03	69	44	114	56	113	169	282
2003–04	99	66	165	155	60	215	381
2004–05	101	62	164	208	65	273	437
2005–06	100	63	162	287	39	326	488
2006–07	41	8	49	305	28	333	382
2007–08	63	12	75	359	17	376	451
2008–09	73	25	98	313	177	490	588
2009–10	89	63	151	328	26	353	505
2010–11	69	106	175	495	–	495	670
2011–12	64	165	229	451	52	503	732
2012–13	86	209	296	601	129	729	1025
2013–14	209	241	450	659	26	684	1134
2014–15	231	380	611	678	–	678	1289
2015–16[b]	314	511	825	776	25	801	1626
Total	1833	2099	3932	6160	921	7081	11,030

Source: *Ministry of Finance*, Expenditure Budget—http://indiabudget.nic.in/previousub.asp, accessed on 15 December 2015

[a]Rupee figures converted at average annual rupee-dollar exchange rates

[b]Budget estimates

Table 9.5 Loans and grants to South Asia, 1984–2016

Year	*South Asia total ($ million)*[a]
1984–85	107
1985–86	105
1986–87	110
1987–88	77
1988–89	82
1989–90	54
1990–91	77
1991–92	39
1992–93	47
1993–94	45
1994–95	34
1995–96	63
1996–97	59
1997–98	89
1998–99	79
1999–00	78
2000–01	84
2001–02	95
2002–03	92
2003–04	102
2004–05	116
2005–06	145
2006–07	188
2007–08	199
2008–09	328
2009–10	349
2010–11	463
2011–12	562
2012–13	788
2013–14	902
2014–15	929
2015–16[b]	1184

Source: *Government of India, Ministry of Finance*: Expenditure Budget—http://indiabudget.nic.in/previousub.asp, accessed on 17 September 2015

[a]South Asia includes Nepal, Bangladesh, Bhutan, Maldives, Sri Lanka

[b]Budget estimates

2004–05 and more so over 2008–15. Table 9.5 gives the amount of grant and loan assistance, other than Exim Bank, to South Asia.

Of the grand total, since 1997, of $9404 million, 67 percent was given as grants and 33 percent as loans. Of this, $5588 million, or 59 percent

(Tables 9.4 and 9.5), went to its South Asian neighbors. Thus, India's non-Exim Bank grants and loans have gone mainly as grants, and primarily to its South Asian neighbors (see Tables 9.4 and 9.5), with Afghanistan registering a presence since 2008–09 and Africa since 2005–06. Infrastructure, health and education are the main focus of Indian development assistance in South Asia while assistance tied to purchases of Indian goods and services and technical training of civil servants and public sector managers is the main focus in Africa. An Indian company, usually a public sector company, has to be the lead contractor and 75 percent of goods and services should be sourced from India. However, there is an open bidding process among Indian companies and the choice of contractor among them is the host government prerogative. The LOCs, however, are not characterized by resource-for-loan conditions and are not bundled with private investment and trade.

Consolidated data on the number of scholarships and training slots offered under the ITEC program and allied programs like the Technical Cooperation Scheme (TCS) of the Colombo Plan, and the Special Commonwealth Assistance to Africa Programme (SCAAP), and the amounts spent on these, are still unavailable. However, for capacity building the 2013–14 allocation is Rs. 1700 million ($28 million) and is tremendously diverse, consisting of 8780 civilian training slots, 1500 defense training slots consisting of 280 different training courses in 47 institutions in India for 161 partner countries.

Overall, it is not surprising, as we shall see later, that South Asia, as well as the "near abroad", including Myanmar and Afghanistan, has dominated Indian foreign assistance. However, Africa has emerged as a major focus particularly since 2008 (Duclos, 2012; Kragelund, 2010; Naidu, 2008).

India's foreign assistance policy does not seem to be related to trade and investment relationships as far as its major thrust, South Asia, is concerned (Reserve Bank of India database for all data in the rest of this section). India's trade with the countries of the South Asian region, a major focus of Indian assistance with 28 percent of Exim Bank credit, amounts to only 3.1 percent of its overall trade in 2014–15, up from 2.6 percent in 2000–01, and only 6.6 percent of its exports in 2014–15, from only 5.5 percent in 2004–05. India's trade with, and exports to, Afghanistan, remain tiny at 0.09 percent and 0.14 percent respectively as at 2014. Likewise, India's trade with, and exports to Myanmar remain tiny at 0.29 percent and 0.27 percent respectively as at 2014.

As far as Africa is concerned, total trade with Africa was about \$62 billion in 2014–15, equal to trade with China also at \$62 billion, of which Nigeria with \$18.53 billion and South Africa with \$11.72 billion, accounted for about half with \$30.25 billion. However, out of total assistance to Africa, these two countries are not at all dominant in the assistance profile, the overwhelming bulk of the assistance going to less developed or less resource-rich countries.

Likewise, the bulk of Indian outward foreign direct investment (FDI) since 2010 has gone to developed Western Europe and North America, and to Southeast Asia (mainly, developed Singapore), oil-rich West Asia, resource-rich South America, and not to the main aided regions.

Recent Institutional and Policy Evolution: The Development Partnership Administration

Since January 2012, a Development Partnership Administration (DPA) has been formed within the MEA, and started functioning from June 2012 in effect, coordinating the implementation of India's development partnership program. It is a multi-division department. The DPA currently has a staff strength of 75–80. This was a somewhat belated response to India's development assistance program since 2003–04 outpacing the support infrastructure in the MEA.

The core DPA mandate consists of (a) focused attention on projects, the flagship project of the DPA being the construction of 50,000 houses for displaced persons in the North and East of Sri Lanka; (b) developing a skill base; and (c) helping in policy formulation. However, it is an implementation agency, not a policy-making agency and does not propagate any particular development philosophy or strategy. Policy is handled by the country desk in the relevant political (territorial) division in the MEA. The traditional mechanism continues, that is, requests for assistance originate from the would-be recipient country. The Indian embassy, usually the ambassador or deputy chief of mission, is approached by the foreign government. This also happens very commonly on high-level visits by heads of government or foreign ministers, or other cabinet ministers such as trade ministers, to India or when Indian leaders undertake high-level visits.

Four major examples are the India-Africa Forum summits of 2008 and 2011, the Afghan president's visit to India in 2011 and the Indian prime minister's visit to Bangladesh in 2011, all of which were followed by major increases in assistance commitments. Assistance requests and hence, assistance decisions reflected in annual numbers are not—and cannot realistically be expected to be—a smooth affair but jerky and politically punctuated.

Once a policy decision is made by the relevant political division of the MEA, the DPA is then charged with implementing the decision. After the shift to Exim Bank LOCs for project loans, including import of Indian equipment, the MEA now gives 95 percent of the total assistance, reflected in Statement 11 of the Government of India's Expenditure Budget, with about 5 percent coming from some other ministries such as Science and Technology, Health, and Renewable Energy.

Internal issues that the DPA is currently addressing include (a) budget allocations—funds are needed early in the financial year; (b) the approval process—an empowered committee is proposed to be set up to speed up LOCs selected by host countries; (c) efforts to move away from the monopolization of projects by a few companies and reduce overdependence on public enterprises; and (d) streamlining contracting/procurement procedures.

India is striving to emerge as a South-South cooperation leader, cofounding the Global Network of Exim Banks and Development Finance Institutions in 2006, promoting the establishment of the Development Cooperation Forum in 2007, and becoming one of the largest contributors to the Commonwealth Fund for Technical Cooperation, and has now joined the New Development Bank (NDB) and the Asian Infrastructure Investment Bank (AIIB). There has been some cooperation with DAC donor agencies which have expressed a desire to train Afghans and Africans in India as it is more cost-effective; this has been welcomed by DPA. Some DAC agencies have also expressed interest in joint project implementation in third countries. DPA has resisted this, fearing brand equity dilution and also wanting to avoid the terms and conditions of DAC aid.

Discernible Patterns and an Overall Assessment

If trade and investment relations have not been the prime drivers what have been the motivations behind India's development partnership program? The following patterns are discernible based on detailed confidential interviews.[4]

First, in the cases of Bhutan and Nepal, India bulks large in their trade, inward investment and tourism profiles, while they are of marginal significance in India's trade and outward investment profile. They matter to India's security calculations in a major way as they are neighbors with porous borders and buffer states between India and China. Hence, India's assistance to them is primarily motivated by political and security considerations but is important to the recipients in economic terms. Also, that India being the principal destination for higher studies and training creates an alumni network in both countries.

Second, Bangladesh and Sri Lanka, which are neighbors in which India perceives competition for diplomatic influence from Pakistan and China, are both insignificant to India's trade and outward investment profile but of considerable importance to the recipients' trade, inward investment, remittances (for Bangladesh) and tourism (for Sri Lanka) profile. In both cases, Indian assistance is fairly recent, becoming significant over the past half-decade, and relatively concentrated in large lines of credit. Scholarships and training are significant in both cases.

Third, Afghanistan and Myanmar are again recent cases of assistance, motivated primarily by political and security considerations with perceived competition for political influence from Pakistan and China respectively. In both cases, the recipient country is of marginal economic but major geopolitical significance to India, although both can be of significance for India's natural resource needs in the future. The pattern of assistance is one of large lines of credit rather than small projects although this is beginning to happen in Afghanistan, where scholarships and training are also significant.

Fourth, in the case of Africa, assistance again is recent in its growth, particularly after the India-Africa summits of 2008 and 2011 (a third summit in 2015 took the process forward). It consists of 139 of 193 operative LOCs, with an average worth of $49 million, with only 17 of over $100 million, to 36 countries and the Economic Community of West African States (ECOWAS) Bank of Investment spread across the continent, and is concentrated in fairly large to medium projects in infrastructure and agriculture, although scholarships and training are important. Within Africa, there has been a shift of Indian assistance from Eastern and Southern Africa to West Africa, recognized to be energy- and mineral-rich. Assistance is not driven by immediate trade and resource considerations but by long-term relationship-building, plus close to 50 UN General Assembly votes factored in.

Four major points emerge from an overall assessment of the Indian development partnership program.

First, India eschews terms like aid and donor, and prefers to use the term "development partner" as a fellow developing country and DAC aid recipient. It is only with the formation of the DPA, that India's "demand-driven" and politically punctuated assistance can be said to have acquired the character of a program. As the amounts increased it gradually acquired the character of a program in two shifts—the shift to LOCs through the Exim Bank from 2004, and the formation of the DPA as an implementation agency in 2012.

Second, while the purpose of partnership is admittedly political, it is meant to cultivate goodwill toward India and long-term relationships rather than immediate payoffs, either political or economic, particularly in the case of Africa.

Third, the MEA considers the ITEC program the most cost-effective and the one that had yielded the best returns in terms of long-term goodwill because it trains key personnel in India and builds long-term human relationships.

Fourth, there is no clear economic development philosophy or macroeconomic policy prescription that emerges from a scrutiny of the development partnership program.

Overall, from a practitioner's standpoint, as emphasized in interviews, the Indian program is about building long-term relationships and not about immediate benefit. This is particularly the case in South Asia but also applies to Africa.

Notes

1. See Chaturvedi (2012a, pp. 171–177) for a historical account until the 2000s.
2. Source: https://www.dea.gov.in/divisionbranch/ideas, accessed on 15 December 2015.
3. Source: http://newsletters.cii.in/Newsletters/mailer/LAC_Newsletter/february/Opportunities/locbooklet.pdf, accessed on 15 December 2015.
4. All facts and figures in the country accounts in this section are from Indian Ministry of External Affairs, *Annual Reports*, various years and anonymous conversations with nine senior Indian diplomats with experience of the various countries and regions covered, including two former heads of the DPA, and a former chairman and managing director of the Exim Bank of India.

References

Agrawal, S. (2007). *Emerging Donors in International Development Assistance: The India Case*. Canada: IDRC-CDI.

Chanana, D. (2009). India as an Emerging Donor. *Economic and Political Weekly, 44*(12), 11–14.

Chaturvedi, S. (2012a). India and Development Cooperation: Expressing Southern Solidarity. In S. Chaturvedi, T. Fues, & E. Sidoropoulos (Eds.), *Development Cooperation and Emerging Powers: New Partners or Old Patterns* (pp. 169–189). London: Zed Books.

Chaturvedi, S. (2012b). India's Development Partnership: Key Policy Shifts and Institutional Evolution. *Cambridge Review of International Affairs, 25*(4), 557–577.

Duclos, V. (2012). Building Capacities: The Resurgence of Indo-African Technoeconomic Cooperation. *India Review, 11*(4), 209–225.

India, Govt. of. (2015). *Government of India Portal on Development Assistance*. Retrieved April 2, 2016, from http://www.externalassistance.gov.in/portal/

India, Ministry of External Affairs. *Annual Reports*, 1991–92 to 2014–15. Retrieved December 15, 2015, from http://www.mea.gov.in/annual-reports.htm?57/Annual_Reports

India, Ministry of Finance. *Economic Survey*, 1984–85 to 2014–15. Retrieved December 15, 2015, from http://finmin.nic.in/the_ministry/dept_eco_affairs/dea.asp

India, Ministry of Finance. *Annual Budget*, 1991–92 to 2014–15. Retrieved December 15, 2015, from http://indiabudget.nic.in/glance.asp

Kragelund, P. (2010). India's African Engagement. *Elcano Newsletter, 63*, 6.

Mullen, R. D. (2012). India Flexes Its Foreign Aid Muscle. *Current History, 111*(744), 154.

Naidu, S. (2008). India's Growing African Strategy. *Review of African Political Economy, 35*(115), 116–128.

Price, G. (2005). Diversity in Donorship: The Changing Landscape of Official Humanitarian Aid: India's Official Aid Programme. *Overseas Development Institute*. Retrieved from http://www.odi.org

CHAPTER 10

Chinese Foreign Aid and Financing: An Example of New Development Assistance?

Denghua Zhang

Introduction

China's rise has been prominent in contemporary history. It overtook Japan as the world's second largest economy in 2010, and its growth has continued though at a slower pace. China's impact is increasingly felt by the international community in sectors including development assistance. As a recent example, during the inaugural Belt and Road Forum for International Cooperation in Beijing in May 2017, the Chinese government pledged substantial financing to the developing world. Some of the measures include: China will provide US$8.81 billion (RMB 60 billion)[1] of aid over the next three years to developing countries (and international organizations) participating in the Belt and Road; The China Development Bank will set up a special lending scheme of US$36.7 billion (RMB 250 billion) to support the Belt and Road; The China Export-Import Bank (China Exim Bank) will set up a similar scheme of US$14.6 billion (RMB 100 billion) and an additional US$4.4 billion (RMB 30 billion)

D. Zhang (✉)
Australian National University, Canberra, ACT, Australia
e-mail: denghua.zhang@anu.edu.au

Y. Jing et al. (eds.), *New Development Assistance*, Governing China in the 21st Century,
https://doi.org/10.1007/978-981-13-7232-2_10

Infrastructure Development Fund (Xinhua, 2017). By 2016, Chinese enterprises had invested US$18.55 billion in countries along the Belt and Road and created 177,000 employments for them (MOFCOM, 2017).

This is just a small part of the whole story with respect to Chinese development assistance that could trace back to 1950 when Beijing started to provide foreign aid. Chinese aid spending has become remarkably notable in the past decade. China-funded projects especially large-scale infrastructures have spread across the developing world. In addition to its impressive scale, Chinese aid has demonstrated distinctive features. Against this backdrop, this country report seeks to deconstruct Chinese aid program and briefly explore seven main aspects which include aid amount, destinations, patterns, motivations, organizations, impact and future directions. Some sections will also discuss the broader term of Chinese financing. It draws upon an extensive literature review and the author's research on China's foreign aid over the past 15 years, in particular more than 140 interviews with aid officials, practitioners and researchers in China, traditional donor states and development partner countries. The main purpose of this report is to enrich the debate on Chinese aid, a significant part of new development assistance highlighted by the research project, and its impact on the global landscape of development assistance.

Aid Amount

China does not release its annual country-based aid data. To obtain an accurate figure of Chinese foreign aid is an extremely challenging, if not impossible, task, or a game of "putting together a jigsaw puzzle" (Grimm, Rank, McDonald, & Schickerling, 2011, p. 22). According to the two white papers on foreign aid released by China in April 2011 and July 2014, Chinese aggregate aid amounted to US$37.6 billion (RMB 256.29 billion) between 1950 and 2009, while the figure for 2010–2012 totaled US$13.1 billion (RMB 89.34 billion), more than one-third of its aid for the six decades prior to 2010 (State Council, 2011, p. 22, 2014, p. 22). These official figures could have been understated for three main reasons. First, China still has a large population living under the poverty line. It makes sense for Beijing to downplay the magnitude of its foreign aid program to mute domestic discontent. Second, a total of 33 ministerial-level agencies are involved in Chinese aid delivery, which exacerbates the difficulty in coordinating and producing reliable aid data, even for China itself.[2]

A third reason relates to the differences between China and traditional donors in aid definitions. Some elements of Chinese aid such as military aid and construction of sports facilities do not align with official development assistance (ODA), a term used by members of OECD Development Assistance Committee. More importantly, concessional loans and other types of loans, which are more commercial in nature, such as preferential buyers' credit, preferential exporters' credit and mixed credit, have constituted the majority of Chinese financing overseas. Traditional donors exclude commercial loans from ODA, and some officials and experts in recipient countries even take issue with the concessionality of Chinese concessional loans.[3] In practice, China is placing far more emphasis on these broad financial facilities than foreign aid to materialize its financial pledges to other developing countries. China's commitment to African allies through the Forum on China-Africa Cooperation and the measures it announced to support the Belt and Road are two examples.[4] From this perspective, new development assistance could serve as a better term to depict Chinese economic and financial assistance to recipient countries.

Figure 10.1 offers a summary of Chinese annual aid budget released by the Ministry of Finance (MoF), which combines its grant, interest-free loans and interest gap[5] of concessional loans, but excludes the principal of concessional loans (MoF, 2017). Even so, Chinese aid budget had grown steadily over the years between 2005 and 2015 except for a slight decline in 2014.

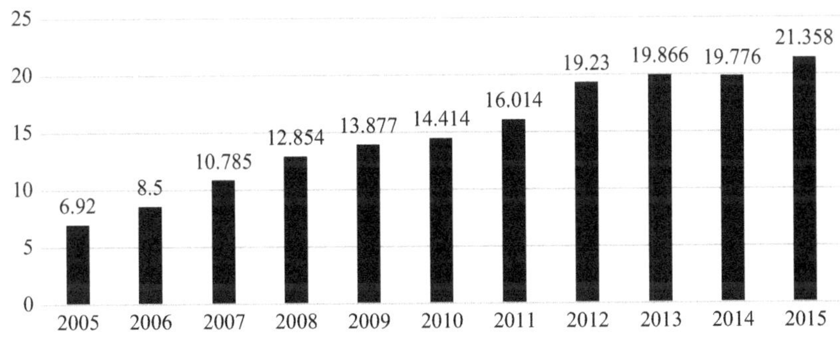

Fig. 10.1 Chinese annual aid budget (2005–2015), billion RMB. Source: Compiled by author based on MoF data

Table 10.1 China's financial flows overseas for development cooperation

Category		*Volume, US$ million*
China's gross concessional flows overseas[a]	2011	2785
	2012	3123
	2013	2997
	2014	3401
	2015	3113
China's development-oriented contributions to and through multilateral organizations in 2015[b]	United Nations	206.6
	Regional Development Banks	21.3
	World Bank Group	/
	Other multilateral organizations	5.0
China's official financial flows in 2015[c]	To recipient countries bilaterally	10,746.1
	To multilateral organizations	132.3

Source: Compiled by author based on *OECD* and *World Bank* dataset

[a]See http://www.oecd.org/development/stats/non-dac-reporting.htm

[b]See http://www.oecd.org/development/stats/non-dac-reporting.htm

[c]See http://wdi.worldbank.org/table/6.10

Drawing upon the data from OECD and the World Bank, Table 10.1 estimates China's gross concessional financing overseas at US$15,419 million between 2011 and 2015. In 2015, China's official financial flows to recipient countries bilaterally reached US$10,746 million. AidData's Chinese development finance database is another useful source to track Chinese aid projects in 50 countries for the period of 2000–2013 (AidData, 2017).

Aid Destinations

Beneficiaries of Chinese aid program cover the majority of developing countries. For the period of 1950–2009, 161 countries and over 30 regional and international organizations had received Chinese foreign aid (State Council, 2011, p. 22). In the following three years, China provided aid to 121 countries which include 51 countries in Africa, 30 in Asia, 19 in Latin America and Caribbean, 12 in Europe and 9 in Oceania (State Council, 2014, p. 22). Figure 10.2 presents a snapshot of the geographical distribution of Chinese aid by value. As we can see, Africa and Asia remain the two largest recipients, receiving 45.7% and 32.8% of Chinese aid between 1950 and 2009, and 51.8% and 30.5% between 2010 and 2012 (State Council, 2011, p. 22, 2014, p. 22). This distribution high-

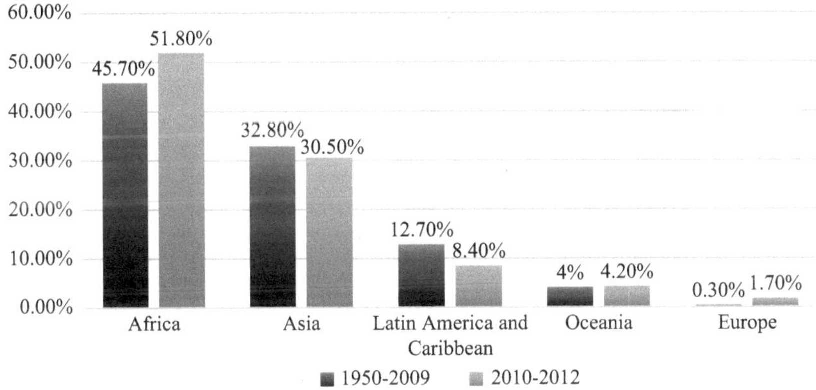

Fig. 10.2 Geographical distribution of Chinese foreign aid. Source: Compiled by author

lights China's emphasis on the two continents for economic and strategic considerations. Countries from other regions including Latin America and Caribbean, Oceania and East Europe also receive Chinese development assistance. For instance, the Pacific island countries, mainly the 8 of the 14 sovereign states recognizing Mainland China, had received 4.2% of Chinese total aid between 2010 and 2012, exceedingly US$550 million. Given the small population in most of these island countries (for instance, Samoa: 187,400; Tonga: 103,400; Cook Islands: 15,200), the per capita of Chinese aid to them is impressive.

Aid Patterns

Chinese aid has been offered in eight forms including complete projects (turn-key project), goods and materials, technical cooperation, human resources development cooperation, medical teams, volunteer programs, emergency humanitarian aid and debt relief. In terms of components, Chinese aid has experienced significant changes. As Fig. 10.3 shows, interest-free loans had been reduced drastically, accounting for less than 10% of Chinese total aid in 2010–2012. The proportion of aid in grants in 2010–2012 remained similar to the period of 1950–2009. Concessional loans increased rapidly, representing more than half of Chinese aid in 2010–2012.

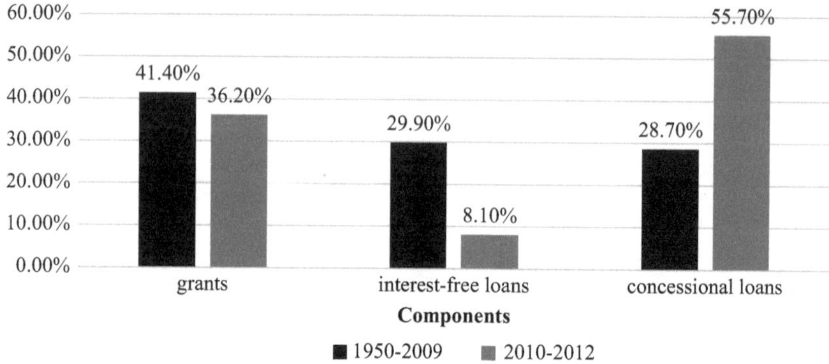

Fig. 10.3 Components of Chinese aid. Source: Compiled by author

In comparison to traditional donors' ODA, China's foreign aid has demonstrated its own features that could enrich the category of new development assistance. These aid practices take root in China's own experience of national development and perception of development path. They are also informed by *China's Eight Principles for Economic Aid and Technical Assistance to Other Countries.*[6] Juxtaposed with traditional donors' ODA, several aspects of Chinese aid deserve attention. First, China boasts the equal donor-recipient relationship between itself and partner countries, labeling its aid as South-South cooperation and mutual assistance between developing countries (*qiong bang qiong*). Second, China insists its aid aims to bring mutual benefits and win-win for both recipient countries and China (*hu li gong ying*) (see also Chandy & Kharas, 2011, p. 742). This philosophy lends support to China's use of foreign aid to facilitate its economic operations (such as resource extraction) in recipient countries. It also justifies China's use of a high proportion of its own workers and materials in the aid projects, concessional loan projects in particular. Third, China argues that it attaches no political strings to recipient governments on the use of Chinese aid, while traditional donors usually set aid conditions in areas such as governance, human rights, democratization and financial rigidity (see also Gore, 2013, p. 774). One exemption, as some analysts argue, is that recipient countries of Chinese aid are required to respect the "one China" policy and refrain from developing official ties with Taiwan. Another important feature is that China's development assistance has primarily focused on the economic growth in recipient countries, which is evidenced by China's preoccupation with infrastructure improvement such as interconnection and intercommunication in Africa and Asia.

Aid Motivations

Providing foreign aid serves China's multidimensional national interests. The focus of China's motivations has shifted over time and will be discussed in three roughly divided periods. From 1950 to the mid-1970s, Chinese aid was dominated by ideology and worked to rally support from other socialist and developing countries, and extend China's diplomatic space against the isolation from western nations and the Soviet Union. Soon after China adopted the reform and opening policy in the late 1970s, it focused the attention on domestic economic development. Chinese foreign aid provision became pragmatic and its aid budget was reined in.

Since the beginning of the new millennium, China has greatly increased its development assistance to the developing world. Chinese aid spending has soared, and its loan facilities have grown even faster. These assistance programs are expected by Beijing to facilitate its achievement of political, economic and image-building purposes. Politically, China aims to consolidate brotherhood with other developing countries, which is valued as the foundation of China's foreign policy (Chen, 2009), and secures their support for China's diplomacy. Economically, China hopes its aid could continue to play its part in facilitating China's access to minerals and natural resources in recipient countries and supporting Chinese enterprises' commercial operations there. China is also keen to build a benign image globally commensurate with its status as a rising great power. Another important motivation behind China's aid program is that China is having more self-confidence and a stronger desire to reshape global governance into a more equitable system in China's eyes. It is providing large amounts of development assistance to woo the support of recipient countries for this objective. This motivation is becoming increasingly notable in President Xi Jinping's administration since 2013, and ambitious programs including the Belt and Road and the Asian Infrastructure Investment Bank (AIIB) were initiated. Equally important, the Chinese government is enthusiastically using BRICS as an important vehicle to "make the international order more just and equitable", as President Xi highlighted at the BRICS Xiamen Summit in September 2017 (MFA, 2017).

Aid Organizations

China did not have a single agency to oversee its foreign aid until the establishment of China International Development Cooperation Agency (CIDCA) in April 2018. CIDCA was largely designed to improve the coordination and supervision of Chinese aid. It leads the inter-agency coordination mechanism which consists of 33 ministerial-level members involved in Chinese aid management, though to varying degrees (Zhang & Smith, 2017). The impact of this loosely structured mechanism should not be exaggerated, and the members meet occasionally to exchange views on broad issues and continue to do business in their own ways. Among these members, CIDCA, China's Ministry of Commerce (MOFCOM), Ministry of Foreign Affairs (MFA), MoF and China Exim Bank are most important players on aid management. CIDCA replaces MOFCOM to control the lion's share of China's aid budget and oversee the majority of Chinese aid projects. It, in consultation with other agencies, assesses and decides on aid requests from recipient countries. As the former guardian of Chinese aid, MOFCOM retains significant influence as its Department of Foreign Aid has become the backbone of CIDCA. Also, Zhou Liujun, deputy director of CIDCA, is MOFCOM's representative in the new agency. MFA is the caretaker of China's foreign policy and provides advice to CIDCA on granting or declining aid requests based on China's diplomatic needs. As CIDCA reports to State Councilor and MFA Minister Wang Yi, and one of its mandates is to use aid to support China's diplomacy, this gives MFA more influence in Chinese aid decision-making. MoF holds the purse strings of Chinese aid budget and keeps aid spending in check. As China is enthusiastically rolling out new initiatives such as the BRICS New Development Bank, Belt and Road and AIIB, MoF is heavily involved and playing a significant role. Therefore, its role in managing Chinese financing overseas will undoubtedly be boosted.

Ever since China's approval of its first concessional loan to Zimbabwe in July 1995, China Exim Bank has played an important role in managing Chinese concessional loans overseas. This responsibility has become heavier in the past decade as Chinese concessional loans increased substantially, and this trend continues. If non-concessional loan facilities are included in the category of new development assistance, the China Development Bank stands out as another significant player in the delivery of Chinese financing overseas. It has played a substantial role in supporting China's "go global strategy". By 2016, the bank's balance of loans oversea reached US$328.5 billion, accounting for more than 30% of the balance of loans provided by Chinese financing organizations (CDB, 2017). It is also actively involved in China's Belt and Road.

Aid Impact

The rapid growth of Chinese aid is starting to yield substantial impact on the global landscape of development assistance. Both positive and negative results are observable. On the positive side, Chinese aid becomes a new option for recipient countries. In particular, as some traditional donors have tightened their control on aid spending after the 2008 global financial crisis, Chinese aid has filled part of the gap. Chinese financing could assist recipient countries in economic development especially infrastructure upgrade. Take AIIB as an example. Inadequate infrastructure has hampered economic growth in many Asian countries. The Asian Development Bank estimates that Asia's infrastructure needs exceed US$1.7 trillion per year from 2016 to 2030 while the region's current investment in infrastructure annually is US$881 billion (ADB, 2017, p. xi), leaving a huge gap of US$819 billion. The newly established AIIB could play a positive role and fill much of the funding gap.

China's development assistance also brings about opportunities to share its technologies and development experience with developing countries, a point that has been increasingly discussed by senior development experts such as David Dollar, Justin Lin Yifu and Martin Ravallion (De-Haan, 2011, pp. 894–895). Take agricultural aid. China has established a number of agricultural demonstration farms in recipient countries. Not without problems,[7] these farms have provided opportunities for local farmers to learn from Chinese agricultural technologies and practices. As an official from China's Ministry of Agriculture stated proudly, what China is sharing with partner countries is "parallel experience" born out of China's own development, and Chinese agricultural technologies, less sophisticated and advanced than of traditional donors, could be more adaptive and pragmatic to recipient countries.[8] Similarly, China has been dispatching medical teams to other developing countries. China's medical expertise such as in malaria eradication becomes useful reference for these countries. It is noteworthy that China's growing aid could potentially play a significant role in assisting developing countries which have embarked on the journey of implementing the UN 2030 Sustainable Development Goals (SDGs). With its achievements on the Millennium Development Goals including being the first developing country to achieve poverty alleviation targets, China is well positioned to share its development experience with other developing countries on SDGs. The Chinese government has strongly committed to this endeavor and released four policy papers on SDGs.[9]

Recipient countries' perceptions of Chinese aid are diversified. For instance, Marek Hanusch (2012) argued that African countries think positively of China's impact on poverty reduction, which however is counterbalanced by their negative attitudes toward China's huge export to Africa, and by a less favorable view of Chinese aid held by those who value civic and political human rights. Monica DeHart painted a mixed picture of local's perceptions of Chinese aid in Costa Rica: former President Oscar Arias argued that his country's establishment of official relations with China does not indicate a deviation from its market-based economic principles or liberal values, but for the purpose of economic development; in the eyes of many local people who observed Chinese aid operations especially infrastructure construction, "China appears simultaneously as a First World donor and the quintessential Third World labourer" (DeHart, 2012, pp. 1365, 1371).

On the other hand, China's aid and financing is complicating the traditional architecture of development assistance. As recipient countries turn to China as an alternative source of foreign aid, Chinese aid practices, many of which differ from traditional aid, has undeniably reduced the appeal of traditional donors in areas such as governance and human rights, and compromised their impact. Another growing concern of Chinese aid relates to the proliferation of concessional loans. Some disagree with the requirement that recipient countries of Chinese concessional loans purchase at least half of the goods and materials from China. They have also expressed concerns with the use of a large number of Chinese staff in concessional loans projects. It merits clarification that some Chinese contractors have actually employed a tolerable proportion of local staff. On many occasions, these contractors have to employ staff especially skilled technicians from China because of the unavailability of qualified local staff and communication difficulties due to language differences.[10] Rising debt risk is another grave concern attributable to Chinese loans (Dornan & Brant, 2014, p. 355; Samy, 2010, p. 86), both concessional and commercial. With China's deeper pocket, it has increased its loans overseas which appeal to recipient countries for reasons including non-political conditionality and a quicker approval process relative to loans from traditional donors. As a result, many recipient countries have applied for the use of Chinese loans, which play a positive role in promoting their economic development and infrastructure upgrade. However, on some occasions, insufficient attention has been given to recipient countries' repaying capacity and thus contributed to deteriorating indebtedness in these countries.

Challenges also arise from within. With the involvement of more actors including companies in aid delivery, the competition between China's commercial concerns and diplomatic strategy becomes more acute (see also Breslin, 2013, p. 1273). While China is quick at approving and delivering aid commitment, its aid apparatus has remained insufficient such as in overseeing and maintaining aid projects after completion. This point has been repeated by Chinese aid officials and analysts, and whether and to what extent CIDCA could address this challenge is debatable.[11] Another major challenge is that China's aid professional team is awfully understaffed to handle the explosive workload. As an example, the number of staff specializing in foreign aid is only around 200–300 (Zhang & Smith, 2017), which has combined the staff at CIDCA and MOFCOM's three executing aid affiliations.[12] Chinese aid officials have worked around the clock to keep pace with the fast-growing aid commitment made by the government. To honor these aid pledges in time could have been exhausting, let alone spending time on Chinese aid reform.

Future Directions

China would continue to provide substantial amounts of foreign aid in the near future, as long as it could sustain economic growth. Interest-free loans could further dwindle in Chinese aid structure while China could provide larger volumes of grants in response to the outcry for more grant aid from recipient countries. China would likely provide more humanitarian assistance to improve its global image. More importantly, the scale and proportion of loans could unsurprisingly continue to dominate Chinese foreign aid and broad-term financing. If AIIB and Belt and Road, which are in their infancy, proceed well, China's confidence in reshaping global governance would be further boosted, and Beijing would probably expand its financing into the two programs and put forward similar initiatives. China's foreign aid and financing will enrich the concept of new development assistance.

To accommodate its rapidly increasing aid budget, China could make efforts to address the weakness in its aid delivery including bolstering the oversight and maintenance of aid projects in the post-construction stage. Chinese aid agencies could sensibly increase engagement with traditional donors and learn from their aid practices, which will open up new opportunities for the two sides to promote mutual understanding and conduct more aid coordination and cooperation. A typical example is, in recent years China has demonstrated readiness to undertake experimental trilateral cooperation with traditional donors including the US, the UK,

Australia and New Zealand in third countries, which also offers opportunities for traditional donors to maintain their relevance in the changing landscape of development assistance (Abdenur & João Moura Estevão Marques, 2013, p. 1485; Zhang, 2017, p. 753). This is a new phenomenon in Chinese aid delivery and a departure from its insistence on bilateral aid modality.

In the foreseeable future, we could expect to observe dual features of Chinese aid. On one hand, China would maintain engagement with traditional donors in selected areas such as project maintenance and seek opportunities for cooperation. For instance, it will continue to pilot trilateral aid cooperation in a prudent manner. MOFCOM's Foreign Aid Department proactively approached development partners such as the UNDP to explore opportunities for trilateral cooperation and materialize China's South-South Cooperation Fund pledged by President Xi at the UN summit in September 2015, which is in stark contrast to the Department's reluctance to such cooperation.[13] On the other hand, China could continue to insist on many of its aid and financing practices, flex the muscles and promote reform in global governance. As the tug-of-war between traditional donors and emerging economies will continue "through and around the main institutions of global aid regime" (Chin & Quadir, 2012, p. 504), China could play an active role in this process.

Notes

1. One US dollar bought 6.81 Chinese RMB on 31 May 2017. This rate is used in the paper.
2. MOFCOM has experienced such difficulty in collecting aid data from other Chinese agencies to produce the two white papers on Chinese foreign aid.
3. For example, a senior official from Papua New Guinea's Department of Central Planning and Monitoring expressed such views during interview with the author, Port Moresby, November 2015.
4. For more details, see http://www.focac.org/eng/; https://eng.yidaiyilu.gov.cn.
5. The principal of concessional loans is borrowed by the China Exim Bank from the market at commercial rates. The interest gap here refers to the interest difference between concessional and commercial loan rates.
6. See http://www.chinadaily.com.cn/china/2010-08/13/content_11149131.htm.

7. For instance, some criticize the commercial operation of these farms in Africa and the tensions between Chinese management and local staff.
8. Author's interview, Canberra, July 2016.
9. See http://www.fmprc.gov.cn/mfa_eng/.
10. This is based on the author's research and observation during fieldwork in countries including Cambodia, Timor-Leste, Papua New Guinea and other Pacific island countries.
11. Author's interviews, November 2013–September 2015.
12. The three agencies include the Executive Bureau of International Economic Cooperation (Agency for International Economic Cooperation), China International Centre for Economic and Technical Exchanges and the Academy for International Business Officials.
13. Author's interview with UNDP official, Canberra, June 2016.

References

Abdenur, A. E., & João Moura Estevão Marques, D. A. F. (2013). The North's Growing Role in South-South Cooperation: Keeping the Foothold. *Third World Quarterly, 34*(8), 1475–1491.

ADB. (2017). *Meeting Asia's Infrastructure Needs.* Manila: Asian Development Bank (ADB).

AidData. (2017). *Tracking Chinese Development Finance-BETA.* Retrieved from http://china.aiddata.org

Breslin, S. (2013). China and the South: Objectives, Actors and Interactions. *Development and Change, 44*(6), 1273–1294.

CDB. (2017). *Guo kai hang: tuchu fuwu "yi dai yi lu" jianshe* [China Development Bank: To Prioritize the Service for Belt and Road]. Retrieved from http://www.cdb.com.cn/xwzx/khdt/201702/t20170204_4068.html

Chandy, L., & Kharas, H. (2011). Why Can't We All Just Get Along? The Practical Limits to International Development Cooperation. *Journal of International Development, 23*(5), 739–751.

Chen, X. (2009). *Xinshiqi zhongguo da waijiao de fangxiang* [Direction for China's Big Diplomacy in a New Era]. Retrieved from http://lw.xinhuanet.com/htm/content_4954.htm

Chin, G., & Quadir, F. (2012). Introduction: Rising States, Rising Donors and the Global Aid Regime. *Cambridge Review of International Affairs, 25*(4), 493–506.

De-Haan, A. (2011). Will China Change International Development as We Know It? *Journal of International Development, 23*(7), 881–908.

DeHart, M. (2012). Remodelling the Global Development Landscape: The China Model and South-South Cooperation in Latin America. *Third World Quarterly, 33*(7), 1359–1375.

Dornan, M., & Brant, P. (2014). Chinese Assistance in the Pacific: Agency, Effectiveness and the Role of Pacific Island Governments. *Asia & the Pacific Policy Studies, 1*(2), 349–363.

Gore, C. (2013). The New Development Cooperation Landscape: Actors, Approaches, Architecture. *Journal of International Development, 25*(6), 769–786.

Grimm, S., Rank, R., McDonald, M., & Schickerling, E. (2011). *Transparency of Chinese Aid – An Analysis of the Published Information on Chinese External Financial Flows*. Stellenbosch, South Africa: Center for Chinese Studies, University of Stellenbosch.

Hanusch, M. (2012). African Perspectives on China-Africa: Modelling Popular Perceptions and their Economic and Political Determinants. *Oxford Development Studies, 40*(4), 492–516.

MFA. (2017). *Full Text of President Xi's Remarks at Plenary Session of BRICS Xiamen Summit*. Retrieved from http://www.fmprc.gov.cn/mfa_eng/topics_665678/XJPZCJZGJLDRDJCHWHXXSCGJYFZZGJDHH/t1489862.shtml

MoF. (2017). *Zhonghua renmin gongheguo caizhengbu yusuansi: caizheng shuju* [Department of Budget, Ministry of Finance, People's Republic of China: Financial Statistics]. Retrieved from http://yss.mof.gov.cn/zhengwuxinxi/caizhengshuju/index.html

MOFCOM. (2017). *Shangwubu hezuosi fuzeren tan 2016 nian woguo duiwai touzi hezuo qingkuang* [Official in Charge of MOFCOM's Department of International Trade and Economic Affairs Talked About Chinese Overseas Investment in 2016]. Retrieved from http://www.mofcom.gov.cn/article/ae/ag/201701/20170102502097.shtml

OECD. *Development Finance of Countries Beyond the DAC* [Data file]. Retrieved from http://www.oecd.org/development/stats/non-dac-reporting.htm

Samy, Y. (2010). China's Aid Policies in Africa: Opportunities and Challenges. *The Round Table, 99*(406), 75–90.

State Council. (2011, April 22). Zhongguo de duiwai yuanzhu [China's Foreign Aid]. *People's Daily*, p. 22.

State Council. (2014, July 11). Zhongguo de duiwai yuanzhu (2014) [China's Foreign Aid (2014)]. *People's Daily*, p. 22.

The World Bank. *World Development Indicators: Net Official Financial Flows* [Data file]. Retrieved from http://wdi.worldbank.org/table/6.10

Xinhua. (2017). *Full Text: List of Deliverables of Belt and Road Forum*. Retrieved from http://news.xinhuanet.com/english/2017-05/15/c_136286376.htm

Zhang, D. (2017). Why Cooperate with Others? Demystifying China's Trilateral Aid Cooperation. *The Pacific Review, 30*(5), 750–768.

Zhang, D., & Smith, G. (2017). China's Foreign Aid System: Structure, Agencies, and Identities. *Third World Quarterly, 38*(10), 2330–2346.

CHAPTER 11

South African Development Assistance in Africa

Chris Tapscott

Introduction

South Africa's emergence as a player in the new landscape of development assistance has been a complex one, shaped by the negative legacy of its past, its broad commitment to a Southern agenda, and its own economic and geo-political interests. Reconciling these different dynamics has been challenging and, as will be argued in this chapter, it has led to a somewhat inchoate development assistance programme, committed to a new paradigm of partnership, yet embodying elements of a conventional Northern model of donor assistance particularly when effected through trilateral arrangements. Unlike its BRICS (the consortium of Brazil, Russia, India, China and South Africa) partners, moreover, South Africa's development assistance is primarily directed towards African countries, in a context where it has both a comparative advantage over conventional donors and where, at the same time, it faces a range of challenges unique to its status as a member of this community of states.

South Africa's development assistance engagement on the African continent can be traced back to the late 1960s when, as a consequence of

C. Tapscott (✉)
School of Government, University of the Western Cape, Bellville, South Africa
e-mail: ctapscott@uwc.ac.za

Y. Jing et al. (eds.), *New Development Assistance*, Governing China in the 21st Century,
https://doi.org/10.1007/978-981-13-7232-2_11

increasing international isolation (and the growing pressure of sanctions), the then Apartheid government launched a number of foreign policy initiatives intended to forge alliances with what it considered to be moderate African states. The first was the establishment in 1968 of the Economic Cooperation Promotion Loan Fund, which was used by the Department of Foreign Affairs as a slush fund to buy support through a variety of, often nefarious, financial aid programmes (Besharati, 2013). The second was the short-lived attempt to establish a commonwealth in the region, a so-called Constellation of Southern African States (CONSAS), which was intended to strengthen economic links (and, by implication, dependency) between South Africa and its neighbours (Grundy, 1983). This was to be pursued through joint infrastructural projects and by means of financial aid to be channelled through the soon to be established Development Bank of Southern Africa (DBSA). Whilst the CONSAS initiative failed to take root, the DBSA, which was established in 1983, proceeded to provide loans and technical assistance to its neighbours for a range of infrastructural and other development programmes and it continues to do so to this day. Notwithstanding these initiatives, South Africa was widely viewed internationally, and in Africa in particular, as a destructive rogue state.

On its re-entry to the global community following the advent of democracy in 1994, the South African government embarked on a number of diplomatic initiatives to improve the country's standing on the African continent. These included joining prominent African institutions, such as the African Union (AU) and the Southern Africa Development Community (SADC), and aligning itself to the broad African development agenda (Besharati, 2013). Under the presidency of Thabo Mbeki, steps were also taken to support the AU's goal of Pan-Africanism and greater regional integration and these were given expression in the ideas of an African Renaissance and in the establishment of the New Partnership for Economic Development (NEPAD). As part of this broad Pan-African vision, at the turn of the millennium the South African government began extending development assistance to various emerging economies and particularly to those struggling to recover in post-conflict situations. In doing so it was, from the outset, keen to portray itself as an alternative donor voice from the South and, as Lucey maintains, "as a 'development partner', rather than a donor, thus distancing itself from the colonial connotations suggested by North-South relationships" (Lucey, 2015, p. 4). Further differentiating itself from the well established Organisation for Economic Cooperation and Development's (OECD) Development

Assistance Committee (DAC) donors is the seeming anomaly that South Africa is both a recipient and dispenser of development assistance.

Although not unique, its status as both a recipient and donor of aid has been described as an attempt to have the best of both worlds. Viewed from a sceptical perspective, according to Fabricius, "this arrangement implies that Pretoria is asking traditional donors to finance its pretention to join the ranks of the donor countries" (Fabricius, 2013, para. 5). Conversely, it has been argued, South Africa is able to draw on its own experiences as an aid recipient to guard against accusations of political interference and to appreciate the need for ownership of assistance programmes by aid beneficiaries (Lucey & O'Riordan, 2014).

South Africa as a Recipient of Donor Aid

As a pariah state, Apartheid South Africa had received no foreign aid and, increasingly, less and less foreign direct investment as global sanctions took effect. This changed with the advent of democracy and, according to the World Bank, the net official development assistance and official aid received by South Africa increased progressively from US$386.17 million in 1995 to US$1.42 billion in 2015. The bulk of the aid received in 2015 was from the DAC countries (67.2%) and from multilateral agencies (32.7%) and most of this was disbursed in the form of grants (US$808.6 million) and gross loans (US$736.69 million) (World Bank, 2017).

In many respects, however, South Africa's relationship with donors differs from that of most African states in that it has never been reliant on the receipt of foreign funds for the implementation of any of its policies and in 2015 the total aid received amounted to 0.47% of its Gross National Income (GNI), marginally more than the 0.25% received in 1995 (World Bank, 2017). What this has meant, in effect, is that South Africa has never been subjected to the conditionalities of aid imposed on many of its neighbours and it has been able to chart a more independent development path as a consequence. Whilst a considerable amount of funding was received in the early post-1994 era, to assist both in building democratic institutions and, subsequently, in combating an HIV/AIDS pandemic,[1] significant support was provided to non-governmental organisations engaged in community development work or in advocacy work promoting good governance. The decision taken in the last decade by most DAC states to dramatically cut back, or entirely cease, the provision of aid to South Africa on the grounds that it is now classified as a lower middle income country, has had little impact on the government budget, but it has had a significant impact on the non-profit sector and has led to the closure of a substantial number of organisations as a consequence.

South Africa as an Aid Donor

South Africa's first steps in establishing its position as a new donor on the African continent in the post-Apartheid era found expression in the closure of the Economic Cooperation Promotion Loan Fund and the establishment of the African Renaissance and International Co-operation Fund (ARF) in 2000. Amongst the stated objectives of the ARF in its founding statute are to enhance "co-operation between the Republic and other countries, in particular African countries, to promote democracy and good governance, prevent and resolve conflict, promote socio-economic development and integration, and support humanitarian assistance and human resource development" (Republic of South Africa, 2001, p. 3). Reflecting the ideals of an African Renaissance championed by the Mbeki presidency, the fund "was envisioned not as an instrument to provide aid but rather to establish partnerships, demonstrate solidarity and support the economic empowerment of Africa" (Besharati, 2013, p. 19).

From the outset, however, the ARF suffered from a number of weaknesses. As a fund located within the Department of International Relations and Cooperation (DIRCO), it carries none of the status or influence of an independent aid agency such as the Swedish International Development Cooperation Agency (SIDA) or the United Kingdom's Department for International Development) (DFID), and a host of similar national entities elsewhere. As a consequence, it lacks the authority to coordinate South Africa's varied development assistance programmes and this has contributed to the ad hoc nature of much of its approach to development cooperation. The fund has also been criticised for its bureaucratic inertia (on matters of procurement in particular), for poor coordination of its projects and for a lack of strategic direction. Further concerns have been raised that the programmes which it has implemented have lacked proper project management, monitoring and evaluation, and mechanisms for the tracking of expenditure (Lucey & O'Riordan, 2014).

Although plans have been in the offing since 2009 to phase out the ARF and to establish in its place the South African Development Partnership Agency (SADPA) (DIRCO, 2016) this has yet to happen. SADPA is intended to be a more freestanding organisation with a mandate to integrate development assistance and to "manage, coordinate and facilitate all South African official outgoing development cooperation programmes and projects" (Parliament of the Republic of South Africa, 2017, p. 78). The emphasis on "outgoing development cooperation" is of significance in that it differentiates donor aid received by South Africa (which will continue to be overseen by the National Treasury) and that which is disbursed to other development partners and specifically those in Africa.

Unlike its BRICS partners, South Africa's development assistance is fairly narrowly focused on Africa and it is predominantly directed to states in Southern Africa; in the 2013/14 financial year, 70% of its aid support was extended to SADC states (Besharati, 2013). Outside of this region it has engaged in support of states emerging from periods of conflict, notably South Sudan, the Democratic Republic of the Congo, Burundi, Rwanda and Somalia, and it has also provided a limited amount of support to states in West Africa. However, due to the lack of a central development aid agency, it is extremely difficult to estimate, with any precision, how much donor assistance South Africa is providing to states in Africa. This is due largely to the fact that funding and implementation of assistance programmes is fragmented and distributed across different government departments and agencies and, significantly, that there is no integrated system for the collection and collation of data on the aid which has been dispensed. Thus, for example, in addition to the programmes initiated by the ARF and DIRCO, the National School of Government (formerly known as the Public Administration Leadership and Management Academy) has been involved in training in the Congo, the Department of Public Works has been involved in Uganda, and the South African Police Service in South Sudan. However, ambiguity about the levels of assistance disbursed is also due to the way in which aid is classified, internationally, and by the South African government itself.

Development Assistance Flows to and from South Africa

Whilst the OECD countries have a fairly sophisticated mechanism for reporting of donor aid through the DAC, South Africa and the other BRICS countries have elected not to participate in this system. In part this is due to the fact that, notwithstanding its reputed efficiency, the way in which donor aid is computed by the DAC remains highly contentious, notwithstanding recent initiatives to introduce more rigour into this reporting system through the introduction of the Total Official Support for Sustainable Development (TOSSD) measurement system. In that regard, particular concerns have been raised about the fact that in-house expenditure on the marketing, administration, technical assistance, aid-tied services, the monitoring of aid and "publicly mobilized private financing" are routinely counted as part of the total amount disbursed (Besharati, 2017, p. 3), whilst support for political processes like elections and peace building are not. In other words, the dominant measurement system is, for political and ideological reasons, designed in ways which both defend and project the interests of DAC member states domestically and internationally—defending levels of aid dispersed in terms of their contribution to the domestic economy and, at the same time, projecting the extent of their influence in the geo-political order.

The lack of a central database in South Africa aside, it is also difficult to disaggregate the budgets lines of DIRCO and other aid-dispensing departments in order to establish, with any accuracy, how much assistance is provided to African states. Whilst the bulk of what is officially classified as development aid is disbursed through the ARF, it is difficult to determine what proportion of the budgets of the two major programmes, "International Cooperation" and "International Transfers", is assigned specifically to African states. Changes in the composition of these programmes over time also complicate efforts to present longitudinal data on aid flows.

Taking into account inflation, Table 11.1 below indicates that there has been a slight decline in the amount of aid dispensed in the 8-year period from 2009 to 2016. Whilst it is not possible, for the reasons cited above, to compute the amount of Official Development Assistance (ODA) disbursed in 2016 with any accuracy, the data suggests a figure of slightly more than US$100 million.[2] It is likely, furthermore, that faced with weak economic growth and growing government debt, there will be further cut backs in the development assistance funding allocated to the ARF in the next few years (ARF, 2018, p. 16).

A further estimate of the amount donor aid distributed is to be found in Fig. 11.1, prepared by an independent consultant on behalf of the South Africa Treasury, and ostensibly based on OECD data. Although the aid trajectory is similar to that derived from the treasury, it projects significantly higher levels of assistance throughout. The estimate of US$183 million in 2013 is also higher than the US$140 in 2014 cited by the independent US-based research agency, the Hudson Institute, in Table 11.2. Figure 11.1 also presents an interesting divergence in the aid flows into and out of South Africa which suggest that whilst the amount of donor aid received increased significantly in the past decade the amount dispensed remained relatively constant.

Table 11.1 South African treasury data on aid expenditure (millions of Rands)

Financial year	2009/10	2010/11	2011/12	2012/13	2013/14	2014/15	2015/16	2016/17
International Cooperation	406.6	334.4	333.0	370.4	451.7	485.2	523.1	514.3
International Transfers	1115.2	745.9	819.6	937.8	973.9	862.7	766.6	788.4
Total	1521.8	1080.3	1152.6	1308.2	1425.6	1347.9	1289.7	1302.7

Source: South African Treasury/DIRCO

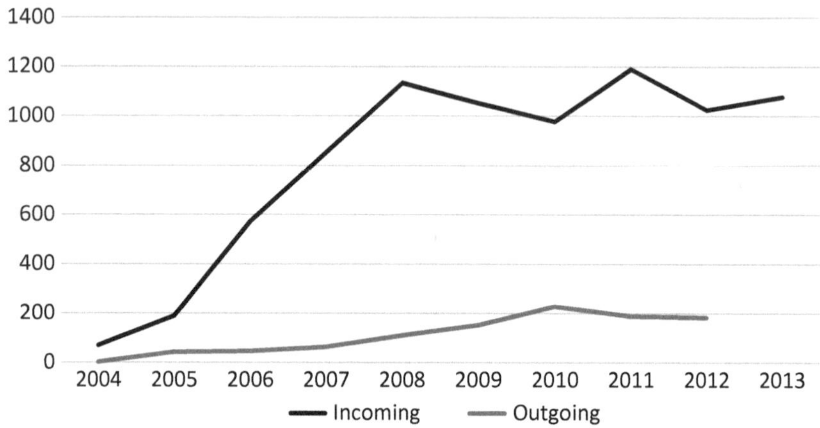

Fig. 11.1 Estimated aid flows to and from South Africa 2004–2013 (US$ millions). Source: Chiwandamira and Smith (2015) (estimates based on OECD data)

Table 11.2 Total economic engagement of four BRICS donor countries in 2014 (US$ millions)

Country	*ODA*	*Private philanthropy*	*Remittances*	*Private capital flows*	*Total*
Brazil	500	34	422	815	1771
China	3401	3.7	1189	1269	5863
India	1398	249	7853	1440	10,940
South Africa	148	23	1374	9987	11,532

Source: Hudson Institute (2016, p. 14)

In addition to the data cited above, there are a number of other forms of aid assistance (which would not be classified as such by the DAC) which are provided for by the South African government (Tjønneland, 2013, p. 3). These include participation in African peacekeeping missions, transfers to regional organisations, the provision of technical assistance and capacity building in state institutions and transfers made through the South African Customs Union (SACU). South Africa's contribution to peace initiatives on the continent, in particular, is significant and by 2017 it had participated in 14 operations, making it the 16th largest supplier of troops and police in the world (Cilliers, 2017, p. 9). In the Democratic Republic of the Congo alone, it is estimated, South Africa contributed over $1 billion in official development assistance (broadly defined) between 2001 and 2015 (Cilliers, 2017).

Under a 2002 SACU agreement the levies from customs, excise and other trade duties from five member states (South Africa, Botswana, Lesotho, Namibia and Swaziland) are collected in a common revenue pool, a portion of which is then paid to a development fund and the remainder is distributed to the partners according to a revenue sharing formula (Goitom, 2011). Although South Africa's trade with its SACU partners is highly asymmetrical and its exports to these countries vastly exceed imports from them, it is also the case that, whilst its contributions to the union have been growing, its partners continue to receive a disproportionately large percentage of the funds dispersed from the common pool. Where South African contributions to SACU were US$3.7 billion in the 2012/13 fiscal year they had risen to US$4.2 billion in 2014/15, an amount which was equivalent to 5.4% of the country's total revenue and 1.3% of its GDP (EIU, 2015). However, despite the fact that the South African contributes 98% of funds going into the pool its partners receive 55% of the proceeds (Mlumbi-Peter, 2015). These transfers amount to a de-facto form of budget support, and in 2011 they were estimated to account for 30% of the national revenue of Botswana, 35% of Namibia, 44% of Lesotho and 50% of Swaziland (Grant & Chapman, 2011).

It is also evident that remittance flows from workers, refugees and illegal immigrants in South Africa to other African states (predominantly Lesotho, Zimbabwe, Nigeria and Mozambique) make a significant contribution to their GNI. In 2014 these remittances amounted to an estimated US$1.37 billion,[3] a considerable increase on the estimated US$710 million remitted in 2011 (Hudson Institute, 2013, p. 30, 2016, p. 14).

Regulation of Aid

South Africa's interaction with states in Africa has, in part, been conditioned by its desire to overcome its image as a would-be hegemon and, at the same time, to strengthen its soft power amongst its development partners. This has meant that much of the aid which has been dispensed has been in response to requests from assistance and its allocation has been unconditional, or, at best, it has been subject to the conditions of high-level memoranda of understanding which are generally unenforceable. Furthermore, due to concerns that it might replicate the hegemonic and prescriptive models of aid distribution associated with some DAC donors, there has been a reluctance to study, let alone adopt some of their hard-earned experience. Moreover, despite the fact that South Africa subscribes to the principles of various international declarations, including the 2003 Paris Declaration on Aid Effectiveness, the 2008 Accra Agenda for Action and the 2011 Busan Partnership Agreement, which emphasise the need for the ownership of development assistance programmes by aid beneficiaries, it is evident that it has yet to develop the skills base and institutional capacity necessary to manage this process effectively. This relates in particular to its ability to analyse the national contexts of it recipient partners and to ensure that the aid which it provides achieves its stated goals (Lucey & O'Riordan, 2014, p. 7). This much appears to be recognised in the National Development Plan which asserts that "South African policy-makers tend to have a weak grasp of African geopolitics. Because of this, foreign relations with African states are often tentative, with policy-makers vacillating between leading and muddling through on issues of integration and cooperation" (NPC, 2012, p. 241).

Amongst the risks identified in the ARF Strategic Plan for 2015–2020 are that "funds distributed (are) not utilised for (their) purposes" and that there might be a "failure to adequately manage project contracts" (DIRCO, 2016, p. 20). Whilst these risks are real and confront most donors, the mitigation strategies proposed are less than convincing. In the case of the former it is proposed that "bi-lateral desks and missions provide monitoring and evaluation services" to ensure proper usage of funds disbursed and, in order to ensure that contracts are adequately managed, it is recommended that "Microsoft Project Office (be used) to manage ARF projects" (DIRCO, 2016). Such pronouncements in an ARF strategy document seem to confirm the views of various commentators that the distribution of South African assistance, hitherto, has been poorly monitored.

Trilateralism

Despite its embrace of South-South cooperation and its criticism of conventional Northern approaches to development assistance, South Africa, unlike some of its BRICS partners, has demonstrated a willingness to participate in trilateral aid partnerships including those with DAC states. In part this has been due to its desire to reintegrate itself into the global community following the demise of Apartheid and in part it is due to ambitions to position itself as a leading player on the continent. Since 1994 it has participated in a variety of triangular cooperation agreements with partners from both the North and the South. On a South-South basis it has worked with India and Brazil, its partners in the erstwhile IBSA consortium (India, Brazil, and South Africa), and with Cuba and Vietnam amongst others. Its North-South partners have included a number of DAC members including Norway, Sweden, Germany, Canada and the United States. It has also partnered with various multilateral organisations and in 2015 its development cooperation with these bodies was primarily channelled through such organisations as the African Development Bank (33%) and the United Nations (23%) (OECD, 2016).

Despite the fact that it has been critical of the donor policies of many DAC countries, South Africa maintains a close working relationship with the OECD. In 2007, together with Brazil, China, India and Indonesia, it was designated one of the five key partners of the OECD. Since then it has become an associate in six OECD bodies and projects, and a participant in 15, and it "has championed several of the OECD's regional initiatives with sub-Saharan Africa" (OECD, 2017a).

Whilst there is a logic to South Africa's participation in such trilateral aid partnership, not least in that it has local knowledge of other African states and an appreciation of their long-term goals and ambitions, the process carries its own risk. As the emerging development donor in a North-South partnership, in particular, it must typically assume responsibility for the direct oversight and support of a project and, at the same time, manage its relationship with the Northern co-funder. As Zondi points out, this places a significant responsibility on the South African agency or department responsible for managing a project (Zondi, 2015). Where this capacity is lacking, as it frequently is, resentment ensues, and this can sour relationships with other partners in the triangle. There is also the risk that as a junior partner in a trilateral programme South Africa could become a mere implementing agent of Northern donors, with relatively little say in shaping the format of the assistance programmes or in mitigating the conditionalities which historically have been the bane of aid recipients in Africa. In such situations, the goodwill and legitimacy which an emerging development donor brings to the partnership will quickly dissipate as the familiar patterns of North-South aid relationship are seen to re-emerge (Zondi, 2015).

Conclusion

In assessing the efficacy of South Africa's aid programme in the two decades since the ending of Apartheid, it is evident that its foreign policy objectives in Africa, and the focus of its development cooperation in particular, have never been clearly articulated and have, at times, appeared contradictory. This may partly be ascribed to the fact that South Africa has striven to maintain a balance between "advancing progressive internationalism while simultaneously acting in solidarity with Africa and the global South" (Cilliers, 2017, p. 3). It may also be attributed to the indeterminacy of South Africa's economic and geo-political ambitions on the Africa continent. Where Thabo Mbeki had championed the idea of Pan-Africanism and partnership and had downplayed South Africa's regional hegemony, under the presidency of Jacob Zuma, the state was less apologetic about the leadership role in Africa to which it aspires. According to the 2012 National Development Plan (NDP), which remains the government's central strategic document, its policies on African integration "must be based on positioning South Africa as one of the continent's powerhouses that would lead African development and influence in world affairs" (NPC, 2012, p. 241).

South Africa's leadership ambitions (including those in the AU, BRICS and the UN Security Council) have indeed raised unease amongst some African states. These concerns have been heightened by the aggressive expansion of South Africa business interests on the continent, and, more recently by concerns that the government has failed to adequately respond to xenophobic attacks on African nationals living in the country. Reflecting on this the NDP is candid about the country's lack of standing amongst other nations on the continent and, particularly, amongst its neighbours in Southern Africa, and asserts that "there is the perception that South Africa is acting as a bully, a self-interested hegemon that acts in bad faith among neighbouring countries" (NPC, 2012, p. 238). Lamenting this state of affairs, the NDP goes on to state that "South Africa's relative decline in global standing has led to material losses in regional and continental bargaining, and in trade and investment opportunities" (NPC, 2012, p. 238). This perception has led to criticisms from the business sector that the government's foreign policy objectives are too altruistic, if not naïve, and that the donor aid to African states is not being used to leverage the growth of South African companies in the same way in which its BRICS partners (India and China in particular) are stated to be doing

(Besharati, 2013). Questions have also been raised by segments of civil society as to whether a country which has such a high proportion of its population living in poverty and which is still so unequal, can afford, both financially and morally, to dispense development assistance to its neighbours.

It remains to be seen which direction South Africa's foreign policy in Africa will take under new the presidency of Cyril Ramaphosa but, formalistically at least, it is unlikely to deviate from the position articulated in the ARF's revised 2018 Strategic Plan which commits to

> Contribute to continental development by means of developmental assistance in support of democracy and good governance; human resource development; social-economic development and integration; humanitarian assistance and disaster relief; and PCRD (post-conflict reconstruction and development). (ARF, 2018, p. 12)

In pursuit of these objectives it is evident that there is space for South Africa to play an important role in both providing and coordinating development assistance to its neighbours. Whilst this process might be driven by enlightened self-interests (including the establishment of a stable trading environment in Africa), it could continue to provide valuable forms of assistance (in peace building, the strengthening of electoral systems, etc.) which are not typically offered by DAC donors. At the same time, whilst some African states might question its ambitions in Africa, none could point to its programme of development assistance as evidence of any form of expansionism. This is because it typically provides aid in response to requests for assistance and this is dispensed without any conditions attached. This approach, combined with an instance that it is a development partner rather than an aid donor, sets it apart from conventional DAC models of development assistance. Furthermore, as an African country it has both a strong vested interest in the development of the continent, and a comparative advantage in understanding the challenges which this entails. In order to so, however, it will need to move beyond its current ad hoc approach to the dispersal of development aid to a more focussed policy which defines both its areas of expertise and the states which are most likely to benefit from its assistance. It will also need to develop the organisational capacity necessary to support and strengthen its development partners.

Notes

1. This amounted to an estimated US$309 million in 2015 (OECD, 2017b).
2. Based on an exchange rate of US$1 to R12, R1.3 billion equates to US$108 million.
3. Whilst the data do not reveal precisely where all remitted funds are going, the current profile of refugees and migrant workers in South Africa suggests the probability that most are being sent back to other African states.

References

African Renaissance and International Cooperation Fund (ARF). (2018). *Revised Strategic Plan 2015–2020*. Retrieved from https://bit.ly/2Eqv3ky

Besharati, N. (2013). *South African Development Partnership Agency (SADPA): Strategic Aid or Development Packages for Africa?* (Research Report No. 12). Johannesburg: South African Institute for International Affairs (SAIIA). Retrieved from http://www.awepa.org/south-african-development-partnership-agency-sadpa-strategic-aid-or-development-packages-for-africa/

Besharati, N. (2017). New Development Finance Measure Should Be TOSSD Out the Window! *Policy Insights*, 45. Johannesburg: South African Institute for International Affairs (SAIIA).

Chiwandamira, D., & Smith, M. (2015). *Review of South Africa's Trilateral Development Cooperation Activities 2004–2014* [PPT]. Madrid: ACE International Consultants. Retrieved from http://www.igd.org.za/jdownloads/General/Review%20of%20South%20Africas%20Trilateral%20Cooperation%202004%20to%202014%20ppt%20261015.pdf

Cilliers, J. (2017). *Life Beyond BRICS? South Africa's Future Foreign Policy Interests*. Southern African Report No. 9. Pretoria: Institute for Security Studies. Retrieved from https://issafrica.s3.amazonaws.com/site/uploads/sar9.pdf

Department of International Relations and Cooperation (DIRCO). (2016). *Revised Strategic Plan 2015–2020; Annual Performance Plan 2016–2017*. Retrieved from www.dirco.gov.za/department/african_renaissance2015_2020/arf_2015_2020.pdf

EIU. (2015). Reforming SACU's Revenue-Sharing Formula. *The Economist Intelligence Unit*. Retrieved from https://bit.ly/2ClWP0d

Fabricius, P. (2013, September 20). *When the New South African Development Partnership Agency Eventually Gets Going, South Africa's Resistance to Conditionality in Aid Disbursements Will Need to Be Reviewed*. Pretoria: Institute for Strategic Studies. Retrieved from https://issafrica.org/iss-today/south-africas-aid-to-its-neighbours-should-be-explicit-and-conditional

Goitom, H. (2011). *Regulation of Foreign Aid: South Africa*. Retrieved from Library of Congress Website: https://www.loc.gov/law/help/foreign-aid/southafrica.php

Grant, C., & Chapman, G. (2011). *Southern African Customs Union: Myths and Reality*. Johannesburg: South African Institute for International Affairs (SAIIA), Economic. Retrieved from http://www.saiia.org.za/opinion-analysis/southern-african-customs-union-myths-and-reality

Grundy, K. (1983). *The Rise of the South African Security Establishment: An Essay on the Changing Locus of State Power*. Bradlow Series 1. Johannesburg: South African Institute for International Affairs (SAIIA).

Hudson Institute. (2013). *The Index of Global Philanthropies and Remittances, with a Special Focus on Emerging Economies*. Washington, DC: Center for Global Prosperity. Retrieved from https://www.hudson.org/research/9914-2013-index-of-global-philanthropy-and-remittances-with-a-special-report-on-emerging-economies

Hudson Institute. (2016). *The Index of Global Philanthropies and Remittances 2016*. Washington, DC: Center for Global Prosperity. Retrieved from https://www.hudson.org/research/13314-index-of-global-philanthropy-and-remittances-2016

Lucey, A. (2015). *South Africa's Development Cooperation: Opportunities in the Global Arena*. Tokyo, Japan: United Nations University Centre for Policy Research.

Lucey, A., & O'Riordan, A. (2014). *South Africa and Aid Effectiveness. Lessons for SADPA as a Development Partner*. ISS Paper 252. Pretoria: Institute for Strategic Studies.

Mlumbi-Peter, X. (2015, July 29). *South Africa and the Southern African Customs Union* [PPT]. Pretoria: Department of Trade and Industry. Retrieved from https://www.thedti.gov.za/parliament/2015/SACU.pdf

National Planning Commission (NPC). (2012). *National Development Plan 2030. Our Future – Make It Work*. Retrieved from https://www.gov.za/issues/national-development-plan-2030

OECD. (2016). *Development Aid at a Glance, Statistics by Region* (Africa No. 2, 2016th ed.). Retrieved from https://www.oecd.org/dac/stats/documentupload/2%20Africa%20-%20Development%20Aid%20at%20a%20Glance%20 2016.pdf

OECD. (2017a). *South Africa and the OECD*. Retrieved from http://www.oecd.org/southafrica/south-africa-and-oecd.htm

OECD. (2017b). *International Development Statistics (IDS)* [Data file]. Retrieved from http://www.oecd.org/dac/stats/idsonline.htm

Parliament of the Republic of South Africa. (2017, May 17). *Report of the Portfolio Committee on International Relations and Cooperation on Budget Vote 6: International Relations and Cooperation* (Report No. 62-20170). Fourth Session, Fifth Parliament.

Republic of South Africa. (2001). *African Renaissance and International Co-Operation Fund Act*. In *Act No 51 of 2000*. Retrieved from http://us-cdn.

creamermedia.co.za/assets/articles/attachments/03522_africrenandintcoop-funact51.pdf
Tjønneland, E. N. (2013). Providing Development Aid to Africa: Comparing South Africa with China, India and Brazil. Open Society Foundation for South Africa. *SAFPI Policy Brief*, 25.
World Bank. (2017). *Net Official Development Assistance and Official Aid Received (Current US$)* [Data file]. Retrieved from http://data.worldbank.org/indicator/DT.ODA.ALLD.CD
Zondi, S. (2015). Tri-lateral Development Cooperation: How Do Poor Countries Experience It? *Global Insight*, 116. Pretoria: Institute for Global Dialogue. Retrieved from https://www.africaportal.org/publications/trilateral-development-cooperation-how-do-poor-countries-experience-it/

Correction to: New Development Assistance

Yijia Jing, Alvaro Mendez, and Yu Zheng

Correction to:

Y. Jing et al. (eds.), *New Development Assistance*, Governing China in the 21st Century, https://doi.org/10.1007/978-981-13-7232-2

The book was inadvertently published with an incorrect series print and electronic ISSN of 2524-3586 and 2524-3594 respectively, whereas the correct numbers should be 2730-6968 and 2730-6976

The updated online version of this book can be found at https://doi.org/10.1007/978-981-13-7232-2

Y. Jing et al. (eds.), *New Development Assistance*, Governing China in the 21st Century,
https://doi.org/10.1007/978-981-13-7232-2_12

Index

Y. Jing et al. (eds.), *New Development Assistance*, Governing China in the 21st Century,
https://doi.org/10.1007/978-981-13-7232-2

M

N

O

Kolibri 360 GmbH
Ferdinand-Jühlke-Straße 7
99095 Erfurt, Deutschland
produktsicherheit@kolibri360.de